Essence of KANSAS!

Taste...

*Food Experiences
with 4-H Friends*

Appreciation . . .
to 4-H Friends

The **Essence of Kansas!** 4-H cook-book represents the participation of hundreds of individuals across Kansas with a special interest in the 4-H program. Publication of this unique cookbook would not have been possible without the support, advice and assistance of numerous individuals.

It is with sincere appreciation that we thank the many 4-H friends who submitted recipes to be considered for publication in the **Essence of Kansas!** We regret that all the recipes could not be used at this time. Generally, all published recipes were selected by the staff of Favorite Recipes Press under their established guidelines.

The actual production challenge would not have been met without the special efforts of Trisha Cash and Rhonda Atkinson of the Kansas 4-H Foundation staff, as well as the participation of the cookbook planning committee and the efforts of many others.

Most of the Kansas 4-H Foundation staff and many Extension professionals played some part in bringing this project to completion. To everyone, we acknowledge their participation and support with this special publication.

Cookbook Planning Committee

Rhonda Atkinson	Marilyn Corbin	Lois Redman
Trisha Cash	Karen Penner	William M. Riley
Mary Clarke	Jim Ploger	C.R. Salmon

Special Assistance

Ann Daniels	Mildred Walker
Ralf Graham	Ruth Wells
	Bob Pinkall

We have attempted to present these tried-and-true family recipes in a form that allows approximate nutritional values to be computed. Persons with dietary or health problems or whose diets require close monitoring should not rely on the nutritional information provided. They should consult their physicians or a registered dietitian.

Abbreviations for Nutritional Analysis

Cal	Calories	Sod	Sodium
Carbo	Carbohydrates	T Fat	Total Fat
Chol	Cholesterol	gr	gram
Potas	Potassium	mg	milligram
Prot	Protein		

Kansas State University, the Kansas 4-H Foundation, and Favorite Recipes Press are not responsible for the nutritional analysis provided at the end of each recipe if ingredients are substituted. Nor can they be held responsible for the mistaken identity of any plant or animal listed in this book. The recipes are home-tested and are not endorsed by Kansas State University or the Kansas 4-H Foundation.

Published by Favorite Recipes Press, P.O. Box 305142, Nashville, TN 37230
First Printing: 13,000   Second Printing: 10,000
Copyright© Kansas 4-H Foundation, 116 Umberger Hall, KSU, Manhattan, KS 66506
Library of Congress Number: 88-16041
ISBN: 0-87197-233-6

A Step Ahead . . .
The Kansas 4-H Campaign

For eighty years, 4-H has spoken loudly in Kansas. Leaders in every field consistently attribute many of their speaking, management and organizational skills to their 4-H experience.

You've heard them. You know them. You most likely are among them.

Today, the Cooperative Extension Service and Kansas 4-H Foundation partnership builds on that eighty-year history. Together, these dedicated supporters have designed A Step Ahead to build more permanent statewide funding support for the 4-H program in Kansas. A Step Ahead has a goal to raise 2.6 million dollars.

A Step Ahead emphasizes permanent endowments to ensure the future of Kansas 4-H and Youth Programs.

A Step Ahead brings 4-H to the attention of Kansas' corporate and civic leadership.

A Step Ahead reminds all of us that Kansas 4-H does, indeed, have a history, but that its future is important to us, too.

A Step Ahead will do exactly that: Move Kansas 4-H a giant step ahead!

The Kansas 4-H family . . . club members, leaders, parents, volunteers, alumni, friends and staff . . . are demonstrating their commitment to this special campaign effort.

The Essence of Kansas! is designed to be a unique product Kansas 4-H can proudly promote featuring award-winning 4-H photography and recipes of the 4-H family.

Your purchase of this book is a step toward that goal and A Step Ahead for Kansas 4-H!

Kansas 4-H . . .
Reaching Kansas People

For years, 4-H has been shaping leaders . . . leaders in government, business and local communities... leaders who represent what the essence of Kansas is all about.

The heart of Kansas is its people... people who have a positive self-concept, who have the ability to make a decision, and who can develop a positive relationship with others. Kansas people have a genuine concern for their community and look at life with open and inquiring minds . . . qualities encouraged by Kansas 4-H programs.

What makes 4-H special is not just taking a project and winning ribbons at the fair . . . a special part of the 4-H program is the values and principles it teaches and its ability to grow and change to meet the needs of changing families, new job skills and societal pressures.

Although 4-H has a rural beginning, it now touches the lives of one out of every four Kansas youth in both rural and urban settings. Today, over 102,000 members participate in 4-H through traditional community clubs, or the new project clubs, mini-clubs and the school enrichment program.

While 4-H does indeed have a rich history in Kansas, it is the future of the program that is essential. *A Step Ahead*, the 4-H campaign, is designed to build on that history and continue the legacy of shaping strong leaders for Kansas.

C.R. Salmon, State 4-H Leader
Extension 4-H — Youth Programs

Kansas People . . .
Reaching Kansas 4-H

The Kansas 4-H Foundation, Inc., organized in 1952, allows the private sector to assist the continued growth and effectiveness of the Kansas 4-H program through the contributions of private funds.

Governed by a twenty-one member board of trustees, the Foundation and its many donors continue to create and manage facilities and services which add new and exciting dimensions to 4-H programs and activities. It is through donor support and sincere interest in the 4-H program that the Foundation successfully carries out its mission.

Although the primary contact for most 4-H'ers with the Foundation is participation at Rock Springs 4-H Center, the other operational projects of the Foundation, such as the Kansas 4-H Journal and Clovia scholarship houses, have a direct impact on the 4-H experience for thousands of 4-H members.

Annually, over 102,000 Kansas youth have an opportunity to participate in 4-H events funded directly or indirectly by the Foundation which reflects its ongoing support . . . support representing over $200,000 in direct monies for county benefits through numerous statewide opportunities available to all 105 Kansas counties.

The Foundation trustees and staff are dedicated to responding in every available manner to growth and enhancement opportunities of the 4-H experience.

Through its management function in the development of the **Essence of Kansas**! 4-H cookbook, the Foundation continues its cooperative effort to promote Kansas 4-H.

Bill Riley, Executive Director
Kansas 4-H Foundation

The Picturesque . . . State of Kansas

The photography throughout this publication depicts the essence of Kansas through the eyes of Kansas 4-H'ers.

We appreciate the opportunity to use these award-winning state fair photographs, and we salute these 4-H'ers, who, like thousands of others, are dedicated to project excellence.

Sunset Silhouette

Enjoy the calm tranquillity and scenic beauty of Kansas as captured by: Slade Alford, son of Steve and Peggy Alford, Grant County; Brenda Andres, daughter of Dwight and Marylin Andres, Wabaunsee County; Darin Ashworth, son of Robert and Dedria Ashworth, Reno County; John Collins, son of Bob and Mary Collins, Morris County; Jeanie David, daughter of Eugene and Leinad David, Graham County; Chris Floyd, son of Martie and Diane Floyd, Stanton County; Sarah Groh, daughter of Donald and Sharon Groh, Doniphan County; Kris Kobiskie, son of John and Sheryl Kobiskie, Riley County; and Jami Krusemark, daughter of Ken and Connie Krusemark, Reno County.

Reflections

Prairie Petals

Sky Nuggets

Radiant Rays

Remembering

Homegrown in the Heartland

Amber Waves of Grain

Flint Hills Fence Post

Table of Contents

"REFLECTIONS" by Darin Ashworth

Kansas . . .
Clover Classics

Kansas has a rich heritage throughout the state . . . a heritage built over eighty years by dedicated Extension professionals, leaders, 4-H parents and members. The following Clover Classics accentuate the accomplishments of past and present Kansas 4-H'ers.

◆ Otis Hall, Kansas state 4-H leader, wrote the 4-H club pledge in 1918, and it was approved in 1927.

◆ The 4-H club pledge:

> I pledge my head to clearer thinking,
> my heart to greater loyalty,
> my hands to larger service,
> and my health to better living,
> for my club, my community,
> my country, and my world.

◆ Kansas 4-H continues to build on its eighty-year history as members strive to uphold the 4-H motto, "To Make the Best Better."

◆ The 4-H flag is flown with pride by Kansas 4-H'ers. Its colors of green and white are the national 4-H club colors. The white background of the 4-H flag symbolizes purity; the green of the 4-H emblem represents nature's most common color in the great out-of-doors and also is emblematic of youth, life and growth.

◆ During World War II, a 10,500 ton steel cargo ship was named S.S. Otis E. Hall in honor of Otis Hall, the first state 4-H leader in Kansas from 1914 to 1920. In order for 4-H members of a state to name a ship, they were to sell $2,000,000 of war bonds, the cost of one of the Liberty ships. Kansas 4-H'ers sold above the required amount.

◆ Kansas was one of the first states to endorse the community club concept.

◆ Started in 1924, the Junior Sunflowers 4-H Club of Lincoln is the oldest community club in existence in Kansas.

◆ 4-H Club Days is one of the oldest existing special 4-H events. 4-H Club Days began in 1925 as a model meeting contest at Round-up and developed through "Spring Festival" to 4-H Day. County Club Days, as they were called for the first time in 1945, have added many new events over the years. Demonstrations and promotional talks became a part of County Club Days in 1949, and musical games followed in 1950. Project and activity talks debuted in 1958.

◆ Camping as a 4-H activity began in the early 1920s. And because of the popularity, Kansas 4-H'ers

Clover Classics continued

purchased their own camping center early in 1946. The clubs raised the purchase price in just five months and in celebration burned the mortgage in June 1946.

◆ Over the years, Kansans have built the Rock Springs 4-H Center, which is now owned and operated by the Kansas 4-H Foundation, into a nationally recognized camping and conference center. One of every five Kansans has been to the center which features native limestone buildings and spans 415 acres of the Kansas Flint Hills near Junction City.

◆ Founded in November 1952, the Kansas 4-H Foundation is known nationally for its many services and support projects provided to Kansas 4-H.

◆ The Kansas 4-H Journal stands alone as the only statewide 4-H magazine in the nation. This unique communication tool enjoys a circulation of over 15,000 4-H families statewide and is designed to share, promote, introduce and unify those involved in the Kansas 4-H program.

◆ The two Clovia 4-H scholarship houses located at Fort Hays State and Kansas State Universities continue 4-H ideology while providing comfortable accommodations as the young women continue their education.

◆ Annually, the Kansas 4-H Foundation makes available over $100,000 for scholarships and awards promoting higher education and project excellence.

◆ Today, over 102,000 Kansas youth participate in the 4-H program . . .that's one of every four Kansans between seven and seventeen!

◆ The enrollment figures continue to increase as opportunities are offered to more Kansas youth. Nearly forty percent of the enrollment is comprised of young people from central cities and suburbs. School enrichment programs, mini-clubs and project clubs are popular new additions to the Kansas 4-H program.

◆ Traditionally, the animal and poultry science, nutrition and foods, and citizenship and community involvement projects have the highest number of participants.

◆ The bucket calf project originated in Kansas, and the Kansas 4-H Ambassador program is used as an example nationwide as other states design their Ambassador programs.

◆ Nationwide, Kansas 4-H enrollment in international programs ranks first. The state also holds top five ranking in: economics and business (2); beef (3); entomology and bees (3); tractor and machinery safety certification (4); school enrichment (5).

Sunflower Medley
(Open House)

"PRAIRIE PETALS" by Slade Alford

BREAD BASKET DIP

1 (8-inch) round loaf
  French bread
3 cups shredded sharp Cheddar
  cheese
8 ounces cream cheese,
  softened
1 cup sour cream
1 (2½-ounce) package smoked
  beef, chopped
¾ cup canned solid-pack
  pumpkin
½ cup sliced green onions
½ cup chopped parsley
1 tablespoon Worcestershire
  sauce
⅛ teaspoon hot pepper sauce

Hollow out bread, leaving ½-inch shell. Cut bread into cubes. Reserve bread shell and cubes. Combine Cheddar cheese, cream cheese and sour cream in bowl; mix until smooth. Add beef, pumpkin and remaining ingredients; mix well. Spoon into bread shell. Wrap in heavy foil. Place on baking sheet. Bake at 300°F. for 2 hours. Serve with reserved bread cubes or bite-sized vegetables. Yield: 80 tablespoons.

Approx Per Tablespoon: Cal 52; Prot 2.2 gr; T Fat 3.3 gr; Chol 9.3 mg; Carbo 3.5 gr; Sod 114.4 mg; Potas 27.3 mg.

Tina Welch, Lakin

QUICK BEAN DIP

1 (16-ounce) can pork
  and beans
¾ cup shredded Monterey Jack
  cheese with jalapeño peppers
¼ cup chopped green bell
  pepper
¼ cup chopped red bell pepper
1 tablespoon finely chopped
  onion

Place beans in food processor container. Process until smooth. Combine with cheese, peppers and onion in bowl; mix well. Chill until serving time. Serve with crackers and chips. Yield: 32 tablespoons.

Approx Per Tablespoon: Cal 31; Prot 1.7 gr; T Fat 1.3 gr; Chol 3.3 mg; Carbo 3.3 gr; Sod 92.7 mg; Potas 41.4 mg.

Chris Neal, Dexter

NUTTY BLUE CHEESE VEGETABLE DIP

1 cup mayonnaise
1 cup sour cream
¼ cup crumbled blue cheese
1 tablespoon chopped onion
2 teaspoons beef bouillon
¾ cup chopped walnuts

Blend mayonnaise, sour cream and blue cheese in bowl. Add onion and bouillon; mix well. Stir in walnuts. Chill, covered, for 1 hour. Stir dip well. Spoon into serving dish. Garnish with additional walnuts if desired. Serve with bite-sized vegetables. Yield: 48 tablespoons.

Approx Per Tablespoon: Cal 58; Prot 0.6 gr; T Fat 6.1 gr, Chol 6.0 mg; Carbo 0.6 gr; Sod 54.6 mg; Potas 18.0 mg.

Tim Schoepflin, Quenemo

DELUXE CHEESE BALL

16 ounces cream cheese, softened
1 (2½-ounce) package dried beef
1 bunch green onions
2 teaspoons Worcestershire sauce
1 teaspoon MSG
1 cup chopped pecans

Mix cream cheese, dried beef, green onions and seasonings in bowl. Shape into ball. Roll in pecans, coating well. Chill, wrapped in plastic wrap, until serving time. Place on serving plate. Serve with crackers. Yield: 32 tablespoons.

Approx Per Tablespoon: Cal 117; Prot 3.5 gr; T Fat 10.3 gr; Chol 24.9 mg; Carbo 3.0 gr. Sod 229.8 mg. Potas 81.2 mg.

C. R. Salmon, Assistant Director 4-H-Youth Programs, Manhattan

FRUIT DIP

⅓ cup sugar
4 teaspoons cornstarch
¼ teaspoon salt
1 cup unsweetened pineapple juice
¼ cup orange juice
2 tablespoons lemon juice
2 eggs, beaten
6 ounces cream cheese

Combine sugar, cornstarch and salt in small saucepan. Blend in juices. Cook until thickened and bubbly, stirring constantly. Stir a small amount of hot mixture into eggs; stir eggs into hot mixture. Remove from heat. Add cream cheese. Beat until smooth. Chill until serving time. Yield: 32 tablespoons.

Approx Per Tablespoon: Cal 39; Prot 0.9 gr; T Fat 2.4 gr; Chol 21.7 mg; Carbo 3.6 gr; Sod 33.9 mg; Potas 24.9 mg.

Steve Schoepflin, Quenemo

GOUDA CHEESE BALL

1 (8-ounce) Gouda cheese
½ cup sour cream
1½ teaspoons dry Italian
  salad dressing mix
¼ cup chopped pecans

Slice off top of cheese. Scoop out cheese, leaving shell. Combine cheese, sour cream and salad dressing mix in bowl; beat until smooth. Spoon into cheese shell. Top with pecans. Yield: 20 tablespoons.

Approx Per Tablespoon: Cal 68; Prot 3.2 gr; T Fat 5.9 gr; Chol 13.8 mg; Carbo 0.8 gr; Sod 112.7 mg; Potas 27.3 mg.

Tina J. Jackson, Phillipsburg

SALMON PARTY BALL

1 (16-ounce) can salmon
8 ounces cream cheese,
  softened
1 tablespoon lemon juice
2 teaspoons grated onion
1 teaspoon horseradish
¼ teaspoon salt
½ cup chopped pecans

Drain and flake salmon, discarding skin and bones. Combine salmon, cream cheese, lemon juice, onion, horseradish and salt in bowl; mix well. Shape into ball. Chill for 1 hour. Roll cheese ball in pecans, coating well. Place on serving plate. Serve with crackers. Yield: 48 tablespoons.

Approx Per Tablespoon: Cal 40; Prot 2.4 gr; T Fat 3.2 gr; Chol 8.6 mg; Carbo 0.3 gr; Sod 59.6 mg; Potas 46.0 mg.

Sharon Ann Straub, Wamego

HOLIDAY TUNA TREE

1 (12½-ounce) can water-pack
  tuna
1 (6½-ounce) can water-pack
  tuna
16 ounces cream cheese,
  softened
1 tablespoon lemon juice
¼ cup chopped green olives
½ cup chopped walnuts
¼ teaspoon salt
1½ teaspoons dry mustard
⅛ teaspoon pepper
½ teaspoon thyme

Drain and flake tuna. Combine with cream cheese, lemon juice, olives, walnuts and seasonings in bowl; mix well. Spoon into oiled Christmas tree mold. Chill until serving time. Unmold onto serving plate. Garnish with garlands of parsley, sliced cherry tomatoes, lemon slice and pimento star. Yield: 64 tablespoons.

Approx Per Tablespoon: Cal 44; Prot 3.1 gr; T Fat 3.4 gr; Chol 13.3 mg; Carbo 0.3 gr; Sod 115.7 mg; Potas 34.2 mg.

Linda A. Pratt, Colorado Springs, Colorado

BARBECUED MEATBALLS

2 pounds ground beef
1 egg
1¾ cups quick-cooking oats
1 (6-ounce) can evaporated
  milk
½ cup finely chopped onion
¼ teaspoon garlic powder
1¼ teaspoons salt
¼ teaspoon pepper
1½ teaspoons chili powder
1¾ cups catsup
1 cup packed brown sugar
1 tablespoon liquid smoke
¼ cup finely chopped onion
¾ teaspoon garlic powder

Combine ground beef, egg, oats, evaporated milk, ½ cup onion, ¼ teaspoon garlic powder, salt, pepper and chili powder in bowl; mix well. Shape into 1-inch balls. Place in greased 9 x 13-inch baking dish. Combine catsup and remaining ingredients in bowl; mix well. Pour over meatballs. Bake at 350°F. for 1 hour.
Yield: 48 meatballs.

Approx Per Meatball: Cal 96.7; Prot 4.5 gr; T Fat 4.7 gr; Chol 19.2 mg; Carbo 9.4 gr; Sod 166.7 mg; Potas 131.4 mg.

Kelly Morris, Winfield

CRAB MEAT SPREAD

8 ounces cream cheese,
  softened
2 teaspoons mayonnaise
2 teaspoons grated onion
1 tablespoon Worcestershire
  sauce
1 tablespoon lemon juice
⅛ teaspoon garlic salt
½ cup Bookbinders cocktail
  sauce
⅓ pound canned crab meat,
chopped, drained

Blend cream cheese and mayonnaise in mixer bowl. Add onion, Worcestershire sauce, lemon juice and garlic salt; beat until smooth. Spread evenly on serving plate. Spread cocktail sauce over top. Chill, covered, for 6 to 12 hours. Sprinkle crab meat over cocktail sauce. Garnish with parsley. Chill, covered, for 6 to 12 hours. Serve with crackers.
Yield: 32 tablespoons.

Approx Per Tablespoon: Cal 38.5; Prot 1.5 gr; T Fat 3.6 gr; Chol 13.6 mg; Carbo 0.4 gr; Sod 78.5 mg; Potas 15.6 mg.
Nutritional information does not include cocktail sauce.

Nikki S. Currie, Holstein-Friesian Association of Kansas Inc., Gypsum

Nikki S. Currie.

PARTY SAUSAGE SPREAD

1 pound ground chuck
1 pound bulk sausage
1 teaspoon oregano
1 tablespoon Worcestershire
  sauce
1 pound Velveeta cheese,
  chopped

Brown ground chuck and sausage with oregano and Worcestershire sauce in skillet, stirring until crumbly; drain. Add cheese. Cook until cheese is melted, stirring constantly. Serve from chafing dish or slow cooker with crackers. Yield: 128 servings.

Approx Per Serving: Cal 25; Prot 1.8 gr; T Fat 1.9 gr; Chol 6.6 mg; Carbo 0.3 gr; Sod 75.5 mg; Potas 21.7 mg.

Wanda Duncan, Phillipsburg

CRANBERRY TEA

¾ cup sugar
8 cups water
3 cinnamon sticks
3 tablespoons lemon juice
2 cups (16 ounces) orange
  juice
4 cups (32 ounces) cranberry
  juice

Mix sugar, water and cinnamon sticks in large saucepan. Simmer for 25 minutes. Remove cinnamon sticks. Add juices. Heat to serving temperature. Serve warm. Yield: 16 cups.

Approx Per Cup: Cal 92; Prot 0.3 gr; T Fat 0.1 gr; Chol 0.0 mg; Carbo 23.2 gr; Sod 1.1 mg; Potas 72.6 mg.

Mary Clark, Washington

FRUIT FRAPPÉ

1 (10-ounce) package frozen
  strawberries
3 ounces frozen orange juice
  concentrate
3 ounces frozen pineapple
  juice concentrate
1 banana
1 carrot, finely grated

Combine strawberries, juice concentrates, banana and carrot in blender container. Process until smooth. Add several ice cubes. Process until slushy. Pour into glasses. May pour into popsicle molds and freeze if preferred. Yield: 3 cups.

Approx Per Cup: Cal 276; Prot 2.6 gr; T Fat 0.5 gr; Chol 0.0 mg; Carbo 68.8 gr; Sod 14.6 mg; Potas 770.9 mg.

Connie Gebhart, Barnard

HOLIDAY PUNCH

4 cups (32 ounces) apple cider
Juice of 6 oranges
3 cups cranberry juice
¼ cup lemon juice
½ cup honey
3 or 4 cinnamon sticks

Mix apple cider, juices, honey and cinnamon sticks in saucepan. Simmer until flavors are blended. Remove cinnamon sticks. Pour into punch bowl. Garnish with orange slices studded with whole cloves. Serve hot or cold. Yield: 10 servings.

Approx Per Serving: Cal 164; Prot 0.7 gr; T Fat 0.4 gr; Chol 0.0 mg; Carbo 42.5 gr; Sod 4.1 mg; Potas 200.1 mg.

Ann Perl, Manhattan

WASSAIL

8 cups (64 ounces)
  unsweetened apple juice
1 cinnamon stick
1 teaspoon whole cloves
1 cup sugar
1 (46-ounce) can
  unsweetened pineapple
  juice
⅔ cup lemon juice
1 (18-ounce) can frozen orange
  juice concentrate

Combine apple juice with cinnamon stick and cloves in saucepan. Simmer for 5 to 10 minutes. Strain into large container. Add sugar and remaining juices. Heat to serving temperature. Yield: 18 cups.

Approx Per Cup: Cal 162; Prot 1.5 gr; T Fat 0.4 gr; Chol 0.0 mg; Carbo 48.3 gr; Sod 3.8 mg. Potas 466.3 mg.

Michaeline Fox, Kiowa

HOPSCOTCHES

12 ounces butterscotch
  almond bark
½ cup peanut butter
1 (3-ounce) can chow mein
  noodles
2 cups miniature marshmallows

Melt butterscotch almond bark and peanut butter in saucepan over low heat, stirring to blend well. Pour over mixture of noodles and marshmallows in bowl; mix well. Drop by spoonfuls onto waxed paper. Let stand until firm. Yield: 36 servings.

Approx Per Serving: Cal 87; Prot 1.7 gr; T Fat 5.7 gr; Chol 0.3 mg; Carbo 9.5 gr; Sod 46.3 mg; Potas 54.9 mg.

Lisa Nelson, Oketo

PEPPY POPCORN

8 cups popped popcorn
1½ cups canned shoestring
    potatoes
½ cup Parmesan cheese
7 ounces roasted salted peanuts
¼ cup margarine
½ teaspoon onion powder
½ teaspoon chili powder
½ teaspoon garlic salt

Combine popcorn, potatoes, Parmesan cheese and peanuts in large bowl. Melt margarine in saucepan. Add seasonings; mix well. Pour over popcorn mixture, tossing to mix well. Yield: 10 cups.

Approx Per Cup: Cal 244; Prot 8.5 gr; T Fat 19.7 gr; Chol 5.6 mg;
    Carbo 11.0 gr; Sod 449.5 mg; Potas 224.8 mg.

Denise Dunn, Scott City

PERKY POPCORN

6 cups popped popcorn
2 cups pretzel sticks, broken
2 cups peanut M and M's
    chocolate candies
⅓ cup sugar
¼ cup honey
¼ cup light corn syrup
⅓ cup peanut butter
½ teaspoon vanilla extract

Mix popcorn, pretzels and M and M's in large bowl. Combine sugar, honey and corn syrup in heavy 1-quart saucepan. Bring to a full boil, stirring constantly. Boil for 2 minutes, stirring constantly; remove from heat. Stir in peanut butter and vanilla until smooth. Pour over popcorn mixture; toss to coat well. Spread on baking sheet. Bake at 250°F. for 30 minutes, stirring after 15 minutes. Cool. Break into bite-sized pieces. Store in airtight container. Yield: 10 cups.

Approx Per Cup: Cal 346; Prot 5.6 gr; T Fat 12.7 gr; Chol 4.1 mg;
    Carbo 56.1 gr; Sod 371.1 mg; Potas 173.3 mg.

Thad Powell, Washington

PUDDING POPS

1 (3½-ounce) package vanilla
    instant pudding mix
2 cups milk
½ cup whipping cream
½ cup sugar

Combine pudding mix, milk, cream and sugar in bowl; mix until smooth. Pour into popsicle molds. Freeze until firm. Yield: 6 servings.

Approx Per Serving: Cal 263; Prot 3.9 gr; T Fat 10.6 gr. Chol 37.8 mg;
    Carbo 40.6 gr; Sod 133.4 mg; Potas 153.4 mg.

Jennifer Turner, Marysville

WALKING STICKS

1¾ cups all-purpose flour
2½ teaspoons baking powder
¾ teaspoon salt
⅓ cup shortening
¾ cup milk
1 (4-ounce) package sliced
  pepperoni
8 ounces Cheddar cheese

Mix flour, baking powder and salt in bowl. Cut in shortening with pastry blender until crumbly. Stir in just enough milk to form a dough which leaves side of bowl. Knead lightly on floured surface 10 times. Roll into square ½ inch thick. Cut into 4-inch squares. Place 3 pepperoni slices in row down center of each square. Slice cheese into ¼ x 4-inch strips. Place 1 strip on pepperoni on each square. Roll from 1 side to enclose filling; seal edges. Roll on floured surface until smooth. Place seam side down on ungreased baking sheet. Bake at 450°F. for 15 minutes or until golden brown. Yield: 12 servings.

Approx Per Serving: Cal 249; Prot 9.4 gr; T Fat 16.6 gr; Chol 26.9 mg; Carbo 15.3 gr; Sod 458.1 mg; Potas 76.7 mg.

Amanda Duncan, Ottawa

VEGETABLE BARS

1 (8-count) package
  refrigerator crescent rolls
8 ounces cream cheese,
  softened
¼ cup sour cream
6 tablespoons mayonnaise-
  type salad dressing
½ envelope ranch-style salad
  dressing mix
½ cup shredded Cheddar
  cheese
Assorted fresh vegetables

Separate roll dough into rectangles. Place in 9 x 13-inch baking pan, stretching to cover and sealing edges and perforations. Bake at 350°F. for 8 to 9 minutes or until light brown. Cool. Combine cream cheese, sour cream, salad dressing and salad dressing mix in mixer bowl; mix until smooth. Spread over crust. Mix Cheddar cheese with assorted chopped vegetables such as broccoli, carrots, cauliflower, radishes and green peppers in bowl. Sprinkle evenly over cream cheese layer. Cover with plastic wrap, pressing vegetables lightly into cream cheese. Chill, covered, for 3 hours to overnight. Cut into bars. Yield: 24 bars.

Approx Per Bar: Cal 100; Prot 2.0 gr; T Fat 8.2 gr; Chol 15.7 mg; Carbo 4.6 gr; Sod 141.7 mg; Potas 33.5 mg.
Nutritional information does not include vegetables.

Janice K. Motes, Scottsville

Flint Hills Brunch

FRUIT KABOB
page 165

FRUIT DIP
page 14

EGGS ELEGANTE
page 98

PARTY POTATOES
page 115

CINNAMON BREAKFAST APPLES
page 120

SWEDISH COFFEE RING
page 176

CRANBERRY TEA
page 17

"SKY NUGGETS" by Jami Krusemark

SMOKEY BEAN SOUP

1 pound sausage
1 (16-ounce) can kidney beans
1 (16-ounce) can butter beans
2 (16-ounce) cans pork
  and beans
8 ounces bacon, crisp-fried,
  crumbled
1 cup chopped onion
1 cup catsup
3 tablespoons vinegar
¼ cup packed brown sugar
1 tablespoon liquid smoke
½ teaspoon garlic salt

Brown sausage in skillet, stirring until crumbly; drain. Combine with all undrained beans, bacon and onion in Crock•Pot. Add remaining ingredients; mix well. Cook on Low for 4 to 6 hours. Serve with corn bread.
Yield: 10 servings.

Approx Per Serving: Cal 402; Prot 17.5 gr; T Fat 16.4 gr; Chol 29.7 mg; Carbo 47.3 gr; Sod 1194.7 mg; Potas 636.6 mg.

Cindy Adams, Yates Center

TEN-BEAN SOUP

1 pound mixed dried beans
2 cups chopped cooked ham
2 quarts water
1 large onion, chopped
1 (16-ounce) can tomatoes,
  chopped
1 teaspoon chili powder
1 clove of garlic, minced

Combine beans with water to cover in bowl. Let stand overnight. Drain. Combine beans and ham with 2 quarts water in large saucepan. Cook for 2½ to 3 hours. Add remaining ingredients. Simmer for 30 minutes. Season with salt and pepper to taste. Yield: 10 servings.

Approx Per Serving: Cal 252; Prot 16.7 gr; T Fat 7.0 gr; Chol 24.9 mg; Carbo 31.4 gr; Sod 282.0 mg; Potas 736.8 mg.

Merle L. Eyestone, Retired Executive Director Kansas 4-H Foundation, Manhattan

CREAM OF BROCCOLI SOUP

2 cups chopped celery
1 cup finely chopped onion
1 (10-ounce) package frozen
  chopped broccoli
1 cup water
1 cup cottage cheese
2 cups milk
1 (10-ounce) can cream of
  chicken soup
½ teaspoon salt
⅛ teaspoon pepper

Combine celery, onion, broccoli and water in saucepan. Simmer until vegetables are tender. Combine cottage cheese and milk in blender or food processor container; process until smooth. Add to chicken soup in bowl; mix well. Stir cottage cheese mixture into broccoli mixture. Heat just to serving temperature; do not boil. Add salt and pepper. Yield: 6 servings.

Approx Per Serving: Cal 167; Prot 11.9 gr; T Fat 7.2 gr; Chol 23.1 mg;
Carbo 15.0 gr; Sod 774.9 mg; Potas 479.6 mg.

Debbie Lindsten, Kanorado

MICROWAVE CREAM OF BROCCOLI AND CHEESE SOUP

1 (10-ounce) package frozen
  chopped broccoli
2 cups chopped celery
1 cup finely chopped onion
1 cup (8 ounces) cottage cheese
2 cups milk
1 (10-ounce) can cream of
  chicken soup
½ teaspoon salt
⅛ teaspoon white pepper

Mix broccoli, celery and onion in 2½-quart glass dish. Microwave, covered, on HIGH (100% power) for 6 minutes, stirring after 3 minutes. Place cottage cheese in blender container; process until smooth. Add milk gradually, processing until smooth. Add chicken soup; blend well. Stir into broccoli mixture. Microwave on HIGH (100% power) for 3 minutes or just until heated through; do not allow to boil. Add salt and pepper. Yield: 6 servings.

Approx Per Serving: Cal 167; Prot ;11.9 gr; T Fat 7.2 gr; Chol 23.1 mg;
Carbo 15.0 gr; Sod 774.9 mg; Potas 479.6 mg.

Eileen R. Pratt, Selden

CABBAGE SOUP

1 pound ground beef
6 cups water
2 cups chopped peeled potatoes
1 cup chopped celery
1 cup whole kernel corn
2 onions, chopped
2 cups shredded cabbage
4 cups stewed tomatoes
¼ cup uncooked rice
1½ teaspoons salt

Brown ground beef in saucepan, stirring until crumbly; drain. Add water. Bring to a boil. Stir in vegetables. Bring to a boil. Add rice and salt. Simmer for 1½ hours. Yield: 8 servings.

Approx Per Serving: Cal 231; Prot 13.8 gr; T Fat 8.8 gr; Chol 38.3 mg; Carbo 25.5 gr; Sod 649.0 mg; Potas 704.8 mg.

Laura L. Roede, Wichita

CHEESE SOUP

2½ cups chopped peeled
  potatoes
1 cup chopped celery
½ cup chopped onion
4 chicken bouillon cubes
6 cups water
1 (20-ounce) package frozen
  California mix vegetables
2 (10-ounce) cans cream of
  chicken soup
16 ounces Velveeta cheese,
  shredded

Combine potatoes, celery, onion, bouillon and water in saucepan. Cook until vegetables are tender. Add frozen vegetables. Cook for 10 to 15 minutes. Stir in chicken soup and cheese. Cook over medium heat for 20 to 30 minutes longer. Yield: 6 servings.

Approx Per Serving: Cal 444; Prot 22.7 gr; T Fat 23.4 gr; Chol 64.4 mg; Carbo 37.8 gr; Sod 2734.5 mg; Potas 783.1 mg.

Karen Mulligan, St. Marys

CHEDDAR CHOWDER

2 cups chopped peeled potatoes
½ cup sliced carrots
½ cup sliced celery
¼ cup chopped onion
2 cups boiling water
¼ cup margarine
¼ cup all-purpose flour
1½ teaspoons salt
¼ teaspoon pepper
2 cups milk
2 cups (8 ounces) shredded
   Cheddar cheese
1 cup chopped ham

Mix vegetables with boiling water in saucepan. Simmer, covered, for 10 minutes. Set aside. Melt margarine in saucepan. Stir in flour, salt and pepper. Whisk in milk gradually. Cook until thickened, stirring constantly. Stir in cheese until melted. Add vegetables with cooking liquid and ham. Heat just to serving temperature, stirring occasionally; do not boil. Yield: 6 servings.

Approx Per Serving: Cal 404; Prot 19.1 gr; T Fat 27.9 gr; Chol 69.4 mg; Carbo 19.2 gr; Sod 1124.5 mg; Potas 489.8 mg.

Cheryl Thole, Manhattan

GET-TOGETHER HARVEST SOUP

3 cups cubed peeled potatoes
½ cup sliced carrots
½ cup sliced celery
½ cup chopped onion
1 cup water
1 chicken bouillon cube
2 tablespoons all-purpose flour
1½ to 2½ cups milk
2 teaspoons parsley
8 ounces Velveeta cheese

Combine vegetables with water and bouillon in saucepan. Cook for 15 to 20 minutes or until vegetables are tender. Blend flour and milk in bowl. Add to soup. Cook until thickened, stirring constantly. Stir in parsley and cheese. Season with salt and pepper to taste. Cook until cheese is melted. Yield: 6 servings.

Approx Per Serving: Cal 273; Prot 13.8 gr; T Fat 13 gr; Chol 38.2 mg; Carbo 24.9 gr; Sod 680.8 mg; Potas 1594.9 mg.

Angela LeSage, Beloit

GOLDEN CHEESE SOUP

3 cups chopped peeled potatoes
½ cup chopped celery
½ cup chopped carrots
1 cup water
1 chicken bouillon cube
1 teaspoon parsley flakes
1 teaspoon instant
  minced onion
½ teaspoon salt
½ teaspoon pepper
2 cups milk
2 tablespoons all-purpose flour
8 ounces Velveeta cheese,
  cubed

Combine vegetables, water, bouillon, parsley flakes, onion and seasonings in saucepan. Simmer for 20 minutes or until tender. Mash vegetables slightly if desired. Combine milk gradually with flour in bowl. Add to soup. Simmer until thickened, stirring constantly. Stir in cheese until melted. Yield: 6 servings.

Approx Per Serving: Cal 249; Prot 12.5 gr; T Fat 12.1 gr; Chol 39.1 mg; Carbo 23.0 gr; Sod 1001.1 mg; Potas 582.7 mg.

Helen Dillon, Topeka

PEA SOUP

1 (1-pound) package dried
  split peas
1 smoked ham bone
2 quarts cold water
1½ cups chopped onion
1 clove of garlic, minced
½ cup chopped celery
½ cup chopped carrots
3 chicken bouillon cubes
1 teaspoon sugar
1 bay leaf
3 whole cloves
½ teaspoon savory

Mix dried peas, ham bone, water and remaining ingredients in large saucepan. Simmer, covered, for 2 to 3 hours or to desired consistency. Remove bay leaf, cloves and ham bone. Remove meat from bone and return to soup. Season with salt and pepper to taste. Heat to serving temperature. Yield: 8 servings.

Approx Per Serving: Cal 310; Prot 21.6 gr; T Fat 8.5 gr; Chol 32.3 mg; Carbo 37.8 gr; Sod 655.5 mg; Potas 721.0 mg.

Jon Wefald, President, Kansas State University, Manhattan

POTATO SOUP

6 medium potatoes, peeled,
  chopped
1 cup chopped celery
2 tablespoons chopped parsley
1 chicken bouillon cube
¼ teaspoon MSG
½ teaspoon seasoned salt
⅛ teaspoon red pepper
1 medium carrot, shredded
½ cup chopped onion
2 tablespoons butter
2 tablespoons all-purpose flour
6 cups milk

Combine potatoes, celery, parsley, bouillon, seasonings and water to cover in 2-quart saucepan. Cook until vegetables are tender; do not drain. Mash half the potatoes and celery. Sauté carrot and onion in butter in 1-quart saucepan. Stir in flour. Add milk gradually. Cook until thickened, stirring constantly. Add to potato mixture. Heat to serving temperature. Yield: 6 servings.

Approx Per Serving: Cal 361; Prot 13.7 gr; T Fat 12.7 gr; Chol 46.5 mg; Carbo 49.3 gr; Sod 613.6 mg; Potas 1258.5 mg.

Janie Lou Kruse, Morrill

CREAMY POTATO SOUP

3 medium potatoes, peeled,
  cubed
8 slices crisp-fried bacon,
  crumbled
1 cup chopped onion
1 cup water
1 (10-ounce) can cream of
  chicken soup
1 cup sour cream
1½ cups milk
2 tablespoons chopped parsley
½ teaspoon salt
Pepper to taste

Bring potatoes, bacon, onion and water to a boil in saucepan; reduce heat. Simmer for 15 to 20 minutes or until potatoes are tender. Add soup and sour cream; mix well. Stir in milk gradually. Add parsley, salt and pepper. Heat just to serving temperature; do not boil. Yield: 7 cups.

Approx Per Cup: Cal 260; Prot 8.2 gr; T Fat 15.3 gr; Chol 32.8 mg; Carbo 23.0 gr; Sod 633.0 mg; Potas 543.4 mg.

Vivian Bebermeyer Funk, Garden City

POTATO AND CREAM CHEESE SOUP

1 cup shredded carrots
½ cup chopped celery
2 cups shredded potatoes
1 medium onion, chopped
2 cups water
1 teaspoon salt
¼ teaspoon hot pepper sauce
8 ounces cream cheese,
  chopped
2 cups milk
2 tablespoons butter, softened
2 tablespoons all-purpose flour

Bring vegetables, water, salt and pepper sauce to a boil in saucepan; reduce heat. Simmer, covered, for 15 minutes or until vegetables are tender. Add cream cheese and milk. Simmer until cream cheese is melted, stirring constantly. Blend butter and flour in cup. Add to soup. Cook until thickened, stirring constantly. Garnish with parsley. Yield: 6 servings.

Approx Per Serving: Cal 295; Prot 7.9 gr; T Fat 21.1 gr; Chol 65.2 mg; Carbo 19.9 gr; Sod 563.7 mg; Potas 493.3 mg.

Karla Fisher, Manhattan

MEXICAN POTATO SOUP

4 cups chopped peeled potatoes
½ cup chopped onion
2 tablespoons margarine
2 tomatoes, seeded, chopped
2 tablespoons margarine
4 cups hot water
6 chicken bouillon cubes
1 pound ham, chopped
1½ cups (12 ounces) sour
  cream

Cook potatoes in water to cover in saucepan for 12 to 15 minutes or until tender; drain. Sauté chopped onion in 2 tablespoons margarine in skillet. Remove onion with slotted spoon. Sauté tomatoes in 2 tablespoons margarine in skillet. Add onion, tomatoes, hot water, bouillon, ham and sour cream to potatoes. Simmer for 15 minutes; do not boil. Yield: 6 servings.

Approx Per Serving: Cal 354; Prot 10.3 gr; T Fat 25.2 gr; Chol 49.1 mg; Carbo 23.0 gr; Sod 1264.1 mg; Potas 672.8 mg.

Ilene Bunger, Beloit

POTATO SOUP SUPREME

4 cups cubed peeled potatoes
1 small onion, chopped
1 teaspoon salt
¾ cup water
3 cups milk
¼ cup butter
1 teaspoon chives
¼ teaspoon pepper
8 ounces Velveeta cheese
1 (2.5-ounce) package dried
   beef

Combine potatoes, onion, salt and water in 2-quart saucepan; cover. Bring to a boil; reduce heat. Simmer for 20 minutes or until potatoes are tender; drain. Mash potatoes slightly. Add milk, butter, chives and pepper. Simmer until heated through. Stir in cheese and dried beef. Simmer until cheese is melted.
Yield: 4 servings.

Approx Per Serving: Cal 562; Prot 27.3 gr; T Fat 32.8 gr; Chol 113.5 mg; Carbo 40.5 gr; Sod 2439.4 mg; Potas 1076.0 mg.

Alyce Springer, Riley

HEARTY TOMATO SOUP

1 onion, chopped
1 stalk, celery, chopped
1 carrot, chopped
1 clove of garlic, minced
2 tablespoons oil
2 tablespoons whole wheat
   flour
1½ cups cooked rice
1 (28-ounce) can tomatoes,
   chopped
1 tablespoon sugar
1 teaspoon oregano
1 teaspoon basil
2 teaspoons salt
4 white peppercorns
3 cups hot milk
1 tablespoon butter

Sauté onion, celery, carrot and garlic in oil in 4-quart saucepan until onion is golden. Add flour and rice. Sauté until rice is golden. Stir in tomatoes, sugar and seasonings. Simmer for 15 minutes or longer. Purée in blender if desired. Add milk and butter. Heat just to serving temperature; do not boil. Yield: 6 servings.

Approx Per Serving: Cal 253; Prot 7.6 gr; T Fat 11.1 gr; Chol 23.0 mg; Carbo 31.8 gr; Sod 1175.8 mg; Potas 597.5 mg.

Betty Banaka, Manhattan

ASTRONAUT SOUP

12 ounces ground beef
1 cup chopped tomatoes
1 cup frozen carrots
1 cup frozen corn
1 tablespoon instant minced
    onion
1 tablespoon instant beef
    bouillon
2 cups water
¼ teaspoon seasoned salt
⅛ teaspoon pepper
½ cup (2 ounces) shredded
    Cheddar cheese

Place ground beef in glass dish. Separate into pieces with fork. Microwave until no longer pink; drain. Combine ground beef with tomatoes, carrots, corn, onion, bouillon, water and seasonings in saucepan. Bring to a boil; reduce heat. Simmer, covered, for 10 to 15 minutes. Ladle into serving bowls. Sprinkle with cheese. Yield: 4 servings.

Approx Per Serving: Cal 298; Prot 21.1 gr; T Fat 17.6 gr; Chol 73.7 mg;
    Carbo 14.9 gr; Sod 1269.3 mg; Potas 453.7 mg.

Jeremiah Stark, Lenora

CHILI

2 bricks chili
1 cup water
2 pounds ground beef
½ teaspoon salt
1 teaspoon Worcestershire
    sauce
2 (10-ounce) cans nacho
    cheese soup
1 (8-ounce) can tomato sauce

Chop chili into 3-quart saucepan. Add water. Simmer until well mixed. Sauté ground beef with salt in skillet, stirring until crumbly; drain. Stir in Worcestershire sauce. Add to chili. Stir in soup and tomato sauce. Simmer for 20 minutes. Serve with crackers, sandwich and salad. Yield: 20 servings.

Nutritional analysis not available.

Alice Weeks, Freeport

CROCK•POT CHILI

2 pounds coarsely ground beef
1 medium white onion,
  chopped
1 (16-ounce) can red kidney
  beans
1 (32-ounce) can whole
  tomatoes
1 (22-ounce) carton tomato
  sauce
2 tablespoons chili powder
2 tablespoons cumin
1/4 teaspoon oregano
1/4 teaspoon cayenne pepper
1/4 teaspoon black pepper
1/4 teaspoon salt

Cook ground beef with onion in saucepan until browned, stirring until ground beef is crumbly; drain. Drain and rinse beans. Drain and chop tomatoes. Combine ground beef, beans, tomatoes, tomato sauce and seasonings in Crock•Pot. Add water to cover. Cook on High for 2 hours. Yield: 8 servings.

Approx Per Serving: Cal 354; Prot 26.2 gr; T Fat 17.4 gr; Chol 76.6 mg;
    Carbo 24.3 gr; Sod 763.1 mg; Potas 991.8 mg.

Mark A. Ummen, Great Bend

COLD WEATHER STEW

2 pounds ground beef
1 medium onion, chopped
1 (16-ounce) can tomatoes
1 (16-ounce) can whole
  kernel corn
1 (16-ounce) can peas
1 (16-ounce) can carrots
1 (16-ounce) can potatoes
1 (8-ounce) can tomato sauce
1/4 cup Worcestershire sauce
3/4 cup chili sauce
1/2 cup steak sauce
1/4 cup catsup
1/4 cup vinegar
1/4 cup sugar

Brown ground beef in large saucepan, stirring until crumbly; drain. Add onion, undrained vegetables and remaining ingredients; mix well. Simmer for several hours. Flavor improves with longer cooking time. Yield: 8 servings.

Approx Per Serving: Cal 489; Prot 27.4 gr; T Fat 17.9 gr; Chol 76.6 mg;
    Carbo 58.5 gr; Sod 1242.1 mg; Potas 1080.2 mg.

Olive Ann McCormick, Kingman

CONNIE'S SPECIAL CHILI

2 pounds ground beef
1 large onion, chopped
1 large green bell pepper
2 teaspoons sugar
1 envelope chili seasoning mix
Chili powder and garlic powder
  to taste
3 (16-ounce) cans chili beans,
  drained
1 (15-ounce) can tomato sauce
1 (6-ounce) can tomato paste
1 (29-ounce) can tomatoes
2 (2.75-ounce) milk chocolate
  candy bars

Cook ground beef with onion and green pepper in large saucepan until browned, stirring until ground beef is crumbly; drain. Stir in sugar and chili seasoning mix. Season with chili powder, garlic powder, salt and pepper to taste. Add beans, tomato sauce, tomato paste and tomatoes; mix well. Break chocolate bars into center of chili. Heat until chocolate is melted, stirring chocolate away from side of pan. Simmer for 1 hour or longer. Yield: 10 servings.

Approx Per Serving: Cal 513; Prot 28.8 gr; T Fat 22.6 gr; Chol 70.5 mg;
    Carbo 51.0 gr; Sod 1136.5 mg; Potas 1108.8 mg.
Nutritional information does not include chili seasoning mix or seasonings to taste.

Connie Walters, Lawrence

PLAZA III SOUP

1½ pounds ground Kansas
  sirloin
¼ cup melted margarine
½ cup all-purpose flour
4 (10-ounce) cans beef
  consommé
½ cup chopped carrots
½ cup chopped celery
½ cup chopped onion
1 (8-ounce) can tomatoes
2 beef bouillon cubes
1½ teaspoons Kitchen Bouquet
½ teaspoon pepper
½ teaspoon mixed marjoram,
  rosemary and thyme
1 teaspoon MSG
1 (10-ounce) package frozen
  mixed vegetables

Brown ground sirloin in skillet, stirring until crumbly; drain. Blend margarine and flour in 4-quart saucepan. Cook over medium heat for 3 minutes, stirring constantly. Add consommé. Bring to a boil, stirring constantly. Add carrots, celery, onion, tomatoes, bouillon and seasonings. Bring to a boil; reduce heat. Simmer for 30 minutes. Add ground sirloin and frozen vegetables. Simmer for 15 minutes longer. Yield: 6 servings.

Approx Per Serving: Cal 399; Prot 35.9 gr; T Fat 17.7 gr; Chol 118.7 mg;
    Carbo 23.1 gr; Sod 1993.4 mg; Potas 762.0 mg.

Glee S. Smith Jr., Immediate Past Chairman,
Board of Trustees Kansas 4-H Foundation, Larned

DADDY'S CHICKEN GUMBO

¼ cup oil
1 cup all-purpose flour
1 onion, chopped
2 cloves of garlic, chopped
1 large chicken, cut up
2 (6-inch) pieces smoked
  sausage
8 cups water
1 tablespoon salt
1 teaspoon black pepper
1 teaspoon red pepper
½ green bell pepper, chopped

Heat oil in large saucepan. Stir in flour. Cook until medium brown, stirring constantly. Add onion and garlic. Cook until onion is transparent. Add chicken and sausage. Cook for 10 minutes or until brown. Add water and seasonings; reduce heat. Simmer, covered, for 35 minutes. Add green pepper. Simmer for 10 minutes longer. Serve over rice. Yield: 6 servings.

Approx Per Serving: Cal 441; Prot 34.7 gr; T Fat 24.2 gr; Chol 96.9 mg; Carbo 19.2 gr; Sod 1450.7 mg; Potas 394.9 mg.

China DeSpain, Lebo

MOTHER HAROLD'S FAMOUS CHICKEN SOUP

1 (3-pound) chicken, cut up,
  skinned
2 medium onions, chopped
2 potatoes, chopped
6 carrots, chopped
2 medium turnips
5 cloves of garlic, minced
1 (6-ounce) package frozen
  noodles
1 bunch broccoli, chopped
8 ounces fresh mushrooms,
  sliced

Mix chicken, 1 onion, 1 potato, 2 carrots, 1 turnip, garlic and water to cover in large saucepan. Season with salt and pepper to taste. Cook, covered, over medium heat for 45 minutes or until chicken is tender. Remove and bone chicken. Add noodles and remaining vegetables to broth. Chop chicken into bite-sized pieces. Add to soup. Simmer, covered, for 20 minutes or until vegetables are tender-crisp. Yield: 10 servings.

Approx Per Serving: Cal 207; Prot 21.2 gr; T Fat 5.4 gr; Chol 48.7 mg; Carbo 19.4 gr; Sod 78.9 mg; Potas 850.6 mg.
Nutritional information does not include frozen noodles.

Harold A. Stones, Executive Vice President, Kansas Bankers Association, Topeka

BLUEBERRY SALAD

1 (3-ounce) package raspberry
  gelatin
2 cups boiling water
1 envelope unflavored gelatin
½ cup cold water
1 cup half and half
1 cup sugar
1 teaspoon vanilla extract
8 ounces cream cheese,
  softened
½ cup pecans
1 (3-ounce) package raspberry
  gelatin
1 cup boiling water
1 (21-ounce) can blueberry pie
  filling

Combine 1 package raspberry gelatin and 2 cups boiling water in bowl; stir until dissolved. Pour into deep glass dish. Chill until firm. Soften unflavored gelatin in ½ cup cold water in saucepan. Add half and half, sugar and vanilla. Heat until gelatin is dissolved, stirring constantly; do not boil. Remove from heat. Stir in cream cheese until melted. Add pecans. Pour over congealed layer. Chill until firm. Dissolve remaining package raspberry gelatin in 1 cup boiling water in bowl. Stir in pie filling. Pour over cream cheese layer. Chill until firm. Yield: 8 servings.

Approx Per Serving: Cal 468; Prot 6.8 gr; T Fat 19.4 gr; Chol 44.4 mg;
  Carbo 69.2 gr; Sod 153.3 mg; Potas 149.7 mg.

Judy Wiseman, Howard

BLACK CHERRY GELATIN SALAD

1 (8-ounce) can black bing
  cherries
Juice of ½ lemon
1 (3-ounce) package black
  cherry gelatin
1 cup boiling water
¼ cup chopped pecans
4 ounces cream cheese, cubed

Drain cherries, reserving liquid. Add lemon juice and enough water to reserved liquid to measure 1 cup. Dissolve gelatin in boiling water in bowl. Stir in reserved liquid. Chill until partially set. Add cherries, pecans and cream cheese; mix well. Chill until set. Yield: 4 servings.

Approx Per Serving: Cal 290; Prot 5.6 gr; T Fat 16.1 gr; Chol 31.5 mg;
  Carbo 34.1 gr; Sod 139.2 mg; Potas 202.2 mg.

Rosemary Busset, Manhattan

CHERRY SALAD

1 (21-ounce) can cherry pie
  filling
1 (16-ounce) can crushed
  pineapple, drained
1 (14-ounce) can sweetened
  condensed milk
1 cup miniature marshmallows
½ cup chopped pecans
1 (12-ounce) carton frozen
  whipped topping, thawed

Combine pie filling, pineapple, condensed milk, marshmallows and pecans in bowl; mix well. Fold in whipped topping. Chill until serving time. Yield: 6 servings.

Approx Per Serving: Cal 730; Prot 9.4 gr; T Fat 29.0 gr; Chol 30.4 mg; Carbo 112.6 gr; Sod 117.7 mg; Potas 431.3 mg.

Dennis Thurman, Sr., Caldwell

CHERRY GELATIN SALAD

1 (3-ounce) package cherry
  gelatin
1 (3-ounce) package lemon
  gelatin
2 cups boiling water
1 cup cold water
1 (21-ounce) can cherry pie
  filling
1 (20-ounce) can crushed
  pineapple
1 (8-ounce) carton whipped
  topping
½ cup chopped pecans

Dissolve gelatins in boiling water in bowl. Add cold water. Reserve ½ cup mixture for topping. Add pie filling and pineapple to remaining gelatin; mix well. Pour into 8x12-inch dish. Chill until firm. Fold whipped topping and pecans into reserved gelatin mixture. Spread over congealed layer. Chill until serving time. Yield: 10 servings.

Approx Per Serving: Cal 289; Prot 2.7 gr; T Fat 9.9 gr; Chol 0.0 mg; Carbo 49.7 gr; Sod 60.3 mg; Potas 136.5 mg.

Robin Beneda, Oberlin

CRANBERRY FLUFF

1 pound fresh cranberries
2 cups sugar
1 (8-ounce) can juice-pack
    crushed pineapple
1 (11-ounce) can mandarin
    oranges
2 cups miniature marshmallows
1 (8-ounce) carton frozen
    whipped topping, thawed
1 cup chopped pecans

Place cranberries in food processor container; process until ground. Mix cranberries and sugar in bowl. Let stand overnight. Drain pineapple and oranges. Add to cranberries; mix well. Fold in marshmallows, whipped topping and pecans. Chill until serving time. Yield: 10 servings.

Approx Per Serving: Cal 386; Prot 2.0 gr; T Fat 14.5 gr; Chol 0.1 mg; Carbo 66.7 gr; Sod 11.2 mg; Potas 169.6 mg.

Steven Melton Family, Stockton

CRANBERRY-APPLE SALAD

12 ounces cranberries
4 stalks celery
2 apples, cored
1 (8½-ounce) can pineapple
Juice of 2 oranges
1 cup sugar
2 (3-ounce) packages
    strawberry gelatin

Grind cranberries, celery and apples. Drain pineapple, reserving juice. Add pineapple, orange juice and sugar to ground mixture in bowl; mix well. Add enough water to reserved pineapple juice to measure 3 cups. Bring to a boil in saucepan. Add gelatin; stir until gelatin is dissolved. Stir into fruit mixture. Chill overnight. Yield: 8 servings.

Approx Per Serving: Cal 261; Prot 2.7 gr; T Fat 0.7 gr; Chol 0.0 mg; Carbo 64.8 gr; Sod 94.9 mg; Potas 277.4 mg.

Mary Stanley, Manhattan

CRANBERRY MARBLE SWIRL SALAD

2 (3-ounce) packages cherry
    gelatin
2 cups boiling water
1 (16-ounce) can whole
    cranberry sauce
1 (8-ounce) can juice-pack
    crushed pineapple
1 cup sour cream

Dissolve gelatin in boiling water in bowl. Stir in cranberry sauce and pineapple. Chill until partially set. Spoon into 8 x 10-inch dish. Spread sour cream over top; swirl with knife to marbleize. Chill until set. Yield: 10 servings.

Approx Per Serving: Cal 212; Prot 2.5 gr; T Fat 5.0 gr; Chol 10.1 mg; Carbo 41.7 gr; Sod 67.1 mg; Potas 109.9 mg.

Sara Grunder, Winfield

FRUIT RELISH SALAD

1½ cups frozen cranberries
1¼ cups pineapple juice
2 tablespoons lemon juice
¼ cup sugar
1 tablespoon brown sugar
¼ teaspoon cinnamon
⅛ teaspoon cloves
⅛ teaspoon ginger
1 (8-ounce) can unsweetened
  crushed pineapple, drained
1 (11-ounce) can mandarin
  oranges, drained

Combine cranberries, pineapple juice, lemon juice, sugar, brown sugar and spices in saucepan. Bring to a boil over medium heat. Cook for 7 to 10 minutes or until mixture is thickened and cranberries pop, stirring constantly. Remove from heat. Stir in pineapple and oranges. Pour into dish. Chill, covered, for 6 hours to overnight. Yield: 10 servings.

Approx Per Serving: Cal 77; Prot 0.4 gr; T Fat 0.2 gr; Chol 0.0 mg;
    Carbo 19.4 gr; Sod 1.7 mg; Potas 115.2 mg.

Maureen Baity, Burrton

HOLIDAY FROZEN SALAD

1 (8-ounce) can white cherries
1 (8-ounce) can pineapple,
  crushed
16 maraschino cherry halves
1 orange, peeled, chopped
1 banana, sliced
1 tablespoon lemon juice
¼ cup sugar
1 cup (½ pint) whipping cream
⅓ cup mayonnaise

Drain canned cherries and pineapple. Combine with maraschino cherries, orange, banana and lemon juice in bowl. Sprinkle with sugar. Whip cream in bowl until soft peaks form. Fold in mayonnaise and fruit. Pour into freezer tray. Freeze until firm. Cut into squares. Serve on lettuce leaf. Yield: 8 servings.

Approx Per Serving: Cal 287; Prot 1.5 gr; T Fat 18.8 gr; Chol 46.1 mg;
    Carbo 30.9 gr; Sod 66.0 mg; Potas 206.2 mg.

J. Chatterton-Papineau, Gardner

FROZEN FRUITCAKE SALAD

1 cup sour cream
½ (4½-ounce) carton frozen
  whipped topping, thawed
½ cup sugar
2 tablespoons lemon juice
1 teaspoon vanilla extract
1 (13-ounce) can crushed
  pineapple, drained
2 medium bananas, chopped
½ cup chopped red candied
  cherries
½ cup chopped green candied
  cherries
½ cup chopped walnuts

Blend sour cream, whipped topping, sugar, lemon juice and vanilla in bowl. Fold in fruit and walnuts. Spoon into 4½-cup ring mold. Freeze until firm. Unmold onto lettuce-lined serving plate. Garnish with additional candied cherries. Let stand for 10 minutes before serving. Yield: 8 servings.

Approx Per Serving: Cal 307; Prot 2.7 gr; T Fat 12.8 gr; Chol 12.6 mg; Carbo 49.1 gr; Sod 18.5 mg; Potas 274.3 mg.

Linda Coleman, Valley Falls

FROZEN FRUIT SALAD

¾ cup sugar
8 ounces cream cheese,
  softened
1 (10-ounce) package frozen
  strawberries, thawed
1 cup pineapple tidbits
2 bananas, sliced
½ cup chopped pecans
1 (8-ounce) carton frozen
  whipped topping, thawed

Cream sugar and cream cheese in bowl until fluffy. Combine fruit and pecans in bowl; mix well. Fold in whipped topping. Add to creamed mixture; mix well. Spoon into 9 x 13-inch dish. Freeze overnight. Let stand for 30 minutes before serving. Yield: 12 servings.

Approx Per Serving: Cal 270; Prot 2.6 gr; T Fat 15.5 gr; Chol 21.0 mg; Carbo 33.0 gr; Sod 52.7 mg; Potas 167.7 mg.

Edna Richert, Assaria

LIME-CHEESE GELATIN SALAD

1 (3-ounce) package lime
  gelatin
1½ cups boiling water
8 ounces cream cheese,
  chopped
½ (10-ounce) package
  marshmallows
1 (16-ounce) can juice-pack
  crushed pineapple
1 tablespoon mayonnaise
1 (8-ounce) carton frozen
  whipped topping, thawed

Dissolve gelatin in boiling water in bowl. Stir in cream cheese and marshmallows. Chill until partially set. Add pineapple and mayonnaise; mix well. Fold in whipped topping. Pour into 9 x 13-inch dish. Chill until set. Yield: 12 servings.

Approx Per Serving: Cal 234; Prot 2.8 gr; T Fat 12.8 gr; Chol 21.9 mg; Carbo 28.7 gr; Sod 86.4 mg; Potas 74.1 mg.

Bruce M. Rimbaugh, Phillipsburg

CHERRY PEPSI SALAD

¾ cup sugar
¾ cup water
1 (21-ounce) can cherry pie
  filling
2 (3-ounce) packages cherry
  gelatin
1 cup Pepsi-Cola
1 (8-ounce) can juice-pack
  crushed pineapple
½ cup chopped pecans
1 (8-ounce) carton frozen
  whipped topping, thawed
½ cup (2-ounces) shredded
  Cheddar cheese

Bring sugar and water to a boil in saucepan. Stir in pie filling. Bring to a boil; remove from heat. Stir in gelatin until dissolved. Add cola, pineapple and pecans; mix well. Pour into serving dish. Chill until set. Top with whipped topping and cheese. Yield: 8 servings.

Approx Per Serving: Cal 438; Prot 5.0 gr; T Fat 14.6 gr; Chol 7.0 mg; Carbo 74.7 gr; Sod 124.5 mg; Potas 131.1 mg.

Phyllis Mitchell, Burns

RAINBOW GELATIN SALAD

1 (3-ounce) package raspberry
  gelatin
1 cup boiling water
2 cups sour cream
18 tablespoons cold water
1 (3-ounce) package orange
  gelatin
1 (3-ounce) package black
  cherry gelatin
1 (3-ounce) package lemon
  gelatin
1 (3-ounce) package lime
  gelatin
1 (3-ounce) package strawberry
  gelatin

Combine raspberry gelatin and 1 cup boiling water in bowl; stir until dissolved. Combine ½ cup raspberry gelatin with ⅓ cup sour cream in bowl. Pour into 9x13-inch dish. Chill until firm. Mix 3 tablespoons cold water into remaining raspberry gelatin. Pour over congealed layer. Repeat processes with each remaining gelatin flavor, water and sour cream, chilling each layer until firm.
Yield: 20 servings.

Approx Per Serving: Cal 144; Prot 3.1 gr; T Fat 4.8 gr; Chol 10.1 mg;
  Carbo 23.4 gr; Sod 93.3 mg; Potas 86.7 mg.

Todd Gurley, Salina

SEVEN-UP SALAD

2 (3-ounce) packages (any
  flavor) gelatin
2 cups boiling water
2 (10-ounce) bottles of 7-Up
1 (20-ounce) can juice-pack
  crushed pineapple
1 cup miniature marshmallows
3 bananas, sliced
1 egg, beaten
½ cup sugar
2 tablespoons all-purpose flour
1 cup whipped topping
½ cup shredded Cheddar
  cheese

Dissolve gelatin in boiling water in bowl. Add 2 bottles of 7-Up. Cool. Drain pineapple, reserving juice. Fold in pineapple, marshmallows and bananas. Pour into 9x13-inch dish. Chill until set. Combine egg, sugar, flour and reserved pineapple juice in saucepan. Cook until thickened, stirring constantly. Cool. Fold in whipped topping gently. Spread over congealed layer. Top with cheese. Yield: 20 servings.

Approx Per Serving: Cal 136; Prot 2.3 gr; T Fat 2.1 gr; Chol 15.5 mg;
  Carbo 28.5 gr; Sod 52.1 mg; Potas 121.7 mg.

Colleen Budenbender, St. George

CRUNCHY CHICKEN SALAD

⅔ cup mayonnaise
⅔ cup sour cream
⅓ cup pineapple juice
½ teaspoon seasoned salt
1 tablespoon sugar
5 cups chopped cooked chicken
1 cup ¼-inch celery slices
½ cup sliced water chestnuts
1 cup drained pineapple tidbits
6 cantaloupe slices

Blend mayonnaise, sour cream, pineapple juice, seasoned salt and sugar in small bowl. Combine chicken, celery, water chestnuts and pineapple in bowl. Add sour cream mixture; toss lightly. Chill until serving time. Serve on cantaloupe slices on salad plates.
Yield: 6 servings.

Approx Per Serving: Cal 529; Prot 40.7 gr; T Fat 29.7 gr; Chol 124.3 mg; Carbo 25.1 gr; Sod 456.0 mg; Potas 920.2 mg.

Mary Alice Waylan, Delavan

CORNED BEEF SALAD

1 (3-ounce) package lemon gelatin
1¾ cups boiling water
1 cup mayonnaise-type salad dressing
1 cup finely chopped celery
¼ cup finely chopped green bell pepper
¼ cup finely chopped onion
3 hard-boiled eggs, chopped
1 (12-ounce) can corned beef, flaked

Dissolve gelatin in boiling water in bowl. Cool. Add remaining ingredients in order listed, mixing well after each addition. Pour into 9x9-inch dish. Chill until firm.
Yield: 9 servings.

Approx Per Serving: Cal 324; Prot 12.2 gr; T Fat 24.7 gr; Chol 133.1 mg; Carbo 13.4 gr; Sod 581.0 mg; Potas 128.2 mg.

Mable Schroeter, Kinsley

SHRIMP-BROCCOLI SALAD

1 cup bulgur
2 cups water
2 tablespoons butter
1 teaspoon seasoned salt
½ cup mayonnaise
½ cup whole milk yogurt
2 teaspoons lemon juice
1 cup shrimp, cooked
1½ cups broccoli flowerets
1 cup sliced celery
6 cherry tomatoes

Mix bulgur, water, butter and seasoned salt in medium saucepan. Bring to a boil, covered; reduce heat. Simmer for 15 minutes. Cool. Mix bulgur with mayonnaise, yogurt and lemon juice in bowl. Add shrimp, broccoli and celery; toss lightly. Chill, covered, until serving time. Spoon onto salad plates. Add cherry tomatoes. Yield: 6 servings.

Approx Per Serving: Cal 335; Prot 10.7 gr; T Fat 20.2 gr; Chol 59.7 mg; Carbo 29.8 gr; Sod 589.9 mg; Potas 450.3 mg.

Sharon Davis, Kansas Wheat Commission, Manhattan
Sharon Davis

SUPER BROCCOLI SALAD

2 pounds fresh broccoli
1 pound bacon
1 purple onion, chopped
1 cup white raisins
1 cup mayonnaise
2 tablespoons white vinegar
⅓ cup sugar

Cut broccoli into bite-sized pieces. Fry bacon in skillet until crisp; drain. Crumble bacon into bowl. Add broccoli, onion and raisins; toss lightly. Add mixture of mayonnaise, vinegar and sugar; toss until well mixed. Chill, covered, overnight. Yield: 6 servings.

Approx Per Serving: Cal 585; Prot 13.5 gr; T Fat 43.4 gr; Chol 48.4 mg; Carbo 42.0 gr; Sod 510.3 mg; Potas 883.4 mg.

La Verne Johnson, Manhattan

COLESLAW

½ cup salad dressing
1 tablespoon sugar
1 tablespoon cider vinegar
½ teaspoon salt
⅛ teaspoon pepper
4 cups very thinly sliced green
  cabbage
½ cup shredded carrots

Combine salad dressing, sugar, vinegar, salt and pepper in large bowl. Add cabbage; mix until coated. Mix in carrots. Chill, covered, until serving time. Yield: 6 servings.

Approx Per Serving: Cal 126; Prot 1.1 gr; T Fat 8.6 gr; Chol 10.0 mg; Carbo 12.5 gr; Sod 311.2 mg; Potas 175.5 mg.

Melissa Miller, Norcatur

APPLE-CABBAGE SLAW

½ cup mayonnaise
3 tablespoons pineapple juice
1 small head cabbage, shredded
1 (8-ounce) can crushed
  pineapple, drained
1 apple, chopped
½ cup raisins
½ cup chopped celery
3 tablespoons sunflower seed
½ cup chopped coconut
½ cup chopped pecans
1 carrot, grated

Blend mayonnaise with pineapple juice. Toss cabbage with pineapple, apple and raisins. Add celery, sunflower seed, coconut, pecans, carrot and mayonnaise mixture; toss to mix. Chill, covered, until serving time. Yield: 8 servings.
Note: For children top salad with a clown face made of raisin eyes, apple peel nose, apple slice mouth and shredded carrot hair.

Approx Per Serving: Cal 262; Prot 2.6 gr; T Fat 18.4 gr; Chol 9.8 mg;
    Carbo 25.5 gr; Sod 125.1 mg; Potas 430.1 mg.

Marcia Hahn, Hesston

TASTY COLESLAW

1 small head cabbage, finely
  shredded
1 small green bell pepper,
  chopped
1 medium onion, thinly sliced
½ cup sugar
¾ cup oil
½ cup vinegar
¼ cup sugar
2 teaspoons celery seed
2 teaspoons salt
1 teaspoon coarsely ground
  pepper
1 teaspoon dry mustard

Mix cabbage and green pepper in 5-quart bowl. Cover with onion slices. Sprinkle with ½ cup sugar. Combine oil, vinegar, ¼ cup sugar, celery seed, salt, pepper and dry mustard in saucepan. Bring to a full rolling boil. Pour over vegetables; do not stir. Chill, covered, for 4 hours to overnight. Stir just before serving; drain. Yield: 4 servings.
Note: Add ½ head shredded red cabbage and 3 chopped and seeded jalapeño peppers or a small jar of chopped pimentos for color and flavor.

Approx Per Serving: Cal 573; Prot 3.2 gr; T Fat 41.2 gr; Chol 0.0 mg;
    Carbo 53.4 gr; Sod 1109.2 mg; Potas 556.7 mg.
Nutritional information includes entire amount of dressing.

Rachel Elmore, Sedan

MARINATED CAULIFLOWER SALAD

1 medium head cauliflower
1 (8-ounce) bottle of Italian
  salad dressing
1 tablespoon minced onion
½ teaspoon dillweed
2 tablespoons chopped pimento
2 tablespoons sugar

Break cauliflower into flowerets. Cook in a small amount of water in saucepan until tender-crisp; drain well. Place in bowl with a tight-fitting cover. Pour mixture of salad dressing, onion, dillweed, pimento and sugar over cauliflower. Chill, covered, for several hours to overnight, turning bowl over several times or basting cauliflower with dressing frequently. Drain. Serve cauliflower skewered on toothpicks or on lettuce-lined plates. Yield: 6 servings.

Approx Per Serving: Cal 280; Prot 4.1 gr; T Fat 24.3 gr; Chol 0.0 mg; Carbo 15.2 gr; Sod 858.0 mg; Potas 453.0 mg.
Nutritional information includes entire amount of dressing.

Ann Waylan, Delavan

BROCCOLI-CAULIFLOWER SALAD

1 head cauliflower
1 bunch broccoli
1 bunch green onions
6 slices crisp-fried bacon,
  crumbled
½ cup mayonnaise
⅓ cup oil
⅓ cup vinegar
¼ cup sugar
½ teaspoon salt
⅛ teaspoon pepper

Chop cauliflower, broccoli and green onions. Combine with bacon in large bowl. Mix mayonnaise with oil, vinegar, sugar, salt and pepper in small bowl. Pour over vegetable mixture; mix gently until coated. Chill, covered, overnight. Mix gently before serving. Yield: 12 servings.

Approx Per Serving: Cal 198; Prot 4.5 gr; T Fat 15.7 gr; Chol 9.9 mg; Carbo 12.4 gr; Sod 198.7 mg; Potas 409.2 mg.

Stan Suelter Family, Lincoln

MOM'S CAULIFLOWER AND BROCCOLI SALAD

1 head cauliflower
1 pound broccoli
1 cucumber
1 green bell pepper
2 tomatoes
1 red onion, sliced into rings
2 cups sliced fresh mushrooms
¼ cup vinegar
¼ cup oil
2 envelopes buttermilk-recipe
   ranch salad dressing mix,
   prepared

Cut first 5 vegetables into medium pieces. Combine with onion slices and mushrooms. Combine vinegar, oil and ranch dressing in bowl. Pour over vegetables. Chill, covered, for 4 hours to overnight. Yield: 8 servings.

Approx Per Serving: Cal 557; Prot 9.7 gr; T Fat 51.4 gr; Chol 39.3 mg;
   Carbo 20.0 gr; Sod 459.3 mg; Potas 906.2 mg.

Kara Ricker, Scott City

MARINATED CARROTS

5 cups sliced carrots
1 small green bell pepper,
   chopped
1 small onion, chopped
1 (10-ounce) can tomato soup
1 cup sugar
½ cup oil
1 teaspoon Worcestershire
   sauce
1 teaspoon prepared mustard
¾ cup vinegar
½ teaspoon pepper

Place carrots in a small amount of water in saucepan. Cook until tender-crisp; drain and cool. Place in bowl. Add green pepper and onion. Blend soup with sugar, oil, Worcestershire sauce, mustard, vinegar and pepper in bowl. Pour over cooled carrot mixture. Chill, covered, for 12 hours to overnight before serving. Salad may be refrigerated for up to 6 weeks. Yield: 15 servings.

Approx Per Serving: Cal 151; Prot 1.0 gr; T Fat 7.8 gr; Chol 0.0 mg;
   Carbo 20.7 gr; Sod 187.6 mg; Potas 195.0 mg.

Irene Holste, Atwood

SHOE PEG CORN SALAD

1 cup sugar
½ cup vinegar
½ cup oil
1 (16-ounce) can Shoe Peg
  corn, drained
1 (16-ounce) can French-style
  green beans, drained
1 (2-ounce) jar chopped
  pimentos, drained
1 cup chopped celery
1 cup chopped green bell pepper
2 bunches green onions,
  chopped
1 teaspoon salt
1 teaspoon pepper

Mix sugar, vinegar and oil in saucepan. Bring to a boil. Cool. Combine all vegetables in large bowl. Add salt and pepper and cooled mixture; mix well. Chill for 24 hours or longer. Yield: 8 servings.

Approx Per Serving: Cal 294; Prot 2.5 gr; T Fat 14.2 gr; Chol 0.0 mg; Carbo 43.4 gr; Sod 563.5 mg; Potas 320.1 mg.

Debbie Sheldon, Halstead

ELITE SALAD

½ cup oil
3 tablespoons wine vinegar
1 tablespoon lemon juice
2 tablespoons sugar
½ teaspoon salt
½ teaspoon dry mustard
½ teaspoon grated onion
1 (11-ounce) can mandarin
  oranges
1 bunch spinach, torn
1 head iceberg lettuce, torn
¼ red onion, sliced
¼ cup toasted slivered almonds

Combine oil, vinegar, lemon juice, sugar, salt, dry mustard and grated onion in small bowl; mix well. Let stand for 1 hour. Drain oranges. Combine with spinach, lettuce, red onion slices and almonds in salad bowl. Add dressing; toss to coat. Serve immediately. Yield: 8 servings.

Approx Per Serving: Cal 196; Prot 3.4 gr; T Fat 15.9; Chol 0.0 mg; Carbo 13.0 gr; Sod 181.0 mg; Potas 469.4 mg.

Charlotte Wessel, Emporia

JICAMA SALAD

1 large or 2 medium jicamas,
  peeled, cubed
1 medium head cauliflower,
  separated into flowerets
1 medium bunch broccoli,
  separated into flowerets
¼ cup chopped onion
2 carrots, chopped
1 (10-ounce) package frozen
  peas, thawed
2 cups (16 ounces) sour cream
1 envelope Italian salad
  dressing mix
2 teaspoons lemon juice
2 tablespoons oil
8 ounces Cheddar cheese, diced

Combine jicama, cauliflower, broccoli, onion, carrots and peas in salad bowl. Blend sour cream with salad dressing mix, lemon juice and oil in small bowl. Chill vegetables and dressing separately until serving time. Mix vegetables, cheese and dressing just before serving.
Yield: 8 servings.

Approx Per Serving: Cal 365; Prot 15.9 gr; T Fat 26.0 gr; Chol 55.5 mg; Carbo 18.2 gr; Sod 325.4 mg; Potas 757.6 mg.
Nutritional information does not include jicama.

Lois Russell, Overland Park

FRESH SPINACH SALAD

1 pound fresh spinach, torn
1 (20-ounce) can bean sprouts,
  rinsed, drained
1 (8-ounce) can sliced water
  chestnuts, drained
4 hard-boiled eggs, sliced
1 medium onion, thinly sliced
8 ounces bacon, crisp-fried,
  crumbled
¾ cup sugar
¼ cup oil
2 teaspoons salt
¾ cup vinegar
⅓ cup catsup
1 teaspoon Worcestershire
  sauce

Place chilled spinach in large salad bowl. Add chilled bean sprouts, water chestnuts, eggs, onion and bacon. Mix sugar, oil, salt, vinegar, catsup and Worcestershire sauce in small bowl; mix well. Pour over spinach mixture; toss to mix well. Serve immediately. Yield: 8 servings.

Approx Per Serving: Cal 308; Prot 9.8 gr; T Fat 15.5 gr; Chol 134.8 mg; Carbo 35.0 gr; Sod 837.3 mg; Potas 488.0 mg.

Harland E. Priddle, Secretary of Commerce, Kansas Department of Commerce, Topeka

FRESH SPINACH AND LETTUCE SALAD

1 bunch spinach, torn
1 bunch leaf lettuce, torn
1 small onion, chopped
1 bunch green onion tops,
  chopped
1 bunch radishes, chopped
4 hard-boiled eggs, chopped
1 cup oil
⅓ cup sugar
⅓ cup catsup
¼ cup vinegar

Combine vegetables and eggs in salad bowl. Process oil, sugar, catsup and vinegar in blender container until well mixed. Pour over vegetable mixture; toss lightly. Serve immediately. Yield: 8 servings.

Approx Per Serving: Cal 354; Prot 5.0 gr; T Fat 30.3 gr; Chol 126.4 mg; Carbo 18.0 gr; Sod 143.6 mg; Potas 369.3 mg.

Janene George, Elbing

SUMMERY TOMATO SALAD

3 cups chopped tomatoes
1½ cups chopped seeded
  cucumber
¾ cup chopped yellow bell
  pepper
½ cup chopped red onion
½ cup Italian salad dressing

Toss tomatoes with cucumber, yellow pepper and red onion in bowl. Add salad dressing and pepper to taste; toss lightly. Chill, covered, until serving time. Yield: 4 servings.

Approx Per Serving: Cal 206; Prot 1.9 gr; T Fat 18.3 gr; Chol 0.0 mg; Carbo 11.0 gr; Sod 637.6 mg; Potas 379.2 mg.

Darla Windholz, Utica

TOMATO SOUP SALAD

1 (10-ounce) can tomato soup
1 (3-ounce) package lemon
  gelatin
1 cup mayonnaise
1 cup (8-ounce) cottage cheese
1 cup grated carrots
1 cup chopped celery
½ cup chopped stuffed olives

Bring soup to the boiling point in saucepan. Add gelatin; stir until gelatin dissolves. Remove from heat. Blend with mayonnaise in bowl. Chill until partially congealed. Add cottage cheese, carrots, celery and olives; mix well. Chill until firm. Yield: 10 servings.

Approx Per Serving: Cal 256; Prot 5.2 gr; T Fat 20.6 gr; Chol 20.3 mg; Carbo 14.2 gr; Sod 664.2 mg; Potas 186.3 mg.

Edith Werner, Sharon

MRS. BENNETT'S SALAD

1 head lettuce, torn
½ green bell pepper, chopped
½ red bell pepper, chopped
½ cup chopped celery
½ sweet red onion, chopped
1 (10-ounce) package frozen
  peas, thawed
1½ cups mayonnaise
2 tablespoons sugar
1 cup (4 ounces) shredded
  Cheddar cheese
8 slices crisp-fried bacon,
  crumbled

Layer lettuce, peppers, celery, onion and peas in 9x13-inch dish. Blend mayonnaise with sugar in bowl. Spread over vegetable layers, sealing to side of dish. Sprinkle cheese and bacon over top. Chill, covered, overnight. Yield: 10 servings.

Approx Per Serving: Cal 366; Prot 7.1 gr; T Fat 33.8 gr; Chol 40.0 mg;
Carbo 10.4 gr; Sod 391.8 mg; Potas 221.3 mg.

Glenna Wilson, Manhattan

T-SPRING SALAD

¼ cup cider vinegar
1 tablespoon sugar
⅛ teaspoon ginger
1 bunch broccoli, finely
  chopped
¼ cup grated carrot
2 tablespoons finely chopped
  onion
6 slices crisp-fried bacon,
  crumbled
¼ clove of garlic, minced
1 cup raisins
½ cup salted sunflower seed

Mix vinegar, sugar and ginger in small bowl. Let stand for 30 minutes. Combine broccoli, carrot, onion, bacon, garlic, raisins and sunflower seed in salad bowl. Add dressing; toss lightly. Serve immediately. Yield: 6 servings.

Approx Per Serving: Cal 219; Prot 8.3 gr; T Fat 9.9 gr; Chol 6.7 mg;
Carbo 29.2 gr; Sod 189.6 mg; Potas 634.2 mg.

Deanna Stalnaker, Cassoday

NINE-LAYER SALAD

1 head lettuce, torn
3 medium tomatoes, seeded,
  chopped
Pepper to taste
2 hard-boiled eggs, chopped
1 green bell pepper, chopped
1 red onion, sliced into rings
1 cup (4 ounces) shredded
  Monterey Jack cheese
½ cup Parmesan cheese
1 cup mayonnaise

Layer lettuce and tomatoes in 9 x 13-inch dish. Sprinkle with pepper. Add layers of eggs, green pepper, onion, Monterey Jack cheese and Parmesan cheese. Spread mayonnaise in thin layer over top. Chill, covered, until serving time. Garnish with crumbled crisp-fried bacon and croutons. Yield: 12 servings.

Approx Per Serving: Cal 224; Prot 6.4 gr; T Fat 20.3 gr; Chol 69.2 mg;
Carbo 5.1 gr; Sod 231.0 mg; Potas 221.1 mg.

Jennifer Brenneman, Easton

MOM'S LINGUINI SALAD

1 (16-ounce) package linquini
  noodles
1 bunch green onions, chopped
1 cucumber, sliced
1 tomato, chopped
1 green bell pepper, chopped
5 radishes, sliced
12 ounces mozzarella cheese,
  shredded
1 (8-ounce) bottle of zesty
  Italian salad dressing
2 tablespoons Salad Supreme
  seasoning

Cook linguini using package directions; rinse with cool water and drain well. Combine with vegetables and cheese in salad bowl. Add salad dressing and seasoning; toss to mix. Chill, covered, until serving time. Yield: 8 servings.

Approx Per Serving: Cal 537; Prot 17.1 gr; T Fat 29.1 gr; Chol 37.4 mg;
Carbo 50.3 gr; Sod 2913.4 mg; Potas 334.4 mg.
Nutritional information does not include Salad Supreme seasoning.

Rhonda Wessel Atkinson, Manhattan

TACO PASTA SALAD

1 (10-ounce) package spiral
    pasta
1 pound ground beef
1 envelope taco seasoning mix
¾ cup water
2 tomatoes, chopped
1 medium onion, chopped
2 cups shredded Cheddar
    cheese
1 cup pitted black olives, sliced
1½ cups taco sauce
4 cups shredded lettuce

Cook pasta using package directions; rinse with cold water and drain well. Cook ground beef in skillet, stirring until crumbly; drain. Add taco seasoning mix and ¾ cup water. Bring to a boil; reduce heat. Simmer for 10 minutes, stirring occasionally. Combine cooled pasta, ground beef mixture, tomatoes, onion, cheese and olives in salad bowl. Add taco sauce; toss lightly. Spoon onto lettuce-lined salad plates. Garnish salad with crushed corn chips and guacamole. Yield: 10 servings.

Approx Per Serving: Cal 335; Prot 18.0 gr; T Fat 16.6 gr; Chol 48.6 mg; Carbo 27.1 gr; Sod 552.7 mg; Potas 324.7 mg.
Nutritional information does not include the taco sauce.

Carla Morrical, WaKeeney

RICE SALAD

1½ cups cooked rice
3 cups chopped unpeeled apples
1 cup drained crushed
    pineapple
2 cups miniature marshmallows
½ cup sugar
¼ teaspoon salt
½ teaspoon vanilla extract
½ cup chopped pecans
1 envelope whipped topping
    mix, prepared

Combine rice, apples, pineapple and marshmallows in bowl. Add sugar, salt, vanilla and pecans; mix well. Add whipped topping; mix well. Chill until serving time. Yield: 10 servings.

Approx Per Serving: Cal 223; Prot 1.7 gr; T Fat 7.7 gr; Chol 0.1 mg; Carbo 39.0 gr; Sod 175.8 mg; Potas 113.1 mg.

Glenda Taylor, Walnut

COLD SPAGHETTI SALAD

1 (16-ounce) package thin
  spaghetti
1 medium green bell pepper,
  chopped
1 medium red onion, chopped
1 medium cucumber, chopped
2 large tomatoes, chopped
1 (8-ounce) bottle of Italian
  salad dressing
½ to ¾ jar Salad Supreme
  seasoning

Break spaghetti into 3 to 4-inch lengths. Cook using package directions; rinse with cold water and drain well. Combine with vegetables, salad dressing and seasoning; mix well. Chill, covered, until serving time. Yield: 8 servings.

Approx Per Serving: Cal 398; Prot 8.3 gr; T Fat 18.8 gr; Chol 0.0 mg;
  Carbo 49.8 gr; Sod 635.2 mg; Potas 304.4 mg.
Nutritional information does not include Salad Supreme seasoning.

Pauline Brungardt, Kansas City

SUNFLOWER CRUNCH SALAD

1 medium head cabbage,
  shredded
2 green onions, minced
2 packages chicken-flavored
  ramen noodles
¾ cup sunflower oil
6 tablespoons red wine vinegar
2 teaspoons salt
½ teaspoon pepper
5 tablespoons hulled sunflower
  seed
1 cup toasted slivered almonds

Mix cabbage and green onions in large bowl. Chill, covered, in refrigerator. Reserve ramen noodles. Combine flavor packets from noodles with oil, vinegar, salt and pepper in bowl; mix well. Crush ramen noodles. Add noodles, sunflower seed and almonds to cabbage mixture. Add dressing; mix well. Serve immediately. Yield: 10 servings.

Approx Per Serving: Cal 262; Prot 4.4 gr; T Fat 24.8 gr; Chol 0.0 mg;
  Carbo 8.8 gr; Sod 446.3 mg; Potas 354.6 mg.
Nutritional information does not include ramen noodles.

Senator Mike Johnston, Senate Minority Leader, Parsons

SPINACH SALAD

1 tablespoon sesame seed
2 medium bananas
1 (16-ounce) can pineapple
  chunks
1 (11-ounce) can mandarin
  oranges
12 ounces fresh spinach, torn
⅓ cup Dorothy Lynch
  salad dressing

Toast sesame seed in skillet over medium heat until golden brown, stirring constantly. Slice bananas ½-inch thick. Drain pineapple and mandarin oranges. Combine fruit with spinach in salad bowl. Add salad dressing; toss lightly. Sprinkle with toasted sesame seed. Yield: 6 servings.

Approx Per Serving: Cal 139; Prot 3.1 gr; T Fat 1.1 gr; Chol 0.0 mg;
  Carbo 32.9 gr; Sod 43.2 mg; Potas 558.6 mg.
Nutritional information does not include salad dressing.

Colleen Walton, Goddard

BLUE CHEESE DRESSING

5.3 ounces blue cheese
1½ cups mayonnaise
1 teaspoon white vinegar
¼ teaspoon minced garlic
¼ teaspoon Worcestershire
  sauce

Crumble half to three-fourths of the blue cheese into bowl. Add 1 cup mayonnaise; mix until smooth. Crumble remaining cheese into bowl. Add remaining mayonnaise, vinegar, garlic and Worcestershire sauce; mix well. Chill, covered, for 1 hour or longer to blend flavors. Serve on tossed salad or sliced tomatoes and green onions on lettuce. Yield: 48 tablespoons.

Approx Per Tablespoon: Cal 62; Prot 0.7 gr; T Fat 6.5 gr; Chol 7.2 mg;
  Carbo 0.2 gr; Sod 86.3 mg; Potas 10.7 mg.

Betty Lou Denton, Kansas Farmer Magazine, Topeka
Betty Lou Denton

FRUIT SALAD DRESSING

¼ cup sugar
1 teaspoon salt
¼ teaspoon dry mustard
4 egg yolks, well beaten
¼ cup cream
Juice of 1 lemon
Whipped cream

Mix sugar, salt and dry mustard in double boiler. Add egg yolks, cream and lemon juice; blend well. Cook over hot water until mixture coats spoon, stirring constantly. Cool. Fold into desired amount of whipped cream. Use on any combination of fruit. Serve immediately. Yield: 16 tablespoons.

Approx Per Tablespoon: Cal 33; Prot 0.8 gr; T Fat 1.7 gr; Chol 64.5 mg;
  Carbo 3.6 gr; Sod 137.2 mg; Potas 14.5 mg.
Nutritional information does not include whipped cream.

Lorrine Walsh, Collyer

Sunset Sizzle
(Cookout)

"RADIANT RAYS" by John Collins

BEEF STEW

3 pounds stew beef cubes
¼ cup all-purpose flour
¼ cup butter
1 medium onion, chopped
1 (8-ounce) can whole
  tomatoes
3 cups water
2 beef bouillon cubes
2 cloves of garlic, minced
2 tablespoons minced parsley
⅛ teaspoon thyme
1½ teaspoon salt
½ teaspoon pepper
1 cup red wine
6 carrots, cut up
2 stalks celery, chopped
6 potatoes, peeled, cut up
1 medium onion, chopped

Season beef with salt and pepper to taste. Coat well with flour. Brown on all sides in butter in heavy saucepan. Remove beef with slotted spoon. Sauté onion in drippings in saucepan. Add beef, tomatoes, water, bouillon, garlic, parsley and seasonings. Stir in wine. Simmer, covered, for 1½ hours. Add vegetables. Cook for 1 hour longer or until vegetables are tender. Yield: 8 servings.

Approx Per Serving: Cal 537; Prot 38.8 gr; T Fat 24.3 gr; Chol 129.2 mg; Carbo 37.6 gr; Sod 875.9 mg; Potas 1309.6 mg.

Connie Egbert, President, Young Farm Women, McCune

Connie Egbert

BEEF BAVARIAN

2 tablespoons cornstarch
¼ teaspoon garlic powder
2 teaspoons salt
¼ teaspoon pepper
1½ pounds tenderized round
  steak
2 tablespoons oil
1 large onion, sliced
1 (12-ounce) can beer
1 cup beef broth
¼ teaspoon Tabasco sauce
1 tablespoon brown sugar
3 cups hot cooked rice

Mix cornstarch, garlic powder, salt and pepper in shallow dish. Cut steak into 1-inch wide strips. Add to cornstarch mixture, coating steak well. Brown steak in oil in skillet. Add onion. Cook for 2 to 3 minutes. Stir in beer, beef broth, Tabasco sauce and brown sugar. Bring to a boil; reduce heat. Simmer, covered, for 30 minutes or until steak is tender. Serve over rice. Yield: 6 servings.

Approx Per Serving: Cal 423; Prot 27.2 gr; T Fat 16.8 gr; Chol 83.2 mg; Carbo 35.1 gr; Sod 1481.4 mg; Potas 401.0 mg.

Stephanie Lubbers, Kingman

FIFTEEN-MINUTE STROGANOFF

1 pound round steak
2 tablespoons shortening
⅔ cup water
1 (3-ounce) can mushrooms
1 envelope dry onion soup mix
1 cup sour cream
2 tablespoons all-purpose flour

Cut trimmed steak into strips or small cubes. Brown in shortening in heavy skillet. Stir in water, undrained mushrooms and soup mix. Bring to a boil. Blend sour cream and flour in small bowl. Stir into steak mixture. Cook until thickened, stirring constantly. Serve over hot noodles. Yield: 4 servings.

Approx Per Serving: Cal 440; Prot 26.5 gr; T Fat 31.4 gr; Chol 115.0 mg;
Carbo 11.9 gr; Sod 803.3 mg; Potas 397.5 mg.

Linda (Rickter) Walter, Jetmore

GREEN PEPPER STEAK

1 pound beef round steak
¼ cup soy sauce
1 clove of garlic
1½ teaspoons grated ginger
¼ cup oil
1 medium onion, sliced
1 cup red bell pepper strips
3 stalks celery, thinly sliced
1 tablespoon cornstarch
1 cup water

Trim steak; slice cross grain into ⅛-inch slices. Combine with soy sauce, garlic and ginger in bowl. Let stand for several minutes. Stir-fry in hot oil in wok until brown. Cover; reduce heat to low. Cook for 30 to 40 minutes or until tender. Increase heat. Add vegetables. Stir-fry for 10 minutes or until vegetables are tender-crisp. Dissolve cornstarch in water. Stir into skillet. Cook until thickened, stirring constantly. Serve with rice. Yield: 4 servings.

Approx Per Serving: Cal 375; Prot 24.8 gr; T Fat 26.1 gr; Chol 73.8 mg;
Carbo 10.3 gr; Sod 1419.5 mg; Potas 553.5 mg.

Justin Gosch, Rago

SLO-COOK BARBECUED BEEF

1½ pounds round steak,
　1½ inches thick
2 tablespoons oil
½ onion
⅓ cup catsup
1 clove of garlic, minced
1 tablespoon vinegar
2 tablespoons molasses
1 tablespoon Worcestershire
　sauce
½ teaspoon chili powder
1 teaspoon seasoned salt
3 or 4 drops of hot pepper sauce
½ teaspoon dry mustard
1 teaspoon cornstarch

Slice steak cross grain into ¼x2-inch pieces. Brown on all sides in hot oil in skillet. Place in slow-cooker. Process onion in blender or food processor until very fine. Combine with catsup and remaining ingredients in bowl; mix well. Pour over steak. Cook, covered, on Low for 5 to 6 hours, stirring once. Serve on buns, noodles or rice. Yield: 4 servings.

Note: If cooker is less than ⅓ full after adding sauce, place circle of foil on steak and sauce.

Approx Per Serving: Cal 429; Prot 34.6 gr; T Fat 25.1 gr; Chol 110.7 mg;
　Carbo 15.1 gr; Sod 867.9 mg; Potas 620.8 mg.

Carrel Dutt, Topeka

SLOW-COOKER STEAK

½ cup all-purpose flour
2 teaspoons salt
1 teaspoon pepper
4 pounds trimmed round steak,
　2 inches thick
1 small onion, minced
1 (32-ounce) can tomatoes
1 (32-ounce) can tomato juice

Pound mixture of flour, salt and pepper into steak on both sides. Sauté onion in a small amount of shortening in large skillet until brown. Remove onion. Brown steak on both sides in shortening in skillet. Place steak in 4-quart slow-cooker. Pour tomatoes and tomato juice over steak. Add enough water to cover if necessary. Cook, covered, on High for 6 to 8 hours or to desired degree of doneness. Serve with baked or mashed potatoes, using sauce as gravy. Yield: 8 servings.

Approx Per Serving: Cal 487; Prot 48.0 gr; T Fat 24.6 gr; Chol 147.6 mg;
　Carbo 16.4 gr; Sod 1042.8 mg; Potas 1047.6 mg.
Nutritional information does not include shortening necessary for browning onion and steak.

Kathleen Kay Harris Stutts, Bellevue, Nebraska

WESTERN LITE BROIL

2½ cups soy sauce
1¼ cups water
½ cup plus 2 tablespoons
  lemon juice
½ cup plus 2 tablespoons honey
1 tablespoon plus 2 teaspoons
  instant minced onion
1¼ teaspoons garlic powder
7½ pounds beef round, flank
  or sirloin steaks, 1½ inches
  thick

Mix soy sauce, water, lemon juice, honey, onion and garlic powder in large bowl or dish. Add steaks; turn to coat well with marinade. Marinate, covered, in refrigerator for 24 to 48 hours, turning occasionally. Broil until Medium-Rare; do not overcook. Slice thinly across the grain. Garnish with toasted sesame seed. Serve 4 ounces broiled steak with 2 cups of tossed salad and a muffin for a diet plate with a total of less than 400 calories.
Yield: 25 servings.

Approx Per Serving: Cal 293; Prot 28.6 gr; T Fat 14.9 gr; Chol 88.6 mg;
Carbo 10.2 gr; Sod 2176.2 mg; Potas 421.9 mg.

Renee Wassenberg, Kansas Beef Council, Topeka

BROCCOLI BEEF

1 pound lean beef
1 clove of garlic
2 slices fresh gingerroot
1 tablespoon soy sauce
2 tablespoons cornstarch
½ cup water
1 tablespoon oil
3 green onions, sliced into
  1-inch pieces
1 green bell pepper, cut into
  triangles
1 bunch broccoli, sliced
  diagonally
2 carrots, sliced diagonally

Slice beef very thinly cross grain. Marinate in mixture of garlic, gingerroot, soy sauce and 1 tablespoon cornstarch for 10 minutes. Dissolve remaining tablespoon cornstarch in water; set aside. Stir-fry beef in 1 tablespoon hot oil in wok until seared. Remove from wok; keep beef covered. Wipe wok with paper-towel. Stir-fry vegetables in 1 tablespoon hot oil in wok until tender-crisp. Remove from wok; keep vegetables covered. Pour water and cornstarch mixture into wok. Cook until thickened, stirring constantly. Add beef and vegetables; stir until coated. Serve with hot cooked rice.
Yield: 6 servings.

BEEF BRISKET

2 tablespoons liquid smoke
2 tablespoons soy sauce
2 teaspoons celery salt
2 teaspoons pepper
2 teaspoons Worcestershire
　sauce
1½ teaspoons salt
1 teaspoon garlic salt
1 teaspoon onion salt
4 pounds beef brisket

Place liquid smoke, soy sauce, pepper, celery salt, Worcestershire sauce, salt and garlic and onion salts in covered jar; shake until well mixed. Line 9 x 13-inch baking pan with large piece of heavy foil. Place brisket fat side up in foil-lined pan. Pour soy sauce mixture over brisket. Fold foil over brisket; seal. Refrigerate overnight. Bake at 300°F. for 5 hours.
Yield: 12 servings.

Approx Per Serving: Cal 276; Prot 30.1 gr; T Fat 16.2 gr; Chol 98.4 mg;
　Carbo 0.4 gr; Sod 1278.3 mg; Potas 353.0 mg.

Marjorie Moorhouse, Cheney

COCA-COLA CHAMPION BARBECUE BEEF

1 (3-pound) chuck roast
⅓ cup packed brown sugar
⅓ cup water
1 (12-ounce) bottle of catsup
¼ cup Worcestershire sauce
2 tablespoons prepared mustard
2 tablespoons liquid smoke
⅛ teaspoon hot sauce
1 (10-ounce) bottle of
　Coca-Cola

Rub roast with brown sugar; place in roaster. Add water. Bake, covered, at 250°F. for 5 hours. Shred roast; discard fat. Place roast in refrigerator container. Mix remaining ingredients in saucepan. Simmer for 30 minutes, stirring frequently. Pour over shredded beef; mix well. Chill for 1 to 2 days to allow flavors to blend or freeze if desired. Repeat and serve as desired.
Yield: 6 servings.
Note: Do not use diet cola.

Approx Per Serving: Cal 354; Prot 26.9 gr; T Fat 12.7 gr; Chol 80.1 mg;
　Carbo 32.9 gr; Sod 768.8 mg; Potas 492.3 mg.

Trisha Cash, Manhattan

CHILI

2 pounds ground round
Grated onion to taste
1 brick chili
1 (10-ounce) can tomato soup
1 teaspoon cinnamon
1 can Brown Beauty
　Mexican-style beans

Brown ground round with onion in saucepan, stirring until ground round is crumbly; drain. Combine chili and soup in saucepan. Heat until well mixed, stirring frequently. Add to ground round with cinnamon and beans; mix well. Heat to serving temperature.
Yield: 6 servings.

Nutritional analysis not available.

Robert T. "Bob" Stephan, Attorney General of Kansas

Robert T. Stephan

ALL-PURPOSE PASTA SAUCE

1 pound ground beef
½ cup chopped onion
1 (8-ounce) can tomato sauce
2 cups tomato juice
¼ teaspoon salt
¼ teaspoon garlic salt
⅛ teaspoon pepper
½ teaspoon sugar
1 tablespoon chopped parsley
¼ teaspoon oregano
1 bay leaf

Cook ground beef with onion in skillet, stirring until crumbly; drain. Add tomato sauce, tomato juice and seasonings. Simmer for 30 minutes, stirring occasionally. Discard bay leaf. May use as sauce for 1 pound of favorite pasta or omit ground beef and sugar and use as sauce for one 15-inch pizza. Yield: 4 servings.

Approx Per Serving: Cal 382; Prot 22.1 gr; T Fat 16.8 gr; Chol 76.6 mg; Carbo 36.9 gr; Sod 888.6 mg; Potas 768.7 mg.

Jane L. Boyer, Longford

MEXICAN SPAGHETTI

1 pound ground beef
½ cup chopped celery
⅓ cup chopped green bell
   pepper
⅓ cup chopped green olives
1 cup frozen whole kernel corn
1 (10-ounce) can tomato soup
1 tablespoon Worcestershire
   sauce
1 tablespoon A-1 sauce
1 cup cooked spaghetti
1 cup (4 ounces) shredded
   Cheddar cheese

Brown ground beef with celery and green pepper in electric skillet, stirring until crumbly; drain. Add olives, corn, soup, Worcestershire and A-1 sauces. Season with salt and pepper to taste. Mix well. Simmer for 20 minutes. Mix with spaghetti. Top with cheese. Cook in electric skillet over Low heat until heated through. Yield: 4 servings.

Approx Per Serving: Cal 475; Prot 32.3 gr; T Fat 24.1 gr; Chol 97.3 mg; Carbo 35.0 gr; Sod 1301.8 mg; Potas 733.7 mg.

Sharon Bairow, Overland Park

SLOPPY JOES

2 pounds ground beef
1 onion, chopped
1 tablespoon shortening
2 cups tomato juice
1 tablespoon vinegar
¼ cup packed brown sugar
½ teaspoon Worcestershire
   sauce
1 teaspoon oregano
½ teaspoon salt

Brown ground beef and onion in shortening, stirring until ground beef is crumbly; drain. Add tomato juice, vinegar and brown sugar, stirring to mix well. Add remaining ingredients. Simmer for 20 minutes, stirring occasionally. Serve as desired. Yield: 8 servings.

Approx Per Serving: Cal 294; Prot 20.6 gr; T Fat 18.4 gr; Chol 76.6 mg;
   Carbo 11.3 gr; Sod 310.3 mg; Potas 420.2 mg.

Carol Luttig, Emmett

SPANISH RICE

1 pound ground beef
1 medium onion, chopped
1 small green bell pepper,
   chopped
1 cup minute rice
1 (15-ounce) can tomato sauce
1 teaspoon prepared mustard
1¾ cups hot water

Cook ground beef in skillet, stirring until brown and crumbly; drain. Add onion, green pepper, rice, tomato sauce, mustard and water; mix well. Simmer, covered, for 30 minutes. Season with salt and pepper to taste. Yield: 5 servings.

Approx Per Serving: Cal 305; Prot 19.3 gr; T Fat 13.5 gr; Chol 61.3 mg;
   Carbo 26.5 gr; Sod 580.5 mg; Potas 619.9 mg.

Joshua Belland, Garden City

POOR MAN'S STROGANOFF

1 pound ground beef
Chopped green peppers
Sliced water chestnuts
Chopped onions
Diagonally sliced celery
1 (10-ounce) can cream of
   mushroom soup
Chinese red pepper to taste
MSG, to taste

Brown ground beef in saucepan, stirring until crumbly; drain. Add green peppers, water chestnuts, onions and celery; mix well. Stir in soup and seasonings. Simmer, covered, until heated through. Yield: 4 servings.

Nutritional analysis not available.

Sam Brownback, Kansas Secretary of Agriculture

MEXICALI MEAT LOAF

2 pounds ground beef
1 cup quick-cooking oats
⅔ cup tomato juice
1 egg, beaten
2 teaspoons instant onion
    flakes
1 teaspoon salt
¼ teaspoon pepper
1¼ teaspoons chili powder
¼ cup melted margarine
¼ cup all-purpose flour
1 teaspoon salt
1⅔ cups milk
12 (1-ounce) slices American
    cheese
2 (12-ounce) cans corn, drained

Combine ground beef, oats, tomato juice, egg, onion flakes, 1 teaspoon salt, pepper and chili powder in bowl; mix well. Press over bottom of 9 x 13-inch baking pan. Bake at 350°F. for 20 minutes; drain. Blend margarine and flour in saucepan. Add 1 teaspoon salt. Stir in milk gradually. Bring to a boil, stirring constantly. Cook for 1 minute, stirring constantly. Add cheese; stir until cheese melts. Stir in corn. Pour over partially baked meat loaf. Bake for 20 to 30 minutes. Let stand for 10 minutes before cutting. Yield: 10 servings.

Approx Per Serving: Cal 461; Prot 27.6 gr; T Fat 29.1 gr; Chol 116.8 mg;
    Carbo 23.1 gr; Sod 1244.3 mg; Potas 443.2 mg.

Sharon Ann Wilson, Augusta

MICROWAVE LAYERED MEAT LOAF

2 pounds ground beef
2 eggs, slightly beaten
1½ cups cracker crumbs
½ cup chopped onion
2 tablespoons Worcestershire
    sauce
1½ teaspoons salt
½ teaspoon pepper
2 tablespoons margarine
8 ounces fresh mushrooms,
    chopped
1 medium onion, chopped
1 teaspoon thyme
1 teaspoon cumin
1 cup sour cream
1 cup bread crumbs

Mix ground beef, eggs, cracker crumbs, onion, Worcestershire sauce and salt and pepper in bowl; set aside. Microwave margarine in glass baking dish on HIGH until melted. Add mushrooms and onion. Microwave for 3 minutes. Add thyme, cumin, sour cream and bread crumbs; mix well. Pat ⅓ of the ground beef mixture into 2-quart microwave-safe bundt pan. Add layers of mushroom mixture and remaining ground beef mixture ½ at a time, ending with ground beef mixture. Microwave on HIGH (100% power) for 5 minutes. Reduce setting to MEDIUM-HIGH (60% power). Microwave for 10 to 15 minutes or to internal temperature of 140°F., turning pan twice. Invert onto serving plate. Yield: 6 servings.

Approx Per Serving: Cal 683; Prot 34.8 gr; T Fat 48.4 gr; Chol 204.2 mg;
    Carbo 26.0 gr; Sod 1015.0 mg; Potas 816.2 mg.

Clay Neal, Dexter

VERA'S APPLESAUCE MEATBALLS

1 pound ground beef
1 cup unsweetened applesauce
2 cups Special-K cereal
½ onion, chopped
1 egg
1 teaspoon salt
1 teaspoon pepper
1 (10-ounce) can tomato soup
1 (10-ounce) can cream of
  mushroom soup

Mix ground beef with applesauce, cereal, onion, egg, salt and pepper in bowl. Shape into 24 meatballs. Arrange in 9x13-inch baking pan. Pour mixture of tomato and mushroom soups over top. Bake at 350°F. for 1 hour. Yield: 6 servings.
Note: This recipe has been made successfully substituting different cereals for Special-K or cheese soup for mushroom soup.

Approx Per Serving: Cal 313; Prot 18.0 gr; T Fat 17.2 gr; Chol 97.2 mg;
Carbo 22.3 gr; Sod 1260.7 mg; Potas 362.1 mg.

Jan (Fanshier) Day, Houston, Texas

BARBECUED MEATBALLS

3 pounds ground beef
1 (12-ounce) can evaporated
  milk
2 cups quick-cooking oats
2 eggs
1 cup chopped onion
½ teaspoon garlic powder
2 teaspoons salt
½ teaspoon pepper
2 teaspoons chili powder
2 cups catsup
1½ cups packed brown sugar
½ teaspoon garlic powder
½ cup chopped onion
2 tablespoons liquid smoke

Combine ground beef, evaporated milk, oats, eggs, onion, garlic powder, salt, pepper and chili powder in bowl; mix well. Shape into balls. Place in single layer in 9x13-inch baking pan. Combine catsup, brown sugar, garlic powder, onion and liquid smoke in bowl; mix well. Pour over meatballs. Bake at 350°F. for 1 hour. Yield: 60 meatballs.

Approx Per Meatball: Cal 100; Prot 5.3 gr; T Fat 4.3 gr; Chol 25.9 mg;
Carbo 10.3 gr; Sod 177.6 mg; Potas 132.3 mg.

Shawna Jordan, Glen Elder

FRICABILLIES

1½ pounds ground beef
2 eggs
2 slices bread, torn
1 cup milk
1 teaspoon salt
Pepper to taste
1 cup all-purpose flour
1 (10-ounce) can cream of
  mushroom soup
¾ soup can water

Combine ground beef, eggs, bread, milk, salt and pepper in bowl; mix well. Shape into desired sized balls; coat with flour. Brown on all sides in lightly greased skillet; drain. Place meatballs in 9x13-inch baking dish; pour excess drippings from skillet. Pour mixture of soup and water into skillet. Deglaze skillet, stirring to mix soup with browned bits. Mixture will resemble gravy. Pour over meatballs. Bake at 350°F. for 45 minutes. Yield: 12 servings.

Approx Per Serving: Cal 222; Prot 13.6 gr; T Fat 12.2 gr; Chol 85.4 mg; Carbo 13.5 gr; Sod 443.8 mg; Potas 185.7 mg.

Kathy Daharsh, Smith Center

MEATBALLS SUPREME

1 pound ground beef
2 tablespoons minced onion
2 tablespoons minced green
  bell pepper
¼ cup cornmeal
¼ teaspoon chili powder
½ teaspoon dry mustard
1 teaspoon salt
1 egg, beaten
½ cup milk
¼ cup all-purpose flour
¼ cup shortening
1½ cups tomato juice

Combine ground beef, onion, green pepper, cornmeal, chili powder, dry mustard, salt, egg and milk in bowl; mix well. Shape into 12 balls. Roll in flour; reserve any remaining flour. Brown in shortening in oven-proof skillet. Sprinkle with reserved flour. Add tomato juice. Bake, covered, at 375°F. for 1 hour.
Yield: 12 meatballs.
Note: If serving with spaghetti add tomato sauce or additional tomato juice.

Approx Per Meatball: Cal 159; Prot 8.3 gr; T Fat 11.1 gr; Chol 48.0 mg; Carbo 6.3 gr; Sod 265.8 mg; Potas 175.3 mg.

Jason Esslinger, Madison

HAMBURGER CASSEROLE

2 pounds ground beef
1 onion, chopped
2 (10-ounce) cans vegetable
  beef soup
6 medium potatoes,
  peeled, sliced
1 (10-ounce) can cream of
  mushroom soup

Brown ground beef with onion in skillet, stirring until ground beef is crumbly; drain. Season with salt and pepper to taste. Mix vegetable beef soup with ½ soup can water in bowl. Alternate layers of potatoes, ground beef and vegetable soup mixture in greased 3 to 4-quart baking dish. Combine mushroom soup with ½ soup can water in bowl. Pour over layers. Bake at 350°F. for 2 hours. Yield: 6 servings.

Approx Per Serving: Cal 430; Prot 22.7 gr; T Fat 17.0 gr; Chol 74.4 mg;
    Carbo 46.7 gr; Sod 1303.8 mg; Potas 1128.8 mg.

Tara Kipp, Phillipsburg

MEATBALLS STROGANOFF-STYLE

1½ pounds ground beef
1 egg
⅓ cup milk
¼ cup fine dry bread crumbs
1 tablespoon minced onion
1½ teaspoons salt
½ teaspoon pepper
2 tablespoons butter
¼ (10-ounce) can cream of
  mushroom soup
½ cup water
1 teaspoon steak sauce
2 tablespoons minced onion
½ cup sour cream

Combine ground beef, egg, milk, bread crumbs, 1 tablespoon onion, salt and pepper in bowl; mix well. Shape into 18 meatballs. Brown in butter in skillet. Add cream of mushroom soup, water, steak sauce and 2 tablespoons onion. Simmer, covered, for 15 to 20 minutes. Stir in sour cream just before serving. Yield: 18 meatballs.

Approx Per Meatball: Cal 121; Prot 7.6 gr; T Fat 9.0 gr; Chol 47.3 mg;
    Carbo 2.0 gr; Sod 261.4 mg; Potas 101.0 mg.

Kenneth Selby Jr., Manhattan

SWEET AND SOUR MEATBALLS

1 pound ground beef
½ cup milk
1 cup cracker crumbs
¼ cup vinegar
½ cup catsup
3 tablespoons brown sugar
1½ tablespoons Worcestershire
  sauce
½ cup chopped onion
½ cup chopped green
  bell pepper

Mix ground beef with milk and cracker crumbs in bowl; season with salt and pepper to taste. Shape into 1½-inch balls; place in 9 x 9-inch baking dish. Combine vinegar, catsup, brown sugar, Worcestershire sauce, onion and green pepper in saucepan. Bring to a boil; pour over meatballs. Bake at 350°F. for 1 hour, beating occasionally. Yield: 12 meatballs.

Approx Per Meatball: Cal 140; Prot 7.9 gr; T Fat 6.6 gr; Chol 27.0 mg;
  Carbo 12.2 gr; Sod 213.8 mg; Potas 190.6 mg.

Angie Price, Coffeyville

CHALUPAS

½ cup chopped onion
2 tablespoons butter
2 pounds ground beef
2 tablespoons all-purpose flour
3 tablespoons chili powder
1 cup water
1 (10-ounce) can tomato soup
2 cups (8-ounces) shredded
  Cheddar cheese
1½ cups light cream
½ cup chopped onion
1 teaspoon salt
12 corn tortillas

Sauté ½ cup onion in butter in skillet. Add ground beef. Cook until brown and crumbly. Stir in flour and chili powder. Cook for 5 minutes longer. Add water. Cook until thickened, stirring constantly. Combine soup, cheese, cream, ½ cup onion and salt in bowl; mix well. Slice tortillas into strips. Layer tortillas, ground beef mixture and soup mixture ½ at a time in buttered baking dish. Bake at 325°F. for 30 minutes. Yield: 12 servings.

Approx Per Serving: Cal 546; Prot 24.4 gr; T Fat 30.4 gr; Chol 108.8 mg;
  Carbo 44.5 gr; Sod 586.8 mg; Potas 288.5 mg.

Nancy Landon Kassebaum, United States Senator

BIEROCH

1 medium onion, finely
  chopped
2 tablespoons butter
1 pound ground beef
1 medium head cabbage,
  shredded
2 tablespoons butter
1 recipe yeast dough

Sauté onion in 2 tablespoons butter in skillet. Add ground beef. Cook until brown; drain. Steam cabbage in 2 tablespoons butter in saucepan just until tender. Add to ground beef; mix well. Season to taste with salt and pepper. Roll dough ¼ inch thick on floured surface. Cut into 6-inch squares. Place 3 tablespoons cabbage mixture on each square. Pull up corners to enclose filling, sealing edges. Place seam side down in greased baking pan. Bake at 350°F. for 30 minutes. Serve hot. Yield: 6 servings.

Approx Per Serving: Cal 261; Prot 15.0 gr; T Fat 19.1 gr; Chol 73.9 mg;
  Carbo 8.2 gr; Sod 145.4 mg; Potas 453.5 mg.
Nutritional information does not include yeast dough.

Senator Robert J. Dole, United States Senator

CREAM CHEESE-GROUND BEEF CASSEROLE

1 pound ground beef
1 cup chopped onion
8 ounces cream cheese
1 (10-ounce) can cream of
  mushroom soup
½ cup milk
¼ cup catsup
1 teaspoon salt
10 refrigerator biscuits

Brown ground beef with onion in skillet, stirring until ground beef is crumbly; drain. Add cream cheese, soup, milk, catsup and salt; mix well. Spoon into 1-quart baking dish. Bake at 375°F. for 20 minutes. Arrange biscuits over top. Increase temperature to 400°F. Bake until biscuits are golden brown. Yield: 3 servings.

Approx Per Serving: Cal 1096; Prot 45.5 gr; T Fat 67.4 gr; Chol 251.0 mg;
  Carbo 76.0 gr; Sod 3001.4 mg; Potas 728.7 mg.

Valdimer Domeny Bairow, Wamego

GROUND BEEF-PASTA-BROCCOLI CASSEROLE

2 pounds ground chuck
1 teaspoon salt
½ teaspoon pepper
1 cup spaghetti sauce
Flowerets of 1 bunch broccoli
1 (16-ounce) package spiral
  pasta
3 cups heated spaghetti sauce
⅓ cup Parmesan cheese

Combine first 4 ingredients in bowl; mix lightly. Shape into 8 patties. Brown in skillet over medium heat. Steam broccoli just until fork-tender. Cook pasta using package directions just until tender; drain. Alternate layers of patties, broccoli and pasta in 3-quart casserole. Top with sauce and cheese. Bake at 350°F. for 20 minutes. Yield: 8 servings.

Approx Per Serving: Cal 480; Prot 30.6 gr; T Fat 18.7 gr; Chol 81.3 mg;
   Carbo 46.2 gr; Sod 360.3 mg; Potas 556.6 mg.
Nutritional information does not include spaghetti sauce.

Teri Springer, Manhattan

LAYERED GROUND BEEF CASSEROLE

1 pound ground beef
3 tablespoons chopped onion
1½ cups instant potato flakes,
  prepared
1 (16-ounce) can cream-style
  corn

Cook ground beef with onion in skillet, stirring frequently; drain. Season with salt and pepper to taste. Layer ground beef, potatoes and corn in 1½-quart baking dish. Bake at 350°F. for 30 minutes or microwave on HIGH (100% power) for 8 minutes. Yield: 4 servings.

Approx Per Serving: Cal 414; Prot 24.0 gr; T Fat 19.8 gr; Chol 76.6 mg;
   Carbo 37.7 gr; Sod 533.1 mg; Potas 582.9 mg.

Arnette Duerksen, McPherson

ONE-DISH DINNER

1½ pounds ground beef
2 teaspoons salt
1 (8-ounce) package noodles
1 (12-ounce) can whole kernel
  corn, drained
1 (10-ounce) can cream of
  chicken soup
1 (8-ounce) can tomato sauce
1 cup (4 ounces) shredded
  Cheddar cheese

Brown ground beef in skillet, stirring until crumbly; drain. Add salt. Spoon into 9x13-inch baking dish. Cook noodles using package directions. Layer corn, soup, noodles, tomato sauce and cheese over ground beef. Bake at 325°F. for 1 hour. Yield: 6 servings.

Approx Per Serving: Cal 603; Prot 32.6 gr; T Fat 33.3 gr; Chol 99.7 mg;
   Carbo 42.8 gr; Sod 1535.4 mg; Potas 642.0 mg.

Janelle Goossen, Newton

ENCHILADA TORTE

1 pound ground beef
7 large flour tortillas
1 (8-ounce) jar taco sauce
1 large onion, chopped
8 ounces Cheddar cheese,
  shredded
1 (16-ounce) can refried beans
1 (4-ounce) can chopped ripe
  olives
1 (4-ounce) can chopped green
  chilies
1 cup sour cream
1 large green pepper, chopped
8 ounces Monterey Jack cheese,
  shredded
1 (8-ounce) can enchilada
  sauce

Brown ground beef in skillet, stirring until crumbly; drain. Place 1 tortilla on baking sheet. Layer ½ of the taco sauce, ground beef, onion and Cheddar cheese on tortilla. Add second tortilla and press layers gently. Layer ½ of the refried beans, olives and chilies on tortilla. Top with third tortilla, pressing gently. Layer ½ of the sour cream, green pepper and Monterey Jack cheese on tortilla. Top with fourth tortilla, pressing gently. Repeat layers with remaining ingredients. Top with enchilada sauce. Bake at 350°F. for 1 hour. Cut into wedges to serve. Yield: 8 servings.

Approx Per Serving: Cal 556; Prot 28.3 gr; T Fat 40.0 gr; Chol 107.3 mg;
    Carbo 21.3 gr; Sod 527.9 mg; Potas 351.4 mg.
Nutritional information does not include taco sauce, beans or enchilada sauce.

Jeff Walters, Lawrence

MICROWAVE ENCHILADAS

2 pounds ground beef
Onion flakes to taste
1 envelope taco seasoning mix
½ cup water
1 (16-ounce) can refried beans
12 corn tortillas
1 (8-ounce) can tomato sauce
1 (5-ounce) jar taco sauce
10 ounces Cheddar cheese,
  shredded

Brown ground beef in skillet, stirring until crumbly; drain. Add onion flakes, seasoning mix, water and beans; mix well. Simmer for 5 minutes. Spoon onto tortillas; roll to enclose filling. Place seam side down in ungreased 9 x 13-inch glass baking dish. Pour mixture of tomato sauce and taco sauce over top. Sprinkle with cheese. Cover with plastic wrap. Microwave on HIGH (100% power) for 10 to 12 minutes or until heated through. Garnish with lettuce, tomatoes and additional cheese. Serve with hot sauce. Yield: 10 servings.

Approx Per Serving: Cal 439; Prot 26.6 gr; T Fat 25.7 gr; Chol 91.3 mg;
    Carbo 28.8 gr; Sod 345.9 mg; Potas 297.3 mg.
Nutritional information does not include taco seasoning mix, refried beans or taco sauce.

Shana Ayers, Altoona

WEST OF THE PECOS ENCHILADAS

1 pound lean ground beef
½ teaspoon salt
1 cup (4 ounces) shredded
  longhorn cheese
1 cup chopped onion
1 can black olives, chopped
2 (8-ounce) cans tomato sauce
1 (6-ounce) can tomato paste
1 (10-ounce) can tomato soup
2 cups water
½ cup oil
2 tablespoons chili powder
1 teaspoon garlic powder
½ teaspoon salt
12 corn tortillas
1 cup (4-ounces) shredded
  longhorn cheese

Brown ground beef in skillet, stirring until crumbly; drain. Add ½ teaspoon salt, 1 cup cheese, onion and olives; mix well. Combine tomato sauce, tomato paste and next 6 ingredients in saucepan. Heat until mixture is simmering. Dip tortillas in simmering tomato sauce. Place heaping tablespoon ground beef mixture on each tortilla. Roll tortillas to enclose filling. Place seam side down in 9 x 13-inch baking pan. Pour 1 cup tomato mixture over top. Bake at 350°F. for 10 minutes. Top with 1 cup cheese. Bake for 5 minutes longer or until heated through. Serve with remaining tomato sauce. Yield: 12 enchiladas.

Approx Per Enchilada: Cal 408; Prot 16.2 gr; T Fat 24.2 gr; Chol 44.2 mg; Carbo 34.0 gr; Sod 859.6 mg; Potas 453.1 mg.

C. Wayne Coleman, Valley Falls

CAVATINI

4 ounces curly noodles
8 ounces ground beef
16 ounces spaghetti sauce
1 (8-ounce) can tomato sauce
1 (4-ounce) can mushrooms
2 ounces pepperoni, chopped
4 (1-ounce) slices mozzarella
  cheese

Cook noodles using package directions. Cook ground beef in skillet until brown and crumbly; drain. Add spaghetti sauce, tomato sauce, mushrooms and pepperoni. Heat until well mixed. Mix with noodles in 5 x 7-inch casserole. Top with cheese. Bake at 350°F. for 20 minutes or until cheese melts. Yield: 4 servings.

Approx Per Serving: Cal 400; Prot 26.3 gr; T Fat 20.5 gr; Chol 89.7 mg; Carbo 27.1 gr; Sod 688.7 mg; Potas 438.8 mg.
Nutritional information does not include spaghetti sauce.

Shari L. Fankhauser, Madison

LASAGNA

1½ pounds ground beef
8 ounces sausage
1 onion, chopped
½ teaspoon fennel seed
3 or 4 cloves of garlic
2 tablespoons parsley
1 tablespoon salt
1 teaspoon basil
¼ teaspoon cumin
6 (8-ounce) cans tomato sauce
4 eggs, beaten
16 ounces ricotta cheese
1 (2-pound) package lasagna
    noodles
1½ cups (6-ounces) shredded
    mozzarella cheese
1 cup Parmesan cheese

Brown ground beef and sausage with onion in skillet, stirring until crumbly; drain. Add seasonings and tomato sauce. Simmer for 10 minutes. Mix eggs with ricotta cheese in bowl. Cook lasagna noodles using package directions. Alternate layers of sauce, noodles, mozzarella cheese and ricotta cheese mixture in 9 x 13-inch baking pan. Top with Parmesan cheese. Bake at 350°F. for 30 to 40 minutes or until heated through. Yield: 12 servings.

Approx Per Serving: Cal 677; Prot 36.3 gr; T Fat 28.7 gr; Chol 242.1 mg;
    Carbo 67.6 gr; Sod 1500.8 mg; Potas 825.1 mg.

Deborah Aiken, Havana

MICROWAVE LASAGNA ROLLS

4 ounces ground beef
1 tablespoon chopped onion
½ cup tomato juice
2 tablespoons tomato paste
⅛ teaspoon basil
¼ teaspoon oregano
1 teaspoon sugar
¼ teaspoon salt
⅛ teaspoon pepper
¼ cup cottage cheese
2 tablespoons Parmesan cheese
⅛ teaspoon garlic powder
⅛ teaspoon basil
¼ cup (2 ounces) shredded
    mozzarella cheese
2 lasagna noodles, cooked

Microwave ground beef and onion in 1-quart casserole on HIGH (100% power) for 3 minutes or until no longer pink, stirring once. Add tomato juice, tomato paste and next 5 seasonings. Microwave for 4 to 7 minutes or until thickened, stirring twice. Reserve ¼ cup mixture. Mix cottage cheese, next 3 ingredients and half the mozzarella cheese in small bowl. Layer remaining ground beef mixture and half the cheese mixture down centers of noodles; roll each as for jelly roll. Place seam side down in 14-ounce oval casserole. Top with reserved ground beef mixture and remaining mozzarella cheese. Microwave, covered, on MEDIUM for 4 minutes or until cheese melts, turning casserole once. Yield: 2 rolls.

Approx Per Roll: Cal 358; Prot 23.4 gr; T Fat 15.9 gr; Chol 83.3 mg;
    Carbo 29.0 gr; Sod 645.0 mg; Potas 567.2 mg.

Tammy Troutt, Satanta

CHEESEBURGER PIE

2 pounds ground beef
1 large onion, chopped
2 cups (8 ounces) shredded
  Cheddar cheese
1 cup buttermilk baking mix
1¾ cups milk
1 egg

Brown ground beef in skillet, stirring until crumbly; drain. Add onion. Cook until tender. Layer ground beef mixture and cheese in lightly greased 10-inch pie plate. Mix remaining ingredients in bowl until smooth. Pour over ground beef and cheese. Bake at 400°F. for 30 minutes or until golden. Yield: 4 servings.

Approx Per Serving: Cal 924; Prot 61.9 gr; T Fat 60.3 gr; Chol 287.3 mg;
Carbo 30.8 gr; Sod 955.1 mg; Potas 748.7 mg.

Tanya A. Kamm, Abilene

HAMBURGER PIE

1 pound ground beef
½ cup chopped onion
½ teaspoon salt
⅛ teaspoon pepper
1 (16-ounce) can green beans,
  drained
1 (16-ounce) can whole kernel
  corn, drained
1 (16-ounce) can peas, drained
1 (10-ounce) can tomato soup
5 medium potatoes, peeled,
  cooked
½ cup warm milk
1 egg, beaten
½ cup (2 ounces) shredded
  American cheese

Cook ground beef with onion in skillet, stirring until crumbly; drain. Add ½ teaspoon salt, pepper, green beans, corn, peas and soup; mix well. Pour into greased 2½-quart casserole. Drain and mash potatoes, adding milk and egg. Season with salt and pepper to taste. Spoon over ground beef mixture. Sprinkle with cheese. Bake at 350°F. for 25 to 30 minutes or until golden brown. Yield: 6 servings.

Approx per Serving: Cal 497; Prot 26.2 gr; T Fat 17.8 gr; Chol 102.1 mg;
Carbo 60.5 gr; Sod 1272.3 mg; Potas 1143.9 mg.

Katherine Mohler, Formoso

TACO PIZZA

¾ cup cornmeal
1¼ cups all-purpose flour
1 teaspoon baking powder
⅔ cup milk
¼ cup oil
1 teaspoon salt
1 pound ground beef
½ (2.5-ounce) package taco
  seasoning mix
1 (8-ounce) can tomato sauce
1 cup (4 ounces) shredded
  mozzarella cheese
2 cups shredded lettuce
1 tomato, chopped
½ cup (2 ounces) shredded
  American cheese

Combine cornmeal, flour, baking powder, milk, oil and salt in bowl. Mix to form dough. Knead on floured surface. Press into greased pizza pan. Bake at 400°F. for 10 minutes. Brown ground beef in skillet, stirring until crumbly; drain. Add taco seasoning mix and tomato sauce; mix well. Spread in prepared pan. Sprinkle with mozzarella cheese. Bake at 400°F. for 10 minutes. Top with lettuce, tomato and American cheese. Yield: 4 servings.

Approx Per Serving: Cal 862; Prot 38.5 gr; T Fat 51.4 gr; Chol 120.5 mg;
  Carbo 60.4 gr; Sod 1376.7 mg; Potas 838.7 mg.
Nutritional information does not include taco seasoning mix.

Kelly Pagel, Lebanon

GROUND BEEF POTPIE

1 (2-crust) recipe whole wheat
  pie pastry
1 pound lean ground beef
¼ cup minced onion
1 (10-ounce) package frozen
  peas and carrots
2 beef bouillon cubes
1 (14-ounce) can stewed
  tomatoes
½ teaspoon marjoram
1 teaspoon salt
⅛ teaspoon pepper
1 tablespoon cornstarch
1 egg, slightly beaten

Line 9-inch pie plate with half the pastry. Brown ground beef with onion in saucepan, stirring until ground beef is crumbly; drain. Add peas and carrots, bouillon cubes, tomatoes, marjoram, salt and pepper; mix well. Simmer for 5 to 10 minutes, stirring until bouillon is dissolved. Blend cornstarch with 2 to 3 tablespoons water in cup. Add to ground beef mixture; mix well. Pour into prepared pie plate. Top with remaining pastry. Trim pastry and cut steam vents. Brush with egg. Bake at 400°F. for 15 minutes. Reduce temperature to 350°F. Bake for 25 minutes or until golden brown. Let stand for 10 minutes before serving. Yield: 5 servings.

Approx Per Serving: Cal 264; Prot 20.3 gr; T Fat 14.8 gr; Chol 113.1 mg;
  Carbo 12.1 gr; Sod 1032.3 mg; Potas 498.6 mg.
Nutritional information does not include pie pastry.

Tony Esfeld, Great Bend

BROILED LAMB CHOPS

2 loin lamb chops
¼ cup honey
¼ cup orange juice

Place lamb chops on rack in broiler pan. Broil 4 inches from heat source for 5 minutes. Season with salt to taste; turn chops over. Broil for 5 minutes or to desired degree of doneness. Top with mixture of honey and orange juice. Broil for 3 minutes longer. Yield: 2 servings.

Approx Per Serving: Cal 483; Prot 21.2 gr; T Fat 28.0 gr; Chol 93.1 mg; Carbo 37.8 gr; Sod 53.6 mg; Potas 317.5 mg.

Michael and Michelle Clayman, Hutchinson

BARBECUED LAMB MEATBALLS

1 (15-ounce) can tomato sauce
1 pound ground lamb
1 egg
¾ teaspoon lemon pepper
½ teaspoon salt
1 tablespoon barbecue sauce
⅓ cup fine dry bread crumbs

Heat tomato sauce over Low heat in 2-quart saucepan. Combine ground lamb with remaining ingredients in bowl; mix well. Shape into 1-inch meatballs. Brown on all sides in skillet; drain. Add meatballs to simmering tomato sauce. Cook over very Low heat for 30 minutes, stirring occasionally. Yield: 4 servings.

Approx Per Serving: Cal 323; Prot 19.2 gr; T Fat 20.4 gr; Chol 129.8 mg; Carbo 15.9 gr; Sod 1034.4 mg; Potas 655.8 mg.

Rachael Baxter, Emporia

GREEK MEATBALLS

1 pound ground lamb
½ cup dry bread crumbs
¼ cup milk
1 egg
1 medium onion, finely chopped
1 clove of garlic, minced
½ teaspoon crushed dried mint
1 teaspoon salt
½ teaspoon crushed dried oregano leaves
¼ teaspoon pepper

Combine ground lamb with bread crumbs, milk, egg, onion, garlic, mint, salt, oregano and pepper in bowl; mix well. Shape into 1-inch balls. Place in ungreased 9 x 13-inch baking pan. Bake at 350°F. for 25 minutes or until light brown; drain. Yield: 36 meatballs.

Approx Per Meatball: Cal 35; Prot 2.7 gr; T Fat 2.0 gr; Chol 16.0 mg; Carbo 1.4 gr; Sod 77.8 mg; Potas 37.4 mg.

Nancy Nelson, Ellsworth

CLASSIC EGG AND HAM STRATA

1 (10-ounce) package frozen
  chopped broccoli
18 slices white bread, cubed
2 cups chopped cooked ham
3 cups (12 ounces) shredded
  sharp process cheese
6 eggs, slightly beaten
3½ cups milk
2 teaspoons instant onion
¼ teaspoon dry mustard
½ teaspoon salt

Steam broccoli according to package directions; drain. Layer bread cubes, ham, broccoli and cheese ½ at a time in 9 x 13-inch baking dish. Combine eggs, milk, onion and seasonings in bowl; mix well. Pour over layers. Refrigerate, covered, for 6 hours to overnight. Bake at 325°F. for 1 hour. Yield: 12 servings.

Approx Per Serving: Cal 389; Prot 22.1 gr; T Fat 21.1 gr; Chol 186.4 mg; Carbo 27.0 gr; Sod 747.0 mg; Potas 314.3 mg.

Marvin Barkis, House Minority Leader, Louisburg

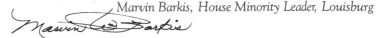

EGG CASSEROLE SOUFFLÉ

8 slices bread
2 tablespoons butter, softened
1 pound cooked ham, chopped
4 (¾-ounce) slices American
  cheese
4 eggs, beaten
2 cups milk

Trim crusts from bread. Spread butter on 1 side of each slice. Place 4 slices, buttered side down, in 8-inch square baking pan. Top with ham, cheese and remaining bread buttered side up. Beat eggs with milk and salt to taste. Pour over layers. Refrigerate overnight. Bake at 325°F. for 1½ hours. Yield: 6 servings.

Approx Per Serving: Cal 506; Prot 29.0 gr; T Fat 31.7 gr; Chol 269.9 mg; Carbo 24.4 gr; Sod 1154.0 mg; Potas 409.3 mg.

Stephanie Trembley, Arlington

HAM BALLS

1 pound ground ham
1 pound ground beef
2 eggs
1½ cups soda cracker crumbs
1 cup packed brown sugar
1 teaspoon dry mustard
½ cup water
½ cup vinegar

Combine ground ham, ground beef, eggs and cracker crumbs in bowl; mix well. Shape into walnut-sized balls; place in baking dish. Pour mixture of brown sugar, dry mustard, water and vinegar over top. Bake at 300°F. for 1½ hours. Yield: 36 ham balls.

Approx Per Ham Ball: Cal 103; Prot 5.4 gr; T Fat 5.3 gr; Chol 33.7 mg; Carbo 8.2 gr; Sod 136.3 mg; Potas 85.3 mg.

Lydia Jaecke, Chapman

HAM AND BROCCOLI CASSEROLE

1 (20-ounce) package frozen
  cut broccoli
½ cup chopped onion
2 tablespoons butter
1 (10-ounce) can cream of
  mushroom soup
1 (10-ounce) can cream of
  celery soup
3 cups cooked ham cubes
1 soup can milk
2 cups minute rice
1 cup (4 ounces) shredded
  American cheese
1 teaspoon Worcestershire
  sauce

Cook broccoli according to package directions; drain. Sauté onion in butter in saucepan. Add mushroom soup, celery soup, ham, milk, rice, cheese and Worcestershire sauce; mix well. Spoon into 2½-quart baking dish. Bake at 350°F. for 45 to 50 minutes or until rice is tender. Yield: 8 servings.

Approx Per Serving: Cal 431; Prot 20.6 gr; T Fat 24.1 gr; Chol 76.6 mg; Carbo 33.2 gr; Sod 1286.0 mg; Potas 470.1 mg.

Shirley Navinsky, Easton

HAM AND POTATO CASSEROLE

1 medium onion, finely
  chopped
3 tablespoons butter
3 tablespoons all-purpose flour
½ teaspoon dry mustard
1½ cups milk
¾ cup (3 ounces) shredded
  Cheddar cheese
4 medium potatoes, peeled,
  sliced
½ cup chopped celery
1½ cups chopped cooked ham
½ cup finely chopped green
  bell pepper

Sauté onion in butter in skillet. Stir in flour and dry mustard; season with salt and pepper to taste. Add milk gradually. Cook until thickened, stirring constantly. Stir in cheese until melted. Alternate layers of potatoes, celery, ham, green pepper and cheese sauce in 9 x 12-inch baking dish until all ingredients are used and ending with cheese sauce. Bake, covered, at 350°F. for 1 hour. Bake, uncovered, for 30 minutes longer. Yield: 4 servings.

Approx Per Serving: Cal 553; Prot 24.8 gr; T Fat 30.6 gr; Chol 107.1 mg; Carbo 45.4 gr; Sod 721.0 mg; Potas 1164.4 mg.

Delores Morgan, Burns

UPSIDE-DOWN HAM LOAF

3 tablespoons butter
5 tablespoons packed brown
  sugar
9 pineapple slices
1 pound ground lean ham
½ pound lean pork, ground
½ cup bread crumbs
¼ teaspoon pepper
2 eggs
¼ cup milk

Melt butter in 8x8-inch baking pan. Stir in brown sugar. Arrange pineapple slices in prepared pan. Combine remaining ingredients in bowl; mix well. Press mixture into baking pan. Bake at 350°F. for 50 to 60 minutes or until cooked through. Invert onto serving platter. Garnish with red cherries. Yield: 9 servings.

Approx Per Serving: Cal 368; Prot 23.4 gr; T Fat 22.5 gr; Chol 144.4 mg; Carbo 17.4 gr; Sod 565.8 mg; Potas 374.3 mg.

Dottie Kraus, Hays

BIGOS (HUNTER'S DISH)

½ medium head cabbage
3 mushrooms, sliced
2 cloves of garlic, minced
4 cups sauerkraut
1 pound lean cooked pork
  cubes
8 ounces Polish sausage, cubed
2 ounces smoked bacon,
  chopped
5 tablespoons tomato paste
1 medium onion, chopped
3 tablespoons shortening
2 tablespoons all-purpose flour

Cook cabbage, mushrooms and garlic in water to cover in uncovered saucepan until tender. Place sauerkraut in large saucepan. Add water to cover. Bring, uncovered, to a boil. Add pork, sausage, bacon, tomato paste and cabbage mixture; mix well. Cook over Low heat, stirring frequently. Sauté onion in shortening in skillet until tender. Mix in flour. Stir onion mixture into cabbage mixture. Cook over Low heat until mixture has very little sauce remaining. Season to taste with salt, pepper, allspice and bay leaf. Yield: 6 servings.

Approx Per Serving: Cal 502; Prot 22.4 gr; T Fat 40.5 gr; Chol 77.3 mg; Carbo 12.5 gr; Sod 1784.3 mg; Potas 701.6 mg.

Suzanne C. Shaw, Vienna, Virginia

ITALIAN PORK CHOPS

4 (1-inch thick) pork chops
½ teaspoon sage
½ teaspoon rosemary
1 teaspoon garlic salt
¼ teaspoon pepper
½ cup white wine

Brown pork chops on both sides in oiled 10-inch skillet. Place in baking dish. Sprinkle with seasonings. Pour wine around pork chops. Bake, covered with foil and baking dish cover, at 300°F. for 2 hours. Check after 30 minutes baking time to see if additional wine is needed. Yield: 4 servings.

Approx Per Serving: Cal 233; Prot 15.0 gr; T Fat 17.4 gr; Chol 54.3 mg; Carbo 0.6 gr; Sod 570.2 mg; Potas 180.8 mg.

Bob Gottschalk, Executive Secretary, Kansas State Fair, Hutchinson

PORK CHOP AND POTATO BAKE

1 (10-ounce) can cream of
    mushroom soup
½ cup milk
½ cup sour cream
½ teaspoon seasoned salt
¼ teaspoon pepper
1 (24-ounce) package frozen
    hashed brown potatoes,
    thawed
1 cup (4 ounces) shredded
    Cheddar cheese
1 (2.8-ounce) can French-fried
    potatoes
6 pork chops
1 tablespoon oil

Mix soup, milk, sour cream, ½ teaspoon seasoned salt and pepper in bowl; mix well. Add potatoes, ½ cup cheese and half the onions. Spoon into 9 x 13-inch baking dish. Brown pork chops on both sides in oil in skillet. Season with salt or seasoned salt to taste. Arrange over potato mixture. Bake, covered, at 350°F. for 40 minutes. Top with remaining cheese and onions. Bake, uncovered, for 5 minutes longer. Yield: 6 servings.

Approx Per Serving: Cal 584; Prot 22.1 gr; T Fat 40.7 gr; Chol 80.8 mg; Carbo 32.8 gr; Sod 646.3 mg; Potas 662.2 mg.

Michelle Klassen, Olathe

OVEN-BAKED BREADED PORK CHOPS

1 cup fine dry bread crumbs
1 tablespoon Parmesan cheese
¼ teaspoon thyme
½ teaspoon paprika
1 teaspoon salt
¼ cup butter
6 (¾-inch thick) lean pork
  chops
1 egg, beaten

Mix bread crumbs, Parmesan cheese and seasonings in bowl. Cut in butter with pastry blender or fork. Dip chops into egg; coat with crumb mixture. Place on wire rack in 10 x 15-inch baking pan. Bake at 375°F. for 20 minutes. Turn chops over. Bake for 20 minutes longer or until cooked through and golden brown. Yield: 6 servings.

Approx Per Serving: Cal 299; Prot 13.6 gr; T Fat 21.3 gr; Chol 104.0 mg;
   Carbo 12.4 gr; Sod 614.7 mg; Potas 151.7 mg.

Karen Maier, Otis

CROCK•POT BARBECUED RIBS

4 pounds spareribs
1 (10-ounce) can tomato soup
½ cup cider vinegar
½ cup packed brown sugar
1 tablespoon celery seed
1 tablespoon soy sauce
1 teaspoon chili powder

Trim excess fat from ribs. Place in Crock•Pot. Mix soup, vinegar, brown sugar, celery seed, soy sauce and chili powder in bowl. Pour over ribs. Cook, covered, on Low for 7 to 8 hours. Yield: 4 servings.

Approx Per Serving: Cal 868; Prot 52.5 gr; T Fat 55.7 gr; Chol 214.0 mg;
   Carbo 38.4 gr; Sod 1107.1 mg; Potas 850.4 mg.

June Setzkorn, Jetmore

SUPER PEPPERONI DISH

8 ounces sliced pepperoni
1 onion, chopped
1 (4-ounce) jar diced pimento
1 (4-ounce) can sliced
  mushrooms
Parsley to taste
4 cups cooked rice
2 cups drained cooked peas
2 tablespoons margarine
¼ cup Parmesan cheese

Combine pepperoni, onion, pimento, mushrooms and parsley in large skillet. Simmer for 5 minutes, stirring frequently. Add rice; toss to mix. Season with salt and pepper to taste. Spoon into ring in serving dish. Heat peas with margarine and cheese in saucepan. Spoon into center of ring. Yield: 6 servings.

Approx Per Serving: Cal 444; Prot 17.1 gr; T Fat 20.1 gr; Chol 29.3 mg;
   Carbo 47.7 gr; Sod 1257.7 mg; Potas 295.0 mg.

Paula G. Webb, Wichita

BREAKFAST PIZZA

1 pound pork sausage
1 (8-ounce) can refrigerator
  crescent dinner rolls
1¼ cups frozen hashed brown
  potatoes, thawed
1 cup (4 ounces) shredded
  Cheddar cheese
1 cup (4 ounces) shredded
  Swiss cheese
5 eggs
1¼ cups milk
½ teaspoon salt
¼ teaspoon pepper
2 tablespoons grated Parmesan
  cheese

Cook sausage in skillet until brown and crumbly; drain. Separate roll dough into triangles. Arrange in ungreased 12-inch pizza pan with points in center; press to seal edges and shape ½-inch edge. Layer sausage, potatoes and cheddar and Swiss cheeses in prepared pan. Beat eggs with milk, salt and pepper. Pour over cheeses. Sprinkle with Parmesan cheese. Bake at 375°F. for 25 to 30 minutes or until golden. Yield: 4 servings.

Approx Per Serving: Cal 870; Prot 40.2 gr; T Fat 62.5 gr; Chol 434.1 mg;
    Carbo 35.1 gr; Sod 1782.0 mg; Potas 591.7 mg.

Bobbi Brooks, Norton

FRENCH BREAD ITALIAN CASSEROLE

½ (16-ounce) loaf French
  bread
4 eggs, beaten
1 cup milk
¼ cup (1 ounce) grated
  Romano cheese
3 drops of Tabasco sauce
1 teaspoon salt
1 pound Italian sausage
Basil to taste
Parsley to taste
1 (15½-ounce) jar spaghetti
  sauce with mushrooms
8 ounces mozzarella cheese,
  shredded

Slice French bread into halves lengthwise. Place cut sides up in greased 8x12-inch glass baking dish. Combine eggs, milk, Romano cheese, Tabasco sauce and salt in bowl; mix well. Pour over bread. Let stand for 30 minutes or longer. Layer sausage over bread. Microwave on HIGH (100% power) for 10 minutes. Sprinkle with basil and parsley. Pour spaghetti sauce over top. Sprinkle with mozzarella cheese. Microwave for 6 to 8 minutes. Let stand for 5 minutes before serving. Yield; 6 servings.

Approx Per Serving: Cal 498; Prot 25.4 gr; T Fat 33.7 gr; Chol 246.0 mg;
    Carbo 45.4 gr; Sod 1387.5 mg; Potas 300.9 mg.
Nutritional information does not include spaghetti sauce.

Jerry Sipes, Manter

SAUSAGE-EGG CASSEROLE

1½ pounds pork sausage
14 slices bread, cubed
8 ounces Cheddar cheese,
    shredded
6 eggs
2½ cups milk
¼ teaspoon salt
1½ teaspoons dry mustard
1 (10½-ounce) can
    mushroom soup
½ cup milk
1 cup chopped fresh
    mushrooms

Cook sausage in skillet until brown and crumbly; drain. Combine with bread and cheese in bowl; mix well. Pour into 9 x 13-inch baking pan. Beat eggs with 2½ cups milk, salt and dry mustard. Pour over sausage mixture. Pour mixture of soup and ½ cup milk over top. Sprinkle with mushrooms. Bake at 300°F. for 1½ hours. Yield: 12 servings.

Approx Per Serving: Cal 401; Prot 18.4 gr; T Fat 25.9 gr; Chol 180.3 mg;
    Carbo 22.7 gr; Sod 858.4 mg; Potas 286.5 mg.

Debbie and Amy Lyons, Manhattar

SCOTCH EGGS

8 hard-boiled eggs
1 pound pork sausage
½ cup all-purpose flour
2 eggs, beaten
1 cup dry bread crumbs
½ teaspoon sage
Oil for deep frying

Peel hard-boiled eggs carefully. Divide sausage into 8 portions. Coat eggs with flour. Shape 1 portion sausage around each egg to cover completely. Dip into beaten eggs; coat with mixture of bread crumbs and sage. Fry 4 eggs at a time in 360°F. oil for 5 to 6 minutes, turning occasionally. Drain on paper towels. Serve hot or cold. Yield: 8 servings.

Approx Per Serving: Cal 306; Prot 15.3 gr; T Fat 19.6 gr; Chol 340.3 mg;
    Carbo 15.7 gr; Sod 423.7 mg; Potas 178.9 mg.
Nutritional information does not include oil for deep-frying.

Craig Dietz, Preston

SAUSAGE CASSEROLE

6 slices bread, trimmed
2 tablespoons butter, softened
1 pound bulk pork sausage
1 cup (4 ounces) shredded
  longhorn cheese
6 eggs, beaten
2 cups half and half
1 teaspoon salt
½ cup (2 ounces) shredded
  longhorn cheese

Spread bread with butter. Place in greased 9 x 13-inch baking dish. Brown sausage in skillet, stirring until crumbly; drain. Layer sausage and 1 cup cheese over bread. Combine eggs, half and half and salt in bowl; mix well. Pour over layers. Sprinkle ½ cup cheese over top. Bake, covered, at 350°F. for 45 minutes. Yield: 6 servings.

Approx Per Serving: Cal 581; Prot 25.0 gr; T Fat 44.7 gr; Chol 359.5 mg; Carbo 19.1 gr; Sod 1181.6 mg; Potas 317.5 mg.

Tom and Jill Docking, Wichita

HOT CHICKEN SALAD

2 cups chopped cooked chicken
2 cups chopped celery
1 (2¼-ounce) package
  slivered almonds
2 tablespoons grated onion
½ teaspoon salt
½ teaspoon garlic powder
1 cup mayonnaise
1 cup crushed potato chips
1 cup (4 ounces) shredded
  Cheddar cheese

Combine chicken, celery, almonds, onion, salt and garlic powder in bowl. Add mayonnaise; mix well. Spoon into greased baking dish. Mix crushed potato chips and cheese in small bowl. Sprinkle over casserole. Bake at 450°F. for 10 minutes. Yield: 4 servings.

Approx Per Serving: Cal 889; Prot 34.1 gr; T Fat 75.3 gr. Chol 120.9 mg; Carbo 22.1 gr; Sod 1015.7 mg; Potas 974.6 mg.

Sandy Lahr, Emporia

BARBECUED CHICKEN

1 frying chicken, cut up
1 cup all-purpose flour
2 tablespoons butter
2 tablespoons shortening
1 cup catsup
1 medium onion, chopped
¼ cup butter
½ cup hot water
⅓ cup lemon juice
1 tablespoon Worcestershire
sauce
1 teaspoon sugar
1 tablespoon paprika
1 teaspoon salt
½ teaspoon pepper

Rinse chicken and pat dry. Shake in bag with flour, coating well. Melt 2 tablespoons butter and shortening in 9 x 13-inch baking dish. Arrange chicken in single layer in prepared dish. Bake at 375°F. for 45 minutes; drain. Turn chicken pieces over. Combine remaining ingredients in saucepan. Bring to a boil. Brush over chicken. Bake for 30 to 45 minutes longer or until chicken is tender, basting frequently with sauce. Yield: 4 servings.

Approx Per Serving: Cal 536; Prot 26.3 gr; T Fat 28.2 gr; Chol 130.0 mg; Carbo 45.2 gr; Sod 1467.3 mg; Potas 602.6 mg.

Dr. Donald W. Wilson, President, Pittsburg State University, Pittsburg

DRESSED CHICKEN AND BROCCOLI

1 medium chicken
2 stalks celery
1 medium onion, cut into
halves
1½ teaspoons salt
1 (10-ounce) package frozen
broccoli, cooked
½ cup melted margarine
3 (heaping) tablespoons flour
3 cups broth
¼ cup Parmesan cheese
½ teaspoon salt
⅛ teaspoon pepper
1 (8-ounce) package herb-
seasoned stuffing mix
½ cup melted margarine
½ cup chicken broth

Place chicken, celery, onion and 1½ teaspoon salt in saucepan. Add water to cover. Simmer until chicken is tender. Remove chicken and chop. Strain broth, reserving 3½ cups. Layer chicken and broccoli in 9 x 13-inch baking dish. Blend ½ cup margarine and flour in saucepan. Add 3 cups reserved broth gradually. Cook until thickened, stirring constantly. Stir in Parmesan cheese, ½ teaspoon salt and pepper. Pour over broccoli. Toss stuffing mix with ½ cup margarine and ½ cup reserved broth in bowl. Spread over casserole. Bake at 350°F. until heated through. Yield: 6 servings.

Approx Per Serving: Cal 598; Prot 31.8 gr; T Fat 36.1 gr; Chol 65.9 mg; Carbo 34.3 gr; Sod 1699.9 mg; Potas 498.5 mg.

Judy McKee, Shawnee Mission

CHICKEN CUSTARD

1 (3½-pound) chicken
1 (8-ounce) package stuffing
   mix
2 eggs, beaten
1 cup milk
1 cup chicken broth
¼ cup melted margarine
½ cup soft bread crumbs

Cook chicken in water to cover in large saucepan until tender; drain, reserving 1 cup broth. Bone chicken; cut into bite-sized pieces. Prepare stuffing mix using package directions. Layer prepared stuffing and boned chicken in 9 x 9-inch baking pan. Combine eggs, milk, reserved broth and margarine in bowl; mix well. Pour over chicken and stuffing. Top with bread crumbs. Bake at 350°F. for 20 to 30 minutes or until custard is set. Yield: 6 servings.

Approx Per Serving: Cal 359; Prot 23.5 gr; T Fat 14.8 gr; Chol 145.2 mg; Carbo 32.3 gr; Sod 820.9 mg; Potas 335.1 mg.
Nutritional information does not include any ingredients necessary to prepare stuffing mix.

Brenda Grace, Haddam

CHICKEN AND RICE

1 (3-pound) frying chicken
½ cup all-purpose flour
¼ cup butter
1 (10-ounce) can cream of
   chicken soup
2½ tablespoons minced onion
1 tablespoon chopped parsley
½ teaspoon instant celery
   flakes
1⅓ cups water
1 teaspoon salt
⅛ teaspoon thyme
1⅓ cups uncooked rice

Season chicken with salt and pepper to taste. Roll in flour, coating well. Brown chicken in butter in skillet. Remove chicken to paper towel to drain. Add soup, onion, parsley, celery flakes, water, salt and thyme to pan drippings; mix well. Bring soup mixture to a boil, stirring to deglaze skillet. Place rice in 9 x 13-inch baking dish. Pour all but ½ cup soup mixture over rice; stir to mix well. Arrange chicken over rice. Spoon remaining ½ cup soup mixture over chicken. Bake, covered with foil, at 325°F. for 2 hours. Yield: 6 servings.

Approx Per Serving: Cal 372; Prot 19.1 gr; T Fat 12.6 gr; Chol 78.8 mg; Carbo 44.0 gr; Sod 892.1 mg; Potas 250.9 mg.

Janet Turner, Marysville

HAWAIIAN CHICKEN

1 (3-pound) chicken, cut up
¼ cup butter, melted
1 (9-ounce) can juice-pack
    crushed pineapple
¼ cup packed brown sugar
2 tablespoons cornstarch
1 teaspoon salt
¼ cup vinegar
½ teaspoon Worcestershire
    sauce
⅓ cup catsup
2 teaspoons chili sauce

Dip each chicken piece into melted butter to coat. Arrange in 9 x 13-inch baking pan. Drain pineapple, reserving juice. Blend reserved juice with brown sugar, cornstarch, salt, vinegar, Worcestershire sauce, catsup and chili sauce. Bring to a boil, stirring constantly. Stir in pineapple. Pour over chicken. Bake, covered, at 325°F. for 1 hour. Turn chicken pieces over; baste. Bake, uncovered, for 30 to 40 minutes longer. Yield: 4 servings.

Approx Per Serving: Cal 361; Prot 21.7 gr; T Fat 15.0 gr; Chol 112.2 mg; Carbo 35.9 gr; Sod 975.6 mg; Potas 454.8 mg.

Scharleen Cross, Bogue

CHICKEN SUPREME

1 frying chicken, cut up
¼ cup oil
1 large green bell pepper, sliced
1 large onion, sliced
1 large orange, sliced
1 (16-ounce) can whole
    tomatoes
¼ cup packed brown sugar
¼ teaspoon Worcestershire
    sauce

Brown chicken in oil in skillet; drain. Add green pepper, onion, orange and tomatoes. Stir in brown sugar, Worcestershire sauce and salt and pepper to taste. Simmer, covered, for 1 hour. Simmer, uncovered, for 15 to 20 minutes or to desired consistency. Serve over rice. Yield: 4 servings.

Approx Per Serving: Cal 353; Prot 23.4 gr; T Fat 17.7 gr; Chol 76.7 mg; Carbo 27.2 gr; Sod 219.8 mg; Potas 711.5 mg.

James D. Braden, Speaker of the House

CHICKEN CHALUPAS

2 (10-ounce) cans cream of
   chicken soup
1½ cups sour cream
1 onion, chopped
1 (4-ounce) can chopped green
   chilies
6 chicken breasts, cooked,
   chopped
12 corn tortillas
2 cups (8 ounces) shredded
   Cheddar cheese
2 cups (8 ounces) shredded
   Monterey Jack cheese

Combine soup, sour cream, onion and green chilies in saucepan; mix well. Cook for 5 minutes. Place 2 to 3 tablespoons chicken on each tortilla. Add 2 tablespoons soup mixture and sprinkle of cheeses. Roll tortillas to enclose filling; secure with toothpicks. Place in 9 x 13-inch baking dish. Top with remaining soup mixture. Bake at 350°F. for 30 minutes.
Yield: 6 servings.

Approx Per Serving: Cal 904; Prot 62.6 gr; T Fat 47.1 gr; Chol 190.8 mg;
   Carbo 58.4 gr; Sod 1432.5 mg; Potas 702.9 mg.

Kari Rogers, Wellsville

CRESCENT CHICKEN

3 chicken breasts
4 ounces sharp Cheddar cheese
2 (8-count) cans refrigerator
   crescent rolls
1 (10-ounce) can cream of
   chicken soup
1 soup can milk

Cook chicken breasts in water to cover in saucepan until tender; drain and bone. Tear chicken breasts into 2½ to 3-inch long strips. Cut cheese into ¼ x 3-inch strips. Separate roll dough into triangles. Place several chicken pieces and 2 cheese strips at wide end of each; roll up. Place in lightly greased 9 x 13-inch baking dish. Pour mixture of soup and milk over top. Bake at 350°F. for 30 minutes or until light brown and bubbly. Yield: 4 servings.

Approx Per Serving: Cal 749; Prot 42.2 gr; T Fat 39.8 gr; Chol 107.1 mg;
   Carbo 53.0 gr; Sod 1868.4 mg; Potas 761.6 mg.

Amy Boehm, Spring Hill

CHICKEN NUGGETS

3 chicken breast filets
½ cup dry bread crumbs
¼ cup Parmesan cheese
2 teaspoons MSG
1 teaspoon dried thyme leaves
1 teaspoon dried basil leaves
½ teaspoon salt
⅓ cup melted butter

Cut chicken breasts into 1 to 1½-inch squares. Press irregular pieces together to approximately the same size. Mix bread crumbs with Parmesan cheese and seasonings in shallow bowl. Dip chicken pieces into butter; coat with crumb mixture. Shape as for nuggets; place in single layer on foil-lined baking sheet. Bake at 400°F. for 15 to 20 minutes. Yield: 4 servings.

Approx Per Serving: Cal 304; Prot 29.2 gr; T Fat 19.8 gr; Chol 116.3 mg; Carbo 0.3 gr; Sod 989.1 mg; Potas 339.1 mg.

Sharon Stauffer Goldsworthy, Germantown, Tennessee

SWEET AND SOUR CHICKEN

12 chicken breasts
1 (8-ounce) can juice-pack
  crushed pineapple
2 tablespoons cornstarch
¾ cup packed brown sugar
½ cup soy sauce
¼ cup vinegar
1 teaspoon garlic powder
½ teaspoon ginger
¼ teaspoon pepper

Bone chicken breasts; arrange skin side down on shallow 3-quart baking dish. Drain pineapple, reserving 2 tablespoons juice. Combine reserved juice with cornstarch, brown sugar, soy sauce, vinegar and seasonings in saucepan. Cook over medium heat until thick and bubbly, stirring constantly. Pour over chicken. Bake at 350°F. for 30 minutes. Turn chicken over. Spread pineapple over top. Bake for 30 minutes longer. Serve over rice. Yield: 12 servings.

Approx Per Serving: Cal 255; Prot 33.9 gr; T Fat 3.7 gr; Chol 82.9 mg; Carbo 20.0 gr; Sod 950.6 mg; Potas 548.2 mg.

Olive W. Garvey, Kansas 4-H Foundation Trustee, Wichita

CHEESY TURKEY LOAF

1 pound ground turkey
1 egg
½ cup milk
¾ cup oats
1 onion, chopped
½ cup (2 ounces) shredded
  Cheddar cheese
3 tablespoons catsup

Combine turkey, egg, milk, oats, onion and cheese in bowl; mix lightly. Shape into loaf in nonstick loaf pan. Spread catsup over top. Bake in preheated 350°F. oven for 1 hour. Yield: 6 servings.

Approx Per Serving: Cal 229; Prot 17.1 gr; T Fat 12.2 gr; Chol 117.3 mg; Carbo 12.5 gr; Sod 167.5 mg; Potas 154.7 mg.

Erika Sweany, St. George

GRANDMA'S CHICKEN BAKE

3 cups chopped cooked chicken
1 cup cooked rice
2 cups soft bread crumbs
1 stalk celery, chopped
1 (4-ounce) jar chopped
  pimento
4 eggs, well beaten
2 cups chicken broth
2 teaspoons salt
¼ teaspoon poultry seasoning
1 (10-ounce) can mushroom
  soup
¼ cup milk

Combine chicken, rice, bread crumbs, celery, pimento, eggs, chicken broth and seasonings in bowl; mix well. Spoon into 8 x 12-inch baking dish. Bake at 350°F. for 1 hour. Combine soup and milk in saucepan. Heat to serving temperature, stirring to mix well. Pour over casserole. Cut into squares. Yield: 6 servings.

Approx Per Serving: Cal 338; Prot 27.5 gr; T Fat 15.6 gr; Chol 234.0 mg; Carbo 20.0 gr; Sod 1625.9 mg; Potas 376.7 mg.

Gloria Stevenson, El Dorado

CHICKEN ENCHILADAS

1 cup chopped onion
½ cup chopped green
  bell pepper
2 tablespoons margarine
2 cups chopped cooked chicken
1 (4-ounce) can chopped
  green chilies
3 tablespoons melted margarine
⅓ cup all-purpose flour
1 teaspoon coriander
¾ teaspoon salt
3 cups chicken broth
1 cup sour cream
½ cup (2 ounces) shredded
  Monterey Jack cheese
12 (6-inch) corn tortillas
1 cup (4 ounces) shredded
  Monterey Jack cheese

Sauté onion and green pepper in 2 tablespoons margarine in skillet until tender. Mix with chicken and green chilies in bowl. Blend 3 tablespoons melted margarine, flour, coriander and salt in saucepan. Stir in broth gradually. Cook until thickened, stirring constantly. Cook for 2 minutes longer. Add sour cream and ½ cup cheese; stir until cheese melts. Add about ½ cup sauce to chicken mixture; mix well. Dip tortillas 1 at a time into sauce. Place ¼ cup chicken mixture on tortilla; roll to enclose filling. Place seam side down in 9 x 13-inch baking pan. Spoon remaining sauce over top. Sprinkle with 1 cup remaining cheese. Bake at 350°F. for 25 minutes.
Yield: 6 servings.

Approx Per Serving: Cal 514; Prot 28.7 gr; T Fat 29.6 gr; Chol 87.9 mg; Carbo 34.4 gr; Sod 997.2 mg; Potas 426.7 mg.

Patricia Booth, Randolph

CHICKEN TETRAZZINI

1 medium onion, chopped
1 stalk celery, chopped
3 tablespoons butter
2 cups chopped cooked chicken
1 (6-ounce) package spaghetti
1 (10-ounce) can cream of
chicken soup
2½ cups chicken broth
¼ teaspoon salt
½ teaspoon pepper
1 cup sliced mushrooms
½ cup Parmesan cheese

Sauté onion and celery in butter in skillet until clear. Layer chicken and uncooked spaghetti over vegetables. Add mixture of soup, broth, salt and pepper. Top with layers of mushrooms and Parmesan cheese. Bring to a boil; reduce heat. Simmer, covered, for 30 minutes or until spaghetti is tender, stirring occasionally. Yield: 6 servings.

Approx Per Serving: Cal 313; Prot 24.7 gr; T Fat 8.2 gr; Chol 65.2 mg;
Carbo 28.4 gr; Sod 944.3 mg; Potas 449.6 mg.

Jill Livingston, Mahaska

ZUCCHINI CHICKEN

4 medium zucchini
¾ cup shredded carrots
½ cup chopped onion
¼ cup margarine
1½ cups herb-seasoned
stuffing mix
1 cup sour cream
1 (10-ounce) can cream of
chicken soup
3 cups chopped cooked chicken
1 cup herb-seasoned
stuffing mix
2 tablespoons melted margarine

Cut zucchini into ½-inch slices. Cook in a small amount of salted water until tender; drain well. Sauté carrots and onion in ¼ cup margarine in skillet until tender; remove from heat. Stir in 1½ cups stuffing mix, sour cream, soup and chicken. Fold in zucchini. Spoon into 2-quart casserole. Toss remaining 1 cup stuffing mix with 2 tablespoons melted margarine. Sprinkle over chicken mixture. Bake at 350°F. for 30 to 40 minutes. Yield: 6 servings.

Approx Per Serving: Cal 501; Prot 30.2 gr; T Fat 25.8 gr; Chol 76.1 mg;
Carbo 37.7 gr; Sod 1118.0 mg; Potas 657.8 mg.

Rita Johnson, Assaria

MAI CHINESE CHICKEN

2 cups chop suey vegetables
1 (10-ounce) can cream of
  chicken soup
2 cups chopped cooked chicken
1 tablespoon dried chives
1 (4-ounce) can water
  chestnuts
1 tablespoon chopped pimento
1 (8-ounce) can chow mein
  noodles

Combine undrained vegetables, soup, chicken, chives, water chestnuts and pimento in bowl; mix well. Spoon into 8x8-inch glass baking dish. Microwave on HIGH (100% power) for 5 minutes. Stir in most of the noodles. Microwave for 3 minutes longer. Bake at 375°F. for 20 minutes. Sprinkle with remaining noodles. Bake for 10 minutes longer. Yield: 6 servings.

> **Approx Per Serving:** Cal 322; Prot 19.5 gr; T Fat 15.3 gr; Chol 38.4 mg; Carbo 37.0 gr; Sod 864.2 mg; Potas 273.7 mg.
> Nutritional information does not include chop suey vegetables.

Nita Mai, Lenora

BAKED CATFISH

1 (12 to 15-pound) catfish
1 to 2 teaspoons liquid smoke
2 to 3 tablespoons margarine
1 package crackers, crushed

Rinse catfish and pat dry. Rub with liquid smoke. Brush with melted margarine. Roll in cracker crumbs, coating well. Place on rack in roasting pan. Bake at 325°F. for 3 to 4 hours or until very tender. Yield: 12 servings.

> Nutritional analysis not available.

Nada E. Thoden, Spring Hill

TUNA CASSEROLE DELIGHT

1 (8-ounce) package noodles
1 (6½-ounce) can water-pack
  tuna
½ cup grated onion
1 (10-ounce) can cream of
  mushroom soup
1 soup can milk
1 cup (4 ounces) shredded
  Cheddar cheese
1 tablespoon vinegar
¼ cup Parmesan cheese

Cook noodles according to package directions; drain. Combine tuna, onion, soup, milk, Cheddar cheese and vinegar in bowl; mix well. Stir in noodles. Spoon into 2-quart baking dish. Sprinkle with Parmesan cheese. Bake at 350°F. for 1 hour. Yield: 8 servings.

> **Approx Per Serving:** Cal 282; Prot 17.2 gr; T Fat 11.4 gr; Chol 67.2 mg; Carbo 26.9 gr; Sod 645.8 mg; Potas 226.1 mg.

Lovetra Harrington, Colony

TUNA AND SHELLS

4 cups shell macaroni
1 (6½-ounce) can water-pack
  tuna
1 cup sliced celery
½ cup sliced sweet pickles
⅓ cup chopped onion
⅓ cup chopped carrot
1 cup mayonnaise
1 tablespoon sweet pickle juice

Cook macaroni according to package directions; drain well. Combine with remaining ingredients in bowl; mix well. Chill until serving time. Garnish with parsley and paprika.
Yield: 6 servings.

Approx Per Serving: Cal 602; Prot 18.9 gr; T Fat 31.0 gr; Chol 45.5 mg;
  Carbo 61.6 gr; Sod 557.0 mg; Potas 357.6 mg.

Karrie Parrack, Mahaska

TUNA CASSEROLE

2 (6½-ounce) cans water-pack
  tuna
1 (6½-ounce) can salmon
1 cup bread crumbs
2 eggs, beaten
⅔ cup milk
3 tablespoons lemon juice
3 tablespoons chopped parsley
1 large onion, chopped
¼ cup butter
½ cup bread crumbs
2 tablespoons melted butter

Drain and flake tuna and salmon. Combine with 1 cup bread crumbs, eggs, milk and lemon juice in bowl; mix well. Sauté parsley and onion in ¼ cup butter in small skillet. Add to tuna mixture; mix well. Spoon into baking dish. Mix remaining ½ cup bread crumbs with 2 tablespoons melted butter in bowl. Sprinkle over casserole. Bake at 350°F. for 25 to 30 minutes or until bubbly and brown.
Yield: 4 servings.

Approx Per Serving: Cal 492; Prot 44.5 gr; T Fat 26.3 gr; Chol 263.2 mg;
  Carbo 17.9 gr; Sod 1392.5 mg; Potas 675.5 mg.

Travis W. Kamm, Abilene

TUNA NOODLE CASSEROLE

1 (10-ounce) package noodles
⅜ teaspoon garlic powder
½ cup melted margarine
2 tablespoons (heaping) flour
2 cups milk
1 (2-inch slice) Velveeta cheese
1 (10-ounce) package frozen
  peas
2 (7-ounce) cans chunk tuna
1 (10-ounce) can cream of
  mushroom soup

Cook noodles with garlic powder according to package directions; drain. Blend margarine and flour in saucepan. Add milk gradually. Cook until thickened, stirring constantly. Stir in cheese until melted. Fold in noodles and peas. Add mixture of tuna and soup; mix gently. Spoon into buttered baking dish. Bake at 325°F. for 1 hour. Yield: 6 servings.

Approx Per Serving: Cal 664; Prot 28.6 gr; T Fat 38.2 gr; Chol 93.0 mg; Carbo 50.5 gr; Sod 1251.9 mg; Potas 454.7 mg.

Andrea Klipp, Hanover

QUICK AND EASY VENISON STRIPS

1 (1¼ to 1½-pound) venison
  round steak
1 green pepper
2 tablespoons (or more) butter
1 large onion, thinly sliced
1 tablespoon Wagner's game
  seasoning

Trim all fat from vension. Cut into paper-thin slices. Slice green pepper into thin rounds; discard membrane and seed. Melt 2 tablespoons butter in heavy skillet over medium heat. Add green pepper and onion. Cook for 5 minutes or until light brown and wilted, stirring frequently. Remove with slotted spoon to heated serving plate. Melt additional butter in skillet if necessary. Add venison strips in single layer. Sprinkle with seasoning. Cook over medium-high heat for 1 minute; turn strips over. Cook for 2 minutes longer. Add green pepper and onion. Heat for several seconds longer, stirring constantly. Do not overcook. Serve immediately on heated plates. Yield: 4 to 6 servings.
Note: Slicing venison or any meat very thinly is much easier if the meat is partially frozen before slicing with very sharp knife.

Nutritional analysis not available.

Janelle Wilmeth, Wichita

ROAST BREAST OF DUCK

4 to 8 duck breasts, skinned
1 medium apple, quartered
Leaves of 5 or 6 celery stalks
1 package instant brown gravy
  mix
1 (6-ounce) can frozen orange
  juice concentrate
1 (6-ounce) jar plum jelly

Place duck, apple and celery in medium roasting bag, following manufacturer's instructions. Place in 9x13-inch baking dish. Purée remaining ingredients in blender container. Spoon over duck in bag; fasten bag securely. Bake at 375°F. for 1 hour or until tender. Remove duck to warm serving platter. Serve with sauce. Yield: 4 to 8 servings.

Nutritional analysis not available.

Melissa Fitzgerald, Pratt

PHEASANT DELUXE

1 large pheasant
1 medium onion, chopped
1½ cups chopped celery
4 cups crushed Ritz crackers
1 (10-ounce) can mushroom
  soup
4 cups broth
3 eggs, beaten
1½ cups (6 ounces) shredded
  American cheese
½ teaspoon pepper
½ teaspoon salt

Simmer pheasant in salted water to cover in saucepan until tender. Chop pheasant into bite-sized pieces. Combine with onion, celery, cracker crumbs, soup, broth, eggs, cheese and seasonings in bowl; mix well. Spoon into shallow baking dish. Bake at 350°F. for 1 hour.

Nutritional analysis not available.

Honorable Mike Hayden, Governor of Kansas

PHANTASTIC PHEASANT

1 cup all-purpose flour
1 cup beer
1 teaspoon Italian seasoning
½ to 1 teaspoon Extra Spicy
  Mrs. Dash seasoning
Cayenne pepper to taste
½ teaspoon salt
2 or 3 pheasant breast filets
Oil for deep frying

Mix flour and beer in bowl. Let stand for 2 to 3 hours. Add seasonings and pepper to taste; mix well. Cut pheasant into bite-sized pieces. Dip in batter, coating well. Deep-fry in 400°F. oil until golden brown; drain. Yield: 4 servings.

Nutritional analysis not available.

Jeannie Engel, Brewster

RABBIT DIVAN

1 (16-ounce) package frozen
　broccoli cuts, partially
　cooked
4 cups chopped cooked rabbit
1 (10-ounce) can cream of
　mushroom soup
½ cup mayonnaise
¼ cup milk
1 teaspoon lemon juice
½ cup (2 ounces) shredded
　Cheddar cheese

Layer broccoli and rabbit in 9x12-inch baking dish. Combine soup, mayonnaise, milk and lemon juice in bowl; mix well. Pour over layers. Sprinkle with cheese. Bake at 350°F. for 30 minutes. Yield: 4 servings.

Nutritional analysis not available.

Jamie Stark, Lenora

SQUIRREL ACADIEN

3 or 4 squirrels, cut up
Salt and pepper to taste
All-purpose flour
Oil
1 cup chopped onion
3 stalks celery, chopped
3 tablespoons chopped green
　bell pepper
2 cups tomatoes
1 can Ro-Tel tomatoes
1 clove of garlic, minced
½ cup red wine
2 tablespoons chopped
　green onions
1 cup sliced mushrooms

Season squirrels with salt and pepper to taste. Roll in flour, coating well. Brown in oil in heavy saucepan; drain. Add onion, celery, green pepper, tomatoes and garlic. Simmer for 1 to 2 hours or until squirrel is tender. Add wine, green onions and mushrooms. Simmer for 30 minutes longer. Serve over hot rice. Yield: 4 servings.

Nutritional analysis not available.

Becky Hopkins, Fredonia

CLASSIC CHEESE STRATA

12 slices day-old bread
3 tablespoons butter, softened
8 ounces Cheddar cheese,
  shredded
4 eggs, beaten
2½ cups milk
¼ cup finely chopped onion
½ teaspoon dry mustard
Paprika to taste

Trim crusts from bread. Spread bread on both sides with butter; arrange in greased 12 x 15-inch baking pan. Sprinkle cheese over top. Beat eggs with milk, onion and dry mustard. Pour over cheese; sprinkle with paprika. Refrigerate overnight. Bake at 325°F. for 1 hour or until golden brown. Let stand for 10 minutes before cutting. Yield: 10 servings.
Note: May sprinkle chopped ham or cooked and well-drained sausage or bacon over bread.

Approx Per Serving: Cal 286; Prot 13.4 gr; T Fat 16.3 gr; Chol 143.7 mg; Carbo 21.2 gr; Sod 428.1 mg; Potas 175.6 mg.

Beverly Aiken, Havana

CHEESE ENCHILADAS

2 medium onions, chopped
2 large green bell peppers,
  chopped
3 tablespoons oil
2 (10-ounce) cans mild
  enchilada sauce
1 cup sour cream
12 corn tortillas
¼ cup oil
1 pound Monterey Jack cheese,
  thickly sliced
2 cups (8 ounces) shredded
  mild Cheddar cheese

Sauté onions and green peppers in 3 tablespoons oil in skillet; do not brown. Combine enchilada sauce and sour cream in saucepan. Simmer for 1 minute. Spread a small amount of sauce in 9 x 13-inch baking dish. Soften tortillas 1 at a time in ¼ cup hot oil in skillet for several seconds; drain on paper towel. Add onion mixture and Monterey Jack cheese; roll to enclose filling. Place seam side down in prepared dish. Repeat with remaining tortillas. Pour remaining enchilada sauce over top. Sprinkle with Cheddar cheese. Bake at 375°F. for 20 to 25 minutes or until heated through.
Yield: 6 servings.

Approx Per Serving: Cal 916; Prot 36.6 gr; T Fat 62.9 gr; Chol 129.0 mg; Carbo 54.9 gr; Sod 823.9 mg; Potas 321.3 mg.

Gail Eyestone, Los Angeles, California

MACARONI AND CHEESE WITH PEAS

1 (7-ounce) package macaroni
and cheese dinner
1 (10-ounce) package frozen
peas
½ cup milk
2 tablespoons margarine
1 (6½-ounce) can water-pack
tuna

Cook macaroni according to package directions, adding peas when water returns to the boil after adding macaroni. Drain. Add milk and margarine; mix well. Stir in tuna. Pour into 1-quart casserole. Bake at 350°F. for 30 minutes. Yield: 4 servings.

Approx Per Serving: Cal 425; Prot 27.3 gr; T Fat 20.0 gr; Chol 71.8 mg; Carbo 33.4 gr; Sod 1195.2 mg; Potas 416.5 mg.

Scott Shepard, Lenora

EGGS ELEGANTE

4 frozen puff pastry shells
2 cups sliced fresh mushrooms
2 medium tomatoes
4 green onions, sliced
¼ cup butter
¼ cup minced fresh parsley
3 egg yolks
1 tablespoon lemon juice
1 tablespoon hot water
1 teaspoon Dijon mustard
½ teaspoon salt
⅛ teaspoon cayenne pepper
1 cup melted butter
4 eggs

Bake pastry shells according to package directions. Sauté mushrooms, tomatoes and green onions in ¼ cup butter in skillet for 2 to 3 minutes. Add parsley. Simmer until liquid has evaporated; keep warm. Combine egg yolks, lemon juice, hot water, mustard, salt and cayenne pepper in blender container. Process on High until well blended. Add 1 cup melted butter in fine stream, processing on Low for 15 to 20 seconds or until mixture thickens. Keep warm. Bring 2 inches water to a boil in skillet. Break eggs into water. Poach to desired degree of doneness. Slice off top ¼ of the pastry shells; remove doughy centers. Place shells on serving plates. Fill with vegetable mixture. Top with poached egg. Replace top of pastry shells. Spoon Hollandaise sauce over top. Garnish with paprika. Yield: 4 servings.

Approx Per Serving: Cal 668; Prot 10.9 gr; T Fat 67.5 gr; Chol 619.0 mg; Carbo 7.5 gr; Sod 1060.3 mg; Potas 457.2 mg.
Nutritional information does not include pastry shells.

Kansas Poultry Association, Manhattan

REAL-MEN-DO-EAT-QUICHE

½ cup shredded peeled potato
½ cup chopped broccoli
2 tablespoons green onions
1 tablespoon flour
4 eggs, beaten
1½ cups milk
¼ teaspoon oregano
¼ teaspoon coarse pepper
¼ teaspoon salt
Parsley to taste
1 cup (4 ounces) Monterey
 Jack cheese

Steam vegetables until tender-crisp; toss with flour to prevent sticking. Beat eggs with milk and seasonings in bowl. Stir in vegetables. Pour into quiche pan; top with cheese. Place pan in large pan with 1 inch hot water. Bake at 325°F. for 40 to 50 minutes or until knife inserted in center comes out clean. Serve with fresh apple slices, orange sections and a cranberry drink. Yield: 6 servings.

Approx Per Serving: Cal 223; Prot 13.9 gr; T Fat 14.0 gr; Chol 217.6 mg;
 Carbo 10.1 gr; Sod 323.5 mg; Potas 340.3 mg.

Audra Dietz, Preston

CHRISTMAS SANDWICHES

2 (16-ounce) loaves French
 bread
1 (8-ounce) jar peanut butter
1 (12-ounce) can Spam
1 (8-ounce) jar Kosher dill
 pickles

Split loaves lengthwise. Spread cut sides lightly with peanut butter. Slice Spam and pickles very thinly. Layer Spam and pickles on bottom halves of loaves; replace tops. Wrap each in foil. Store in refrigerator. Bake at 350°F. for 35 to 45 minutes or until peanut butter is melted and Spam is heated through. Serve with a relish plate and homemade cookies. Yield: 24 servings.

Approx Per Serving: Cal 214; Prot 8.3 gr; T Fat 10.1 gr; Chol 13.7 mg;
 Carbo 23.1 gr; Sod 591.3 mg; Potas 150.9 mg.

Barbara Siebert, Hutchinson

PLEASANT HILL BIEROCKS

3 packages dry yeast
½ cup sugar
2 cups warm (110 to 115°F.)
   water
½ cup shortening
7 cups all-purpose flour
1 tablespoon salt
1 tablespoon nonfat dry milk
   powder
1½ pounds ground beef
1 medium head cabbage,
   shredded
1 medium onion, chopped
Horseradish and dry mustard
   to taste

Dissolve yeast and sugar in warm water in large mixer bowl. Let stand until bubbly. Add shortening, flour, salt and dry milk powder; mix well. Knead with dough hook for 10 minutes or until smooth and elastic. Brush top of dough with melted shortening. Let rise, covered, until doubled in bulk. Cook ground beef with cabbage and onion in skillet over low heat until brown and crumbly, stirring frequently; drain. Season with salt, pepper and MSG to taste. Add horseradish and dry mustard. Roll dough to ¼-inch thickness; cut into 4-inch squares. Spoon ground beef mixture onto squares. Fold edges together to enclose filling; seal. Place on greased baking sheet. Let rise. Bake at 350°F. for 20 minutes. Brush with melted butter. Serve immediately or cool on wire racks.
Yield: 30 servings.
Note: The Pleasant Hill 4-H Club in Cheyenne County makes and sells Bierocks for German Heritage Day.

Approx Per Serving: Cal 210; Prot 7.8 gr; T Fat 7.4 gr; Chol 15.4 mg;
   Carbo 27.8 gr; Sod 231.0 mg; Potas 164.9 mg.

Ruth Milliken, St. Francis

CABBAGE POCKETS

1 pound ground beef
1 small onion, chopped
3 cups shredded cabbage
1 (16-ounce) package frozen
   bread dough, thawed

Cook ground beef with onion in skillet until brown and crumbly; drain. Add cabbage; season with salt and pepper to taste; mix well. Cook over low heat until cabbage is tender. Cool to lukewarm. Roll bread dough to ¼-inch thickness; cut into 3-inch squares. Place about ¼ cup ground beef mixture in center of each square. Fold corners to center; press to seal. Place sealed side down on lightly greased baking sheet. Let rise for 15 minutes. Bake at 350°F. for 20 minutes or until golden brown.
Yield: 12 servings.

Approx Per Serving: Cal 196; Prot 10.6 gr; T Fat 5.9 gr; Chol 25.9 mg;
   Carbo 24.4 gr; Sod 255.3 mg; Potas 354.8 mg.

Orvell Brunner, Ramona

GROUND BEEF-STUFFED FRENCH BREAD

1 pound ground beef
½ cup chopped green
  bell pepper
½ cup chopped celery
½ teaspoon pepper
1 tablespoon Worcestershire
  sauce
1 teaspoon salt
1 (10½-ounce) can Cheddar
  cheese soup
1 (16-ounce) loaf unsliced
  French bread
4 ounces Cheddar cheese,
  sliced

Brown ground beef in skillet, stirring until crumbly; drain. Add green pepper, celery, pepper, Worcestershire sauce, salt and soup; mix well. Simmer for 5 minutes. Cut top from loaf; scoop out center to form shell. Tear enough scooped out bread into pieces to measure 2 cups. Stir into ground beef mixture. Spoon mixture into bread shell. Top with cheese slices; replace top of loaf. Place on baking sheet. Bake at 350°F. for 5 to 8 minutes or until heated through and cheese is melted. Cut into slices. Yield: 15 servings.

Approx Per Serving: Cal 182; Prot 10.0 gr; T Fat 7.7 gr; Chol 29.3 mg; Carbo 17.1 gr; Sod 407.4 mg; Potas 125.6 mg.
Nutritional information does not include cheese soup.

Heather Frasier, Sharon Springs

QUICK SLOPPY JOES

2 pounds ground beef
1 onion, chopped
1 (10-ounce) can tomato soup
1 teaspoon sugar
1 teaspoon mustard
1 tablespoon catsup
4 hamburger buns

Brown ground beef with onion in skillet, stirring until crumbly; drain. Add soup, sugar, mustard and catsup; mix well. Simmer for 5 to 10 minutes. Serve on buns. Yield: 4 servings.

Approx Per Serving: Cal 665; Prot 44.4 gr; T Fat 36.8 gr; Chol 153.2 mg; Carbo 36.4 gr; Sod 961.5 mg; Potas 705.1 mg.

Eva Mae Mount, Bucyrus

PIZZA-WICHES

1 pound ground beef
1 pound Cheddar cheese,
   shredded
1 medium onion, ground
1 (10-ounce) can tomato soup
½ soup can oil
1 teaspoon garlic salt
½ teaspoon oregano
1 (16-ounce) loaf unsliced
   Italian bread

Brown ground beef in skillet, stirring until crumbly; drain. Combine with cheese, onion, soup, oil, garlic salt and oregano in bowl; mix well. Season with salt and pepper to taste. Chill for several hours. Slice bread. Spread with ground beef mixture; place on baking sheet. Broil about 3 inches from heat source for 3 minutes. Yield: 15 servings.

Approx Per Serving: Cal 368; Prot 16.2 gr; T Fat 23.9 gr; Chol 50.6 mg;
   Carbo 22.0 gr; Sod 715.1 mg; Potas 158.9 mg.

Neil Manville, Valley Falls

SANDWICH STROGANOFF

1 teaspoon salt
1 pound ground beef
¼ cup chopped onion
¼ teaspoon garlic juice
¼ teaspoon pepper
½ teaspoon Worcestershire
   sauce
2 tablespoons all-purpose flour
¼ cup chili sauce
¾ cup sour cream
½ loaf French bread, sliced
   lengthwise
4 (¾-ounce) slices American
   cheese
4 tomato slices
4 green bell pepper rings

Sprinkle salt into preheated skillet. Add ground beef and onion. Cook until brown and crumbly, stirring frequently; drain. Add garlic juice, pepper and Worcestershire sauce; mix well. Sprinkle with flour. Stir in chili sauce; reduce heat. Add sour cream; mix well. Heat to serving temperature. Spoon onto bread. Add cheese slices, tomato slices and pepper rings. Broil until cheese melts. Serve immediately. Yield: 4 servings.

Approx Per Serving: Cal 641; Prot 33.0 gr; T Fat 33.0 gr; Chol 113.0 mg;
   Carbo 52.0 gr; Sod 1515.1 mg; Potas 569.3 mg.

Wreatha Streeter Tenney, Phoenix, Arizona
Joyce Plyter, Milton Freewater, Oregon

GRILLED PORKBURGERS

1 (8-ounce) can mushrooms
4 pounds ground pork
2 tablespoons onion flakes
1½ tablespoons paprika
1 tablespoon celery salt
1 tablespoon garlic powder
½ teaspoon pepper
1 cup (4 ounces) shredded
   Cheddar cheese

Drain mushrooms, reserving liquid. Combine ground pork, reserved liquid, onion flakes, paprika, celery salt, garlic powder and pepper in bowl; mix well. Shape into sixteen ½ inch thick patties. Place cheese and mushrooms on 8 patties; top with remaining patties. Seal edges to enclose filling. Grill 6 inches above medium coals for 25 minutes or until cooked through. Serve as desired. Yield: 8 servings.

Approx Per Serving: Cal 506; Prot 33.9 gr; T Fat 39.4 gr; Chol 122.6 mg; Carbo 1.6 gr; Sod 972.0 mg; Potas 354.8 mg.

Marita Ronnau, St. Marys

RIBBON SANDWICHES

½ (16-ounce) loaf unsliced
   white bread
½ (16-ounce) loaf unsliced
   whole wheat bread
¾ cup cottage cheese
¾ cups margarine, softened
2 tablespoons chopped green
   bell pepper
1 tablespoon chopped onion
2 tablespoons chopped pimento
⅛ teaspoon thyme
⅛ teaspoon celery salt

Trim crusts from bread loaves; set aside. Beat cottage cheese in mixer bowl until creamy. Add margarine, green pepper, onion, pimento and seasonings; beat until well mixed. Spread top of each loaf with cottage cheese mixture. Cut thin lengthwise slice from top of each. Repeat process as many times as desired. Assemble loaf alternating slices of white and whole wheat bread beginning and ending with white slices. Press together lightly. Chill, wrapped in waxed paper until serving time. Slice through layers carefully. Yield: 24 servings.

Approx Per Serving: Cal 106; Prot 2.8 gr; T Fat 6.6 gr; Chol 2.0 mg; Carbo 9.1 gr; Sod 191.4 mg; Potas 45.9 mg.

Martha Risley, Wichita

SALMON CROISSANTS

4 croissants, split
2 cups red salmon, drained
3 ounces cream cheese,
   softened
3 tablespoons lemon juice
1½ teaspoons dried dillweed
1 cucumber

Bake croissants in preheated 325°F. oven for 10 minutes. Cool. Combine next 4 ingredients in bowl; toss gently. Score cucumber with fork; slice thinly. Fill croissants with salmon mixture and cucumber slices. Garnish with fresh dill sprigs or parsley. Yield: 4 servings.

Nutritional analysis not available.

Amy Walton, Goddard

ROBOT ROUNDS

1 (10-ounce) package
   refrigerator hot loaf
1 egg, beaten
1 teaspoon water
4 (1-ounce) slices American
   cheese
1 (2½-ounce) package wafer
   thin turkey
12 slices dill pickle
4 (1-ounce) slices process
   Swiss cheese

Divide dough into 8 portions; roll each into 5-inch circle. Moisten edges of circles with egg beaten with water. Mound American cheese, turkey, 3 pickle slices and Swiss cheese on 4 circles; top with remaining circles egg side down. Seal edges with fork. Place on greased baking sheet. Prick tops with fork; brush with remaining egg mixture. Bake at 375°F. for 15 to 20 minutes or until golden. Serve warm or cold. Yield: 4 servings.

Approx Per Serving: Cal 264; Prot 21.0 gr; T Fat 16.9 gr; Chol 125.5 mg;
    Carbo 6.6 gr; Sod 834.9 mg; Potas 228.1 mg.
Nutritional information does not include hot loaf.

Joelle Schweitzer, Osborne

TUNA SCHOONERS

1 (3¼-ounce) can water-pack
   tuna, drained, flaked
¼ cup salad dressing
¼ cup chopped apple
2 tablespoons sunflower seed
2 whole grain English muffins
8 triangular tortilla chips

Combine tuna, salad dressing, apple and sunflower seed in bowl; mix well. Chill if desired. Split and toast English muffins. Spread with tuna mixture. Insert 2 tortilla chips in each muffin to resemble sails. Yield: 4 servings.

Approx Per Serving: Cal 149; Prot 8.2 gr; T Fat 9.9 gr; Chol 22.0 mg;
    Carbo 8.0 gr; Sod 290.6 mg; Potas 117.5 mg.
Nutritional information does not include English muffins.

Lindsay Stockebrand, Halstead

Summer Celebration
(Picnic)

QUICK BEAN DIP
page 13

SHOE PEG CORN SALAD
page 47

SALMON CROISSANTS
page 103

ROBOT ROUNDS
page 104

DEVILED EGGS
page 121

SWEDISH APPLE CAKE
page 126

LOLLIPOP COOKIES
page 151

"REMEMBERING" by Brenda Andres

MARINATED ASPARAGUS

4 cups asparagus pieces
¾ cup olive oil
¼ cup lemon juice
1 teaspoon minced garlic
1 (2-ounce) jar sliced pimento
1 teaspoon Worcestershire
  sauce
1 teaspoon basil leaves
½ teaspoon salt
½ teaspoon pepper

Combine asparagus with a small amount of water in saucepan. Cook for 3 to 4 minutes or just until tender-crisp. Drain and cool. Combine olive oil, lemon juice, garlic, pimento, Worcestershire sauce and seasonings in bowl; mix well. Add asparagus. Marinate, covered, in refrigerator for 24 hours. Yield: 4 servings.

Approx Per Serving: Cal 438; Prot 4.2 gr; T Fat 41.0 gr; Chol 0.0 mg;
    Carbo 17.0 gr; Sod 286.0 mg; Potas 594.2 mg.
Nutritional information includes entire amount of marinade.

Gregory Pease, Maple Hill

CHANCELLOR'S FAVORITE RANCH BEANS

2 medium white onions,
  chopped
2 large green bell peppers,
  chopped
½ cup butter
2 (15-ounce) cans pork and
  beans, drained
1 (15-ounce) can ranch-style
  beans
½ cup catsup
½ cup Worcestershire sauce
⅛ teaspoon Tabasco sauce
1 tablespoon garlic salt
⅛ teaspoon cayenne pepper
1 pound Velveeta cheese, cubed

Sauté onions and green peppers in butter in saucepan. Add beans, catsup, Worcestershire sauce, Tabasco sauce, seasonings and ¾ of the cheese; mix well. Spoon into bean pot. Sprinkle remaining cheese on top. Bake at 350°F. for 1 hour; do not stir. Yield: 8 servings.

Approx Per Serving: Cal 571; Prot 24.7 gr; T Fat 30.3 gr; Chol 84.0 mg;
    Carbo 52.4 gr; Sod 3044.1 mg; Potas 879.2 mg.

Gene A. Budig, Chancellor, University of Kansas, Lawrence

Gene A. Budig

SAVORY BAKED BEANS

2 (29-ounce) cans pork
 and beans
1 pound bacon, chopped
2 large green bell peppers,
 chopped
2 medium onions, chopped
2 teaspoons Worcestershire
 sauce
1 cup catsup
1 cup packed brown sugar

Combine beans, bacon, green peppers, on-ions, Worcestershire sauce, catsup and brown sugar in bowl; mix well. Pour into casserole. Bake, covered, at 325°F. for 2½ hours, stirring occasionally. Bake, uncovered, for 30 minutes longer. Yield: 20 servings.

> **Approx Per Serving:** Cal 320; Prot 7.9 gr; T Fat 18.1 gr; Chol 19.4 mg;
> Carbo 32.4 gr; Sod 702.9 mg; Potas 338.0 mg.

Tommy Green Family, LaCygne

BARBECUED GREEN BEANS

8 ounces bacon, chopped
1 medium onion, chopped
1 cup catsup
1 cup packed brown sugar
3 (16-ounce) cans green beans,
 drained

Brown bacon and onion in skillet. Add catsup and brown sugar; mix well. Place green beans in baking dish. Pour bacon mixture over beans. Bake at 250°F. for 3 hours. Yield: 8 servings.

> **Approx Per Serving:** Cal 359; Prot 4.9 gr; T Fat 19.9 gr; Chol 19.8 mg;
> Carbo 42.7 gr; Sod 903.7 mg; Potas 421.8 mg.

Marie Larson, Chapman

GREEN BEAN CASSEROLE

1 (10-ounce) can Cheddar
 cheese soup
½ cup milk
8 cups green beans, drained
½ cup slivered almonds
1 (3-ounce) can French-fried
 onions

Mix soup and milk in bowl. Add beans, al-monds and onions; mix well. Spoon into bak-ing dish. Bake at 375°F. for 1 hour. Yield: 10 servings.

> **Approx Per Serving:** Cal 108; Prot 3.0 gr; T Fat 5.5 gr; Chol 1.7 mg;
> Carbo 13.1 gr; Sod 391.7 mg; Potas 164.6 mg.
> Nutritional information does not include cheese soup.

Mary K. Hermesch, Goff

SWEET AND SOUR GREEN BEANS

3 slices bacon
2 tablespoons brown sugar
2 tablespoons cornstarch
4 cups canned green beans
¼ cup vinegar

Fry bacon in skillet until crisp. Reserve half the drippings. Stir brown sugar and cornstarch in reserved drippings. Cook until thickened, stirring constantly. Drain beans, reserving liquid. Stir bean liquid and vinegar into skillet. Bring to a boil. Add green beans. Simmer for 20 minutes. Crumble bacon over top. Yield: 8 servings.

Approx Per Serving: Cal 94; Prot 1.7 gr; T Fat 6.0 gr; Chol 6.0 mg; Carbo 9.2 gr; Sod 218.3 mg; Potas 95.0 mg.

Ruth Colgin, Colony

THREE-BEAN CASSEROLE

1 pound ground beef
4 ounces bacon, chopped
1 medium onion, chopped
1 (29-ounce) can pork
 and beans
1 (16-ounce) can kidney beans
1 (16-ounce) can butter beans
½ cup packed brown sugar
½ cup catsup
2 tablespoons vinegar
½ teaspoon salt

Brown ground beef, bacon and onion in skillet, stirring until ground beef is crumbly; drain. Add drained beans, brown sugar, catsup, vinegar and salt; mix well. Spoon into greased 2-quart baking dish. Bake at 350°F. for 1 hour. Yield: 8 servings.

Approx Per Serving: Cal 452; Prot 24.4 gr; T Fat 14.1 gr; Chol 46.9 mg; Carbo 58.3 gr; Sod 986.1 mg; Potas 749.0 mg.

Janice Pauls, McPherson

BEETS WITH PINEAPPLE

2 tablespoons brown sugar
1 tablespoon cornstarch
¼ teaspoon salt
1 cup pineapple tidbits
1 tablespoon butter
1 tablespoon lemon juice
2 cups sliced cooked beets

Mix brown sugar, cornstarch and salt in saucepan. Add pineapple with syrup; mix well. Cook until thickened and bubbly, stirring constantly. Add butter, lemon juice and beets. Cook over medium heat for 5 minutes or until heated through. Yield: 4 servings.

Approx Per Serving: Cal 135; Prot 1.2 gr; T Fat 3.0 gr; Chol 8.9 mg; Carbo 27.5 gr; Sod 408.2 mg; Potas 268.8 mg.

Kami Huxman, Ransom

BROCCOLI-MUSHROOM SCALLOP

1½ pounds fresh broccoli
2 tablespoons butter
1 cup sliced fresh mushrooms
1 teaspoon grated onion
2 tablespoons all-purpose flour
¼ teaspoon salt
⅛ teaspoon pepper
1 cup milk
1 cup (4 ounces) shredded
  sharp Cheddar cheese
Paprika to taste

Cut broccoli into 2-inch pieces. Place in 2½-quart glass dish. Microwave, covered, on HIGH (100% power) for 8 to 9 minutes or until tender. Combine butter, mushrooms and onion in small glass dish. Microwave on HIGH (100% power) for 3 minutes, stirring occasionally. Stir in flour, salt and pepper. Microwave for 3 minutes, stirring after 1½ minutes. Add milk gradually, stirring to mix well. Microwave for 3 minutes, stirring every minute. Pour over broccoli. Sprinkle with cheese and paprika. Microwave on HIGH (100% power) for 4 minutes or until cheese is melted. Yield: 4 servings.

Approx Per Serving: Cal 277; Prot 16.3 gr; T Fat 17.6 gr; Chol 54.3 mg;
  Carbo 17.5 gr; Sod 459.8 mg; Potas 838.7 mg.

Joyce (Lubbers) Baalman, Oakley

BROCCOLI AND RICE

¼ cup chopped onion
1 cup chopped celery
3 tablespoons butter
1 (20-ounce) package
  frozen broccoli
1¼ cups minute rice
1 (7-ounce) can sliced
  water chestnuts
1 (10-ounce) can cream of
  chicken soup
½ cup milk
1 (16-ounce) jar Cheez Whiz

Sauté onion and celery in butter in skillet. Add broccoli, rice, water chestnuts, soup, milk and Cheez Whiz; mix well. Spoon into 9x13-inch baking dish. Bake at 350°F. for 50 minutes. Yield: 10 servings.

Approx Per Serving: Cal 294; Prot 13.5 gr; T Fat 16.4 gr; Chol 47.4 mg;
  Carbo 24.1 gr; Sod 1040.7 mg; Potas 358.3 mg.

Samantha Duncan, Phillipsburg

SKILLET CABBAGE

2 tablespoons butter
4 cups shredded cabbage
½ cup chopped onion
1 cup chopped green
  bell pepper
1 cup sliced celery
2 cups chopped canned
  tomatoes
1 teaspoon sugar
1½ teaspoons salt
⅛ teaspoon pepper

Melt butter in heavy skillet. Add fresh vegetables, canned tomatoes, sugar and seasonings; mix well. Cook, covered, for 10 to 15 minutes or until cabbage is tender. Yield: 6 servings.

Approx Per Serving: Cal 82; Prot 2.3 gr; T Fat 4.2 gr; Chol 11.8 mg; Carbo 10.6 gr; Sod 725.9 mg; Potas 459.0 mg.

Marilyn Larson, Tescott

CHEEZY CARROTS

2 pounds carrots
¼ cup chopped onion
½ cup margarine
10 ounces Velveeta cheese,
  chopped
1 cup crushed potato chips

Peel and slice carrots. Cook in water to cover in saucepan until tender; drain. Sauté onion in margarine in saucepan. Add cheese. Cook over low heat until cheese is melted, stirring constantly. Stir in carrots. Spoon into 1¾-quart baking dish. Top with potato chips. Bake at 350°F. for 20 to 30 minutes or until bubbly. Yield: 12 servings.

Approx Per Serving: Cal 231; Prot 6.1 gr; T Fat 17.3 gr; Chol 17.0 mg; Carbo 14.1 gr; Sod 538.5 mg; Potas 426.4 mg.

Brenda Shipley, Norwich

CORNMEAL BAKED CORN

1 (16-ounce) can cream-style
  corn
1 tablespoon butter
1 egg, beaten
3 tablespoons cornmeal
1 tablespoon sugar
¼ cup milk

Combine corn, butter, egg, cornmeal, sugar and milk in bowl; mix well. Season with salt and white pepper to taste. Pour into greased baking dish. Bake at 350°F. for 45 minutes. Yield: 8 servings.

Approx Per Serving: Cal 98; Prot 2.7 gr; T Fat 2.8 gr; Chol 37.1 mg; Carbo 17.3 gr; Sod 180.1 mg; Potas 85.5 mg.

Eva Mae Mount, Bucyrus

CREAM CHEESE CORN

2 cups whole kernel corn
1 (4-ounce) can mushroom
 stems and pieces
8 ounces cream cheese,
 chopped
2 tablespoons all-purpose flour
1 tablespoon sugar
½ teaspoon salt
1 teaspoon pepper
1 cup milk

Drain corn and mushrooms. Combine with cream cheese in bowl. Stir in flour, sugar, salt and pepper. Spoon into 1¾-quart baking dish. Pour milk over top; stir in well. Bake at 350°F. for 40 minutes. Let stand for 10 minutes before serving. Yield: 8 servings.

Approx Per Serving: Cal 282; Prot 7.8 gr; T Fat 12.4 gr; Chol 35.7 mg; Carbo 35.8 gr; Sod 317.3 mg; Potas 134.7 mg.

Joyce Allen, Manhattan

CREAMY CORN-MUSHROOM BAKE

8 ounces cream cheese,
 softened
¼ cup all-purpose flour
1 teaspoon salt
1 (16-ounce) can cream-style
 corn
8 fresh mushrooms, sliced
½ cup chopped onion
2 tablespoons butter
1 (16-ounce) can whole
 kernel corn, drained
½ cup (2 ounces) shredded
 Swiss cheese
1½ cups soft bread crumbs
3 tablespoons melted butter

Whip cream cheese with fork in bowl until fluffy. Whip in flour and salt. Add cream-style corn gradually, mixing well. Sauté mushrooms and onion in 2 tablespoons butter in skillet. Add to corn mixture; mix well. Stir in whole kernel corn and Swiss cheese. Spoon into 1½-quart baking dish. Toss bread crumbs with 3 tablespoons melted butter in bowl. Sprinkle over casserole. Bake at 350°F. for 35 to 40 minutes or until brown and bubbly.
Yield: 8 servings.

Approx Per Serving: Cal 380; Prot 9.9 gr; T Fat 21.4 gr; Chol 61.1 mg; Carbo 42.5 gr; Sod 968.3 mg; Potas 313.4 mg.

Kathie Kersten, Kiowa

SWISS CORN CASSEROLE

1 (16-ounce) can cream-style corn
¼ cup all-purpose flour
3 ounces cream cheese, softened
½ teaspoon onion salt
1 (16-ounce) can whole kernel corn
1 (6-ounce) can sliced mushrooms
¾ cup (3 ounces) shredded Swiss cheese
1½ cups bread crumbs
2 tablespoons melted butter

Mix cream-style corn and flour in saucepan. Add cream cheese and onion salt. Cook over medium heat until cream cheese is melted, stirring constantly. Stir in whole kernel corn, mushrooms and Swiss cheese. Spoon into 1½-quart baking dish. Bake, covered, at 400°F. for 30 minutes. Toss bread crumbs with melted butter in bowl. Sprinkle over casserole. Bake, uncovered, for 20 minutes longer.
Yield: 6 servings.

Approx Per Serving: Cal 306; Prot 9.9 gr; T Fat 14.5 gr; Chol 42.0 mg; Carbo 38.6 gr; Sod 787.4 mg; Potas 199.4 mg.

Sharon Wienck, Barnes

EGGPLANT PARMESAN

½ cup finely chopped onion
2 tablespoons olive oil
1 (20-ounce) can solid-pack tomatoes
6 tablespoons tomato sauce
1 teaspoon basil
1 teaspoon sugar
½ teaspoon salt
¼ teaspoon pepper
1 (1½-pound) eggplant
½ cup all-purpose flour
¼ cup olive oil
8 ounces mozzarella cheese, thinly sliced
½ cup Parmesan cheese
2 teaspoons basil

Sauté onion in 2 tablespoons olive oil in saucepan. Drain tomatoes, reserving juice; chop tomatoes. Add chopped tomatoes, reserved juice, tomato sauce, 1 teaspoon basil, sugar, ½ teaspoon salt and pepper to onion in saucepan; mix well. Simmer for 40 minutes. Peel eggplant; cut into ½-inch thick slices. Arrange in single layer on platter. Season with salt. Let stand for 30 minutes. Pat dry with paper towel. Coat slices with flour, shaking off excess. Brown slices a few at a time in ¼ cup olive oil in skillet; drain on paper towel. Spread ½ cup tomato sauce in greased 2-quart baking dish. Arrange layers of eggplant and mozzarella cheese over sauce. Sprinkle with a small amount of Parmesan cheese and basil. Repeat layers until all ingredients are used, ending with tomato sauce. Bake at 350°F. for 30 minutes.
Yield: 6 servings.

Approx Per Serving: Cal 367; Prot 15.2 gr; T Fat 25.8 gr; Chol 42.6 mg; Carbo 20.4 gr; Sod 883.1 mg; Potas 519.9 mg.

Sharon Jordan, Glen Elder

PEA AND POTATO SAUTÉ

6 potatoes
¼ cup olive oil
8 ounces fresh mushrooms
¼ cup butter
1 clove of garlic, minced
2 tablespoons chopped parsley
1 (10-ounce) package frozen
   peas, cooked
2 tablespoons lemon juice
1 tablespoon basil
¼ teaspoon nutmeg

Peel potatoes and cut into cubes. Cook in water to cover in saucepan for 4 to 5 minutes; drain. Sauté potatoes in olive oil in heavy skillet until evenly browned. Slice mushrooms. Sauté in butter in skillet. Add garlic and parsley. Cook for 30 seconds. Combine potatoes, peas, mushrooms, lemon juice, basil and nutmeg in serving bowl; toss lightly to mix well. Serve immediately. Yield: 8 servings.

Approx Per Serving: Cal 253; Prot 5.8 gr; T Fat 12.8 gr; Chol 17.7 mg;
   Carbo 30.4 gr; Sod 124.8 mg; Potas 758.3 mg.

Diana Carlin, Topeka

AU GRATIN POTATOES

¼ cup melted butter
¼ cup all-purpose flour
2 cups milk
¼ teaspoon salt
1 tablespoon prepared mustard
2 cups (8 ounces) shredded
   Velveeta cheese
5 cups chopped cooked potatoes

Blend butter and flour in saucepan. Stir in milk. Cook over low heat until thickened, stirring constantly; remove from heat. Add salt, mustard and half the cheese; stir until cheese is melted. Pour over hot potatoes in serving bowl. Sprinkle with remaining cheese.
Yield: 8 servings.

Approx Per Serving: Cal 271; Prot 10.3 gr; T Fat 14.9 gr; Chol 46.7 mg;
   Carbo 24.7 gr; Sod 646.1 mg; Potas 554.8 mg.

Heidi R. Hartman, Clifton

OVEN-FRIED POTATOES

4 large potatoes
¼ cup oil
1 tablespoon Parmesan cheese
½ teaspoon salt
¼ teaspoon garlic powder
¼ teaspoon paprika
⅛ teaspoon pepper

Cut unpeeled potatoes into wedges. Place skin side down in 9x13-inch baking dish. Combine remaining ingredients in small bowl. Brush over potatoes. Bake at 375°F. for 45 minutes, brushing with oil mixture every 15 minutes. Turn potatoes over. Bake for 15 minutes longer. Yield: 4 servings.

Approx Per Serving: Cal 380; Prot 14.6 gr; T Fat 21.5 gr; Chol 28.3 mg;
   Carbo 32.9 gr; Sod 489.6 mg; Potas 807.4 mg.

Chasity Denner, Eureka

PARTY POTATOES

1 (32-ounce) package frozen hashed brown potatoes
1 cup (8 ounces) sour cream
1 (10-ounce) can cream of chicken soup
2 cups (8 ounces) shredded Cheddar cheese
⅓ cup melted butter
2 cups milk
2 tablespoons minced onion
1 teaspoon salt
½ teaspoon pepper
2 cups cornflakes
¼ cup melted butter

Combine potatoes, sour cream, soup, cheese, ⅓ cup butter, milk, onion, salt and pepper in bowl; mix well. Spoon into 9x13-inch baking dish. Toss cornflakes with ¼ cup butter in bowl. Sprinkle over potato mixture. Bake at 350°F. for 1 hour. Yield: 15 servings.

Approx Per Serving: Cal 250; Prot 6.9 gr; T Fat 17.3 gr; Chol 49.8 mg; Carbo 17.4 gr; Sod 558.1 mg; Potas 205.6 mg.

Teresa Briney, Brewster

CROCK•POT SCALLOPED POTATOES

12 medium potatoes
¼ cup chopped onion
1 cup (8 ounces) sour cream
1 (10-ounce) can cream of chicken soup
1 cup (4 ounces) shredded Cheddar cheese
½ cup margarine
1 teaspoon salt
½ teaspoon pepper

Peel and chop potatoes. Cook in water to cover in saucepan for 3 minutes; drain. Add remaining ingredients; mix well. Spoon into Crock•Pot. Cook on High for 3 hours. Yield: 10 servings.

Approx Per Serving: Cal 372; Prot 9.1 gr; T Fat 19.3 gr; Chol 23.7 mg; Carbo 42.1 gr; Sod 664.8 mg; Potas 987.1 mg.

Darlene Schwarz, Baldwin

SCALLOPED POTATOES

1 (32-ounce) package frozen
  hashed brown potatoes
½ cup chopped onion
½ cup melted margarine
1 (10-ounce) can cream of
  chicken soup
2 cups (8 ounces) shredded
  Cheddar cheese
1 cup (8 ounces) sour cream
1½ cups milk
1 teaspoon salt
2 cups cornflakes

Combine potatoes, onion, ¼ cup margarine, soup, cheese, sour cream, milk, salt and pepper to taste in bowl; mix well. Spoon into 9x13-inch baking dish. Mix cornflakes with remaining ¼ cup margarine in bowl. Sprinkle over potato mixture. Bake at 350°F. for 45 minutes. Yield: 12 servings.

Approx Per Serving: Cal 298; Prot 8.4 gr; T Fat 20.0 gr; Chol 33.3 mg; Carbo 21.7 gr; Sod 677.8 mg; Potas 250.2 mg.

Mrs. Ross Presnal, Goddard

TATER STICKS

4 baking potatoes, cut into
  wedges
½ cup melted margarine
1 (2⅜-ounce) package taco
  seasoning mix

Dip potato wedges into melted margarine; shake with seasoning mix in plastic bag, coating well. Place skin side down on ungreased baking sheet. Bake at 350°F. for 40 minutes or until tender. Yield: 4 servings.

Approx Per Serving: Cal 347; Prot 4.1 gr; T Fat 23.2 gr; Chol 0.0 mg; Carbo 32.2 gr; Sod 285.9 mg; Potas 769.7 mg.

Mari C. Becker, Osborne

BAKED SOYBEANS

4 cups dried soybeans
8 ounces bacon, chopped
1 medium onion, chopped
1½ cups catsup
⅔ cup molasses
1 cup packed brown sugar
1 teaspoon salt

Combine soybeans and 6 cups water in large saucepan. Let stand for 6 hours to overnight. Cook over medium heat until tender. Skim; drain. Sauté bacon and onion in skillet. Add remaining ingredients. Mix into soybeans. Pour into 9x13-inch baking dish. Bake at 350°F. for 30 minutes. Yield: 15 servings.

Approx Per Serving: Cal 447; Prot 21.0 gr; T Fat 20.5 gr; Chol 10.6 mg; Carbo 49.4 gr; Sod 505.3 mg; Potas 1244.1 mg.

Lois Larson, Hiawatha

SPINACH-CHEESE DELIGHT

2 (10-ounce) packages frozen
  chopped spinach, thawed
2 cups (16 ounces) small curd
  cottage cheese
12 ounces American cheese,
  cubed
3 eggs, beaten
¼ cup butter
¼ cup all-purpose flour

Combine spinach and remaining ingredients in bowl; mix well. Spoon into Crock•Pot. Cook on High for 1 hour. Reduce temperature to Low. Cook for 3 hours longer.
Yield: 12 servings.

Approx Per Serving: Cal 210; Prot 14.6 gr; T Fat 14.0 gr; Chol 103.2 mg;
  Carbo 7.1 gr; Sod 635.0 mg; Potas 286.9 mg.

Sandra Gerhardt, Wichita

SQUASH CASSEROLE

1½ pounds summer squash,
  chopped
½ cup water
½ cup chopped onion
3 cups grated carrots
1 cup sour cream
1 (10-ounce) can cream of
  chicken soup
1 (8-ounce) package crouton
  stuffing mix
¼ cup margarine, sliced
1 cup (4 ounces) shredded
  Cheddar cheese
1 (3-ounce) can French-fried
  onions

Cook squash in water in saucepan until tender. Drain and mash squash. Add chopped onion, carrots, sour cream, soup, stuffing mix, margarine and cheese; mix well. Spoon into 2-quart baking dish. Bake at 350°F. for 20 minutes. Sprinkle with canned onions. Bake for 10 minutes longer. Yield: 8 servings.

Approx Per Serving: Cal 341; Prot 10.6 gr; T Fat 19.4 gr; Chol 30.7 mg;
  Carbo 33.1 gr; Sod 884.5 mg; Potas 457.1 mg.
Nutritional information does not include French-fried onions.

Annie Bunger, Beloit

SQUASH SUPREME

1½ pounds yellow squash
1 (10-ounce) can cream of
  chicken soup
1 cup (8 ounces) sour cream
1 (7-ounce) can sliced water
  chestnuts
2 medium onions, chopped
1 (8-ounce) package
  stuffing mix
½ cup melted margarine
½ cup (2 ounces) shredded
  Cheddar cheese

Cook chopped squash in a small amount of water in saucepan until tender; drain. Add soup, sour cream, water chestnuts and onions; mix well. Prepare stuffing mix according to package directions. Add ¾ of the margarine; mix well. Spoon into 2-quart baking dish. Spoon squash mixture over stuffing. Drizzle with remaining margarine. Top with cheese. Bake at 350°F. for 30 minutes. Yield: 8 servings.

Approx Per Serving: Cal 385; Prot 9.5 gr; T Fat 22.9 gr; Chol 23.8 mg; Carbo 37.5 gr; Sod 891.7 mg; Potas 402.0 mg.

Janette Gerald, Overland Park

CRANBERRY-APPLE SWEET POTATOES

6 medium sweet potatoes
1 (20-ounce) can apple
  pie filling
1 (8-ounce) can whole
  cranberry sauce
2 tablespoons each apricot
  preserves, orange marmalade

Peel and chop sweet potatoes. Cook, covered, in salted water to cover in saucepan for 15 minutes or until tender; drain. Layer pie filling and sweet potatoes in 8 x 8-inch baking pan. Mix remaining ingredients in bowl. Spoon over sweet potatoes. Bake at 350°F. for 25 minutes or until heated through. Yield: 6 servings.

Approx Per Serving: Cal 351; Prot 2.4 gr; T Fat 0.6 gr; Chol 0.0 mg; Carbo 85.5 gr; Sod 15.2 mg; Potas 336.8 mg.

Jim Ploger, Manhattan

MAPLE-PECAN SWEET POTATOES

3½ pounds sweet potatoes
¼ cup butter
⅓ cup maple syrup
¼ teaspoon salt
⅛ teaspoon pepper
¼ cup pecans, toasted

Cook sweet potatoes in water to cover in saucepan until tender; drain, peel and chop. Place in 3-quart baking dish. Boil butter, syrup, salt and pepper in small saucepan for 2 minutes. Pour over sweet potatoes; top with pecans. Bake at 350°F. until heated through. Yield: 10 servings.

Approx Per Serving: Cal 203; Prot 2.1 gr; T Fat 7.1 gr; Chol 14.2 mg; Carbo 33.9 gr; Sod 119.9 mg; Potas 273.5 mg.

June H. Olsen, Council Grove

SWEET POTATO CASSEROLE

1 (30-ounce) can sweet
  potatoes
¾ cup sugar
¾ cup milk
6 tablespoons margarine
½ cup packed light brown sugar
½ teaspoon nutmeg
½ teaspoon cinnamon
¾ cup cornflakes
½ cup packed light brown sugar
½ cup chopped pecans
¼ cup margarine

Mash sweet potatoes in bowl. Add sugar, milk, 6 tablespoons margarine, ½ cup brown sugar, nutmeg and cinnamon; mix well. Spoon into 8 x 10-inch baking dish. Mix cornflakes, ½ cup brown sugar, pecans and ¼ cup margarine in bowl. Sprinkle over casserole. Bake at 400°F. for 10 minutes. Yield: 8 servings.

Approx Per Serving: Cal 485; Prot 3.8 gr; T Fat 20.6 gr; Chol 3.2 mg;
  Carbo 74.3 gr; Sod 266.6 mg; Potas 379.5 mg.

Mildred Sherrard, Winfield

CALICO VEGETABLES

1 (16-ounce) can whole kernel
  corn
2 (16-ounce) cans cut
  green beans
½ cup chopped green
  bell pepper
½ cup chopped onion
½ cup chopped celery
1 cup (4 ounces) shredded
  Cheddar cheese
½ cup sour cream
12 butter crackers, crushed
½ cup melted margarine

Drain corn and green beans. Mix with green pepper, onion and celery in bowl. Add cheese and sour cream; mix well. Season with salt and pepper to taste. Spoon into 9 x 13-inch baking dish. Toss cracker crumbs with margarine in bowl. Sprinkle over vegetables. Bake at 350°F. for 20 to 30 mintues or until bubbly. Yield: 6 servings.

Approx Per Serving: Cal 214; Prot 8.8 gr; T Fat 11.7 gr; Chol 27.1 mg;
  Carbo 22.2 gr; Sod 704.2 mg; Potas 343.2 mg.

Stacy Eaton, Arkansas City

DELICIOUS VEGETABLE CASSEROLE

1 (16-ounce) can white Shoe
   Peg corn
1 (16-ounce) can French-cut
   green beans
½ cup chopped celery
½ cup chopped onion
¼ cup chopped green
   bell pepper
½ cup (2 ounces) shredded
   sharp Cheddar cheese
½ cup (4 ounces) sour cream
1 (10-ounce) can cream of
   celery soup
½ cup slivered almonds
½ box butter crackers,
   crushed
¼ cup melted margarine

Drain corn and beans. Combine with celery, onion, green pepper, cheese, sour cream, soup and almonds in bowl; mix well. Spoon into greased baking dish. Toss cracker crumbs with margarine in bowl. Sprinkle over casserole. Bake at 350°F. for 45 minutes.
Yield: 8 servings.

Approx Per Serving: Cal 316; Prot 8.0 gr; T Fat 16.6 gr; Chol 15.6 mg;
   Carbo 36.7 gr; Sod 900.8 mg; Potas 290.5 mg.

Joan Forrest, Larned

CINNAMON APPLE RINGS

3 medium apples
½ cup red hot candies
¼ cup sugar
2 cups water

Core apples. Slice crosswise into ½-inch rings. Combine candies, sugar and water in large skillet. Cook until candies and sugar are dissolved. Add apple rings. Simmer just until apples are translucent but still firm. Serve warm or cold. Yield: 12 rings.

Approx Per Ring: Cal 40; Prot 0.1 gr; T Fat 0.2 gr; Chol 0.0 mg;
   Carbo 10.0 gr; Sod 1.1 mg; Potas 29.3 mg.

Dan Morford, Oberlin

DEVILED EGGS

6 hard-boiled eggs
¼ cup mayonnaise
1 teaspoon vinegar
1 teaspoon prepared mustard
⅛ teaspoon salt
⅛ teaspoon pepper

Slice eggs into halves lengthwise. Remove yolks. Mash yolks with remaining ingredients in bowl. Spoon yolk mixture into egg whites. Chill until serving time. Yield: 6 servings.

Approx Per Serving: Cal 150; Prot 6.6 gr; T Fat 13.3 gr; Chol 259.3 mg; Carbo 0.9 gr; Sod 170.0 mg; Potas 71.5 mg.

Frank Black, Cottonwood Falls

MACARONI AND CHEESE

2 cups uncooked macaroni
6 quarts boiling water
¾ cup milk
2 cups cubed Velveeta cheese
¼ cup margarine
½ teaspoon pepper

Cook macaroni in boiling water in saucepan for 7 minutes; drain. Add milk, cheese, margarine and pepper. Cook over low heat until cheese is melted, stirring constantly. Serve hot. Yield: 8 servings.

Approx Per Serving: Cal 262; Prot 10.0 gr; T Fat 13.7 gr; Chol 23.6 mg; Carbo 24.5 gr; Sod 534.5 mg; Potas 155.4 mg.

M. Jo Anne Bray, Quinter

HEARTY GOLDEN NOODLE BAKE

1 (16-ounce) package
  ½-inch noodles
⅓ cup chopped onion
¼ cup butter
½ cup (4 ounces) cottage
  cheese
½ cup (4 ounces) sour cream
1 egg, beaten
2 tablespoons sugar
½ teaspoon salt
Pepper to taste
½ cup cornflakes
8 strips crisp-fried bacon

Cook noodles in boiling salted water to cover in saucepan for 5 to 10 minutes or until tender; drain. Sauté onion in butter in skillet just until translucent. Add sautéed onion, cottage cheese, sour cream and egg to noodles; mix well. Stir in sugar, salt and pepper. Spoon into buttered 2-quart baking dish. Bake at 350°F. for 20 minutes. Sprinkle with cornflakes. Bake for 5 to 8 minutes longer or until brown. Top each serving with 2 strips of bacon. Serve with mixed fruit compote. Yield: 4 servings.

Approx Per Serving: Cal 817; Prot 26.3 gr; T Fat 33.3 gr; Chol 237.2 mg; Carbo 101.2 gr; Sod 774.4 mg; Potas 311.6 mg.

Susan C. Love, Lebo

GOLDEN NOODLE BAKE

1 (8-ounce) package wide
  noodles
¼ cup finely chopped onion
3 tablespoons butter
1 cup (8 ounces) sour cream
16 ounces (2 cups) cream-
  style cottage cheese
½ cup milk
2 tablespoons sugar
1 teaspoon salt
1 cup crushed cornflakes
3 tablespoons melted butter

Cook noodles according to package directions; drain. Sauté onion in 3 tablespoons butter in skillet until tender but not brown. Stir in sour cream, cottage cheese, milk, sugar and salt. Add to noodles; mix well. Spoon into greased 7x11-inch baking dish. Toss cornflakes with melted butter in bowl. Sprinkle over noodles. Bake at 350°F. until bubbly. Yield: 8 servings.

Approx Per Serving: Cal 378; Prot 14.4 gr; T Fat 19.1 gr; Chol 79.7 mg; Carbo 37.0 gr; Sod 643.5 mg; Potas 177.7 mg.

Diana Taylor, Manhattan

POPPY SEED NOODLES

1 (12-ounce) package noodles
¼ cup butter
1 tablespoon poppy seed
⅓ cup slivered almonds

Cook noodles according to package directions; drain. Brown butter in skillet. Stir in poppy seed and almonds. Add noodles; toss lightly to mix. Yield: 10 servings.

Approx Per Serving: Cal 228; Prot 6.1 gr; T Fat 11.2 gr; Chol 46.2 mg; Carbo 26.3 gr; Sod 58.1 mg; Potas 118.7 mg.

Willa Deanne Eyestone, Manhattan

WHEAT CASSEROLE

2 cups cooked wheat (bulgur)
1 (10-ounce) can cream of
  mushroom soup
½ cup (4 ounces) sour cream
1 tablespoon instant
  minced onion
4 ounces (1 cup) American
  cheese, shredded
2 ounces chopped pimento
1 cup crushed potato chips

Combine wheat, soup, sour cream, onion, cheese and pimento in bowl; mix well. Spoon into greased 8x8-inch baking dish. Bake at 350°F. for 1 hour. Stir. Top with crushed potato chips. Bake for 10 minutes longer. Yield: 8 servings.

Approx Per Serving: Cal 259; Prot 7.0 gr; T Fat 15.3 gr; Chol 19.5 mg; Carbo 24.5 gr; Sod 782.7 mg; Potas 297.6 mg.

Coralee Thornburg, Utica

County Fair Bake-Off
(Dessert Samplings)

"HOMEGROWN IN THE HEARTLAND" by Sarah Groh

BLUE RIBBON ANGEL FOOD CAKE

2¼ cups sugar
1½ cups cake flour
18 egg whites, at room
  temperature
¾ teaspoon salt
1½ teaspoons cream of tartar
1½ teaspoons almond extract

Sift sugar 6 times. Sift cake flour 6 times. Beat egg whites with salt in large mixer bowl until foamy. Add cream of tartar. Beat until egg whites are stiff and glossy. Beat in sugar 1 tablespoon at a time. Add almond extract. Fold in cake flour with rubber spatula. Rinse tube pan with cold water; let drain until completely dry. Spoon batter slowly into prepared pan. Bake at 300°F. for 50 to 60 minutes or until cake tests done. Invert onto bottle to cool completely. Loosen cake from pan with knife. Remove to serving plate. Yield: 12 servings.

Approx Per Serving: Cal 220; Prot 6.4 gr; T Fat 0.1 gr; Chol 0.0 mg; Carbo 48.6 gr; Sod 231.7 mg; Potas 96.2 mg.

Deana Elston, Hays

ANGEL FOOD CAKE

½ cup sugar
1 cup pastry flour
1¾ cups egg whites
¼ teaspoon salt
2 teaspoons cream of tartar
1 cup sugar
1½ teaspoons vanilla extract
½ teaspoon almond extract

Combine ½ cup sugar and flour in bowl. Sift mixture 3 times. Beat egg whites in mixer bowl until frothy. Add salt and cream of tartar. Beat just until egg whites are stiff enough to hold their shape. Add 1 cup sugar 1 tablespoon at a time, beating constantly. Add flavorings; beat for 2 minutes. Fold in flour mixture gradually, folding for 2 minutes after last addition. Spoon into large tube pan. Bake at 325°F. for 45 to 55 minutes or until cake tests done. Invert in pan to cool completely. Loosen cake from pan with knife. Remove to serving plate. Yield: 12 servings.

Approx Per Serving: Cal 148; Prot 4.5 gr; T Fat 0.1 gr; Chol 0.0 mg; Carbo 32.5 gr; Sod 130.6 mg; Potas 76.4 mg.

Martha Wreath Streeter, Chairman, Kansas 4-H Foundation Trustee, Manhattan

SWEDISH APPLE CAKE

½ cup shortening
1½ cups sugar
2 eggs
1¾ cups all-purpose flour
1 teaspoon soda
1 teaspoon nutmeg
1 teaspoon cinnamon
3 cups grated apples
1 teaspoon vanilla extract
½ cup pecans
½ cup margarine
½ cup packed brown sugar
¼ cup milk
1 cup pecans
½ cup coconut
1 teaspoon vanilla extract

Cream shortening and sugar in mixer bowl until light and fluffy. Blend in eggs. Add sifted flour, soda, nutmeg and cinnamon; mix well. Stir in apples, 1 teaspoon vanilla and ½ cup pecans. Spoon into greased and floured 9x13-inch cake pan. Bake at 350°F. for 25 minutes. Melt margarine in saucepan. Add brown sugar and remaining ingredients; mix well. Pour over hot cake. Broil for several minutes or until golden brown. Serve warm or cold. Yield: 15 servings.

Approx Per Serving: Cal 399; Prot 3.8 gr; T Fat 24.1 gr; Chol 34.3 mg; Carbo 44.7 gr; Sod 148.5 mg; Potas 163.5 mg.

Evelyn Morrical, Beverly

WHOLE GRAIN APPLE CAKE

1½ cups whole wheat flour
1 cup quick-cooking oats
½ cup sugar
1 tablespoon baking powder
½ teaspoon cinnamon
2 eggs
½ cup oil
½ cup apple juice
1½ cups chopped unpeeled apple
½ cup wheat germ

Combine dry ingredients in large bowl. Beat eggs in small bowl. Stir in oil and apple juice. Add to dry ingredients. Mix just until moistened. Stir in apples. Sprinkle ¼ cup wheat germ in greased 6-cup ring mold. Layer half the batter, remaining wheat germ and remaining batter in pan. Bake at 350°F. for 40 minutes or until cake tests done. Invert onto wire rack to cool. Yield: 12 servings.

Approx Per Serving: Cal 232; Prot 5.3 gr; T Fat 11.0 gr; Chol 42.1 mg; Carbo 29.3 gr; Sod 93.4 mg; Potas 156.6 mg.

Marilee Kiser, Manhattan

BANANA CUSTARD CHIFFON CAKE

2¼ cups sifted cake flour
1½ cups sugar
1 tablespoon baking powder
½ teaspoon salt
½ cup oil
5 egg yolks
¾ cup mashed banana
1 tablespoon lemon juice
1 teaspoon vanilla extract
1 cup egg whites
½ teaspoon cream of tartar

Sift cake flour, sugar, baking powder and salt into bowl; make well in center. Add oil, egg yolks, bananas, lemon juice and vanilla. Beat at low speed for 1 minute. Beat egg whites with cream of tartar in bowl until stiff peaks form. Fold in banana mixture gradually, folding just until well mixed. Spoon into ungreased 10-inch tube pan. Cut through batter with spatula. Bake at 325°F. for 50 to 60 minutes or until cake tests done. Invert pan on bottle to cool completely. Loosen cake from pan with knife. Remove to serving plate. Yield: 12 servings.

Approx Per Serving: Cal 299; Prot 5.0 gr; T Fat 11.4 gr; Chol 104.8 mg; Carbo 44.8 gr; Sod 213.5 mg; Potas 114.6 mg.

Carol Russell Lang, APO San Francisco, California

GRAND CHAMPION CARROT CAKE

4 eggs
2 cups sugar
2 teaspoons soda
2 teaspoons cinnamon
1 teaspoon salt
1⅓ cups oil
2 cups all-purpose flour
3 (4½-ounce) jars carrot
  baby food
¼ cup melted margarine
6 ounces cream cheese,
  softened
1 (16-ounce) package
  confectioners' sugar
½ teaspoon vanilla extract
1 cup chopped pecans

Beat eggs in mixer bowl. Add sugar, soda, cinnamon and salt. Blend in oil and flour. Add baby food; mix well. Pour into 2 greased and floured 10-inch cake pans. Bake at 350°F. for 40 minutes. Remove to wire rack to cool. Blend margarine and cream cheese in bowl. Add remaining ingredients; mix well. Spread between layers and over top and side of cooled cake. Yield: 12 servings.

Approx Per Serving: Cal 782; Prot 6.6 gr; T Fat 42.5 gr; Chol 100.0 mg; Carbo 97.9 gr; Sod 472.3 mg; Potas 172.5 mg.

Karen Cain, Kansas City

MAHOGANY CHIFFON CAKE

½ cup baking cocoa
¾ cup boiling water
1¾ cups cake flour
1¾ cups sugar
1½ teaspoons soda
1 teaspoon salt
½ cup oil
7 eggs, separated
2 teaspoons vanilla extract
½ teaspoon cream of tartar

Dissolve cocoa in boiling water. Cool. Sift flour, sugar, soda and salt into bowl; make well in center. Add oil, egg yolks, vanilla and cocoa mixture; mix well. Beat egg whites and cream of tartar in bowl until stiff peaks form. Add chocolate mixture to egg whites in fine stream, folding gently to mix. Spoon into ungreased tube pan. Bake at 325°F. for 1 hour and 10 minutes or until cake tests done. Invert on bottle to cool completely. Loosen cake from pan with knife. Remove to serving plate.
Yield: 12 servings.

Approx Per Serving: Cal 312; Prot 5.7 gr; T Fat 13.3 gr; Chol 147.5 mg; Carbo 44.8 gr; Sod 325.3 mg; Potas 114.2 mg.

Kimberly Rezac, Onaga

CHOCOLATE-CHERRY UPSIDE-DOWN CAKE

1 (21-ounce) can cherry pie
   filling
2¼ cups all-purpose flour
1½ cups sugar
¾ cup baking cocoa
1½ teaspoons soda
¾ teaspoon salt
½ cup oil
¼ cup vinegar
1½ cups water
1½ teaspoons vanilla extract

Spread pie filling in greased 9 x 13-inch baking pan. Sift dry ingredients into large bowl. Mix oil, vinegar, water and vanilla in small bowl. Add to dry ingredients all at once; stir just until moistened. Pour evenly over pie filling. Bake at 350°F. for 30 to 35 minutes or until cake tests done. Cool in pan. Cut into squares. Invert squares on serving plates. Yield: 12 servings.

Approx Per Serving: Cal 332; Prot 3.4 gr; T Fat 10.3 gr; Chol 0.0 mg; Carbo 59.4 gr; Sod 236.9 mg; Potas 110.2 mg.

Cindy Thieme, Nashville

THE DARKEST CHOCOLATE CAKE EVER

1 cup butter, softened
2 cups sugar
4 eggs
2½ cups sifted flour.
1 tablespoon soda
¼ teaspoon salt
1 cup buttermilk
¾ cup baking cocoa
⅔ cup boiling water
2 teaspoons almond extract
2 cups confectioners' sugar
1 tablespoon butter, softened
1 teaspoon vanilla extract
2 to 3 tablespoons milk

Cream 1 cup butter and sugar in mixer bowl until light and fluffy. Blend in eggs. Add sifted flour, soda and salt alternately with buttermilk, mixing well after each addition. Dissolve cocoa in boiling water. Add cocoa mixture and almond extract to batter, blending at low speed. Pour into greased and floured 12-cup bundt pan. Bake at 350°F. for 60 to 70 minutes or until cake tests done. Cool in pan for 10 to 15 minutes. Remove to wire rack to cool completely. Place on serving plate. Combine confectioners' sugar, 1 tablespoon butter, vanilla and milk in bowl, mixing to desired consistency. Spoon over cake. Yield: 12 servings.

Approx Per Serving: Cal 495; Prot 8.5 gr; T Fat 19.8 gr; Chol 224.8 mg; Carbo 78.3 gr; Sod 497.7 mg; Potas 234.1 mg.

Vicky Kruse, Hanover

COUNTY FAIR CHOCOLATE CUPCAKES

⅔ cup packed brown sugar
⅓ cup milk
2 (1-ounce) squares unsweetened baking chocolate
⅓ cup shortening
⅔ cup packed brown sugar
1 teaspoon vanilla extract
2 eggs, beaten
1⅓ cups sifted flour
1 teaspoon soda
½ teaspoon salt
½ cup milk
1 recipe chocolate frosting

Combine ⅔ cup brown sugar, ⅓ cup milk and chocolate in saucepan. Heat until chocolate is melted; mix well. Cool. Cream shortening, ⅔ cup brown sugar and vanilla in mixer bowl until light and fluffy. Blend in eggs. Add sifted flour, soda and salt alternately with ½ cup milk, mixing well after each addition. Beat in chocolate mixture. Spoon into paper-lined muffin cups. Bake at 375°F. for 15 minutes. Frost with chocolate frosting. Yield: 24 servings.

Approx Per Serving: Cal 172; Prot 2.2 gr; T Fat 7.1 gr; Chol 24.4 mg; Carbo 27.1 gr; Sod 100.2 mg; Potas 111.9 mg.
Nutritional information does not include frosting.

Marsha Weaver, Abilene

GRANDMA'S CHOCOLATE CAKE

2¼ cups sifted cake flour
1 cup sugar
⅔ cup cocoa
⅓ teaspoon baking powder
1 teaspoon soda
1 teaspoon salt
⅔ cup shortening
¾ cup packed brown sugar
⅔ cup water
1 teaspoon vanilla extract
⅓ cup water
3 eggs

Sift first 6 dry ingredients together. Cream shortening and brown sugar in mixer bowl until light and fluffy. Add sifted dry ingredients alternately with ⅔ cup water, mixing well after each addition. Blend in vanilla. Beat for 2 minutes. Add ⅓ cup water and eggs. Beat for 2 minutes longer. Spoon into 2 greased and floured cake pans. Bake at 350°F. for 25 minutes or until cake tests done. Remove to wire rack to cool. Frost with favorite fudge frosting. Yield: 10 servings.

Approx Per Serving: Cal 425; Prot 6.2 gr; T Fat 18.1 gr; Chol 75.8 mg; Carbo 62.7 gr; Sod 329.6 mg; Potas 194.3 mg.

Julie Ellerman, Effingham

MILKY WAY CAKE

7½ (2.1-ounce) Milky Way candy bars
½ cup butter
2 cups sugar
1 cup butter, softened
4 eggs, well beaten
2½ cups all-purpose flour
¼ teaspoon soda
1¼ cups buttermilk
1 teaspoon vanilla extract
1 cup chopped pecans
½ cup confectioners' sugar
2½ cups sugar
1 cup evaporated milk
½ cup butter
1 cup marshmallow creme
6 ounces (1 cup) chocolate chips
1 cup pecans, chopped

Melt candy bars with ½ cup butter in saucepan; blend well. Cool slightly. Cream 2 cups sugar and 1 cup butter in mixer bowl until light and fluffy. Blend in eggs and chocolate mixture. Add sifted flour and soda alternately with buttermilk, mixing well after each addition. Stir in vanilla and 1 cup pecans. Grease three 9-inch cake pans and dust with confectioners' sugar. Spoon batter into prepared pans. Bake at 325°F. for 40 to 50 minutes or until cake tests done. Remove to wire rack to cool. Mix 2½ cups sugar and evaporated milk in saucepan. Cook to 234 to 240°F. on candy thermometer, softball stage. Stir in ½ cup butter, marshmallow creme and chocolate chips until melted. Add 1 cup pecans. Spread between layers and over top and side of cake. Yield: 12 servings.

Approx Per Serving: Cal 1139; Prot 11.9 gr; T Fat 59.6 gr; Chol 195.5 mg; Carbo 146.3 gr; Sod 544.4 mg; Potas 420.3 mg.

Amanda Powell, Washington

CHOCOLATE-OATMEAL CAKE

1 cup oats
1½ cups boiling water
½ cup shortening
1½ cups sugar
2 eggs
1 cup all-purpose flour
½ cup baking cocoa
1 teaspoon soda
½ teaspoon salt
1 teaspoon vanilla extract

Mix oats and boiling water in bowl. Let stand until cool. Cream shortening and sugar in mixer bowl until light and fluffy. Blend in eggs. Add sifted dry ingredients, vanilla and oats mixture; mix well. Batter will be thick. Spoon into greased and floured 8 x 12-inch cake pan. Bake at 350°F. for 35 minutes or until cake tests done. Yield: 18 servings.

Approx Per Serving: Cal 177; Prot 2.5 gr; T Fat 7.7 gr; Chol 28.1 mg;
Carbo 26.2 gr; Sod 112.2 mg; Potas 66.5 mg.

Lois Thompson, Hays

CHOCOLATE SHEET CAKE

2 cups sugar
2 cups all-purpose flour
1 teaspoon soda
1 cup butter
¼ cup cocoa
1 cup water
2 eggs
½ cup buttermilk
1 teaspoon vanilla extract

Sift sugar, flour and soda into bowl. Mix butter, cocoa and water in saucepan. Heat until butter is melted; mix well. Bring mixture to a boil. Pour over dry ingredients; beat until smooth. Add eggs, buttermilk and vanilla. Beat for 2 minutes. Pour into greased and floured 12 x 18-inch jelly roll pan. Bake at 350°F. for 12 to 15 minutes or until cake tests done. Pour hot Frosting over hot cake. Cool.
Yield: 16 servings.

FROSTING

½ cup butter
¼ cup cocoa
6 tablespoons milk
1 (16-ounce) package
  confectioner's sugar
1 teaspoon vanilla extract
1 cup chopped pecans

Combine butter, cocoa and milk in saucepan. Bring to a boil, stirring to mix well. Add remaining ingredients; mix well.

Approx Per Serving: Cal 496; Prot 4.2 gr; T Fat 24.1 gr; Chol 85.9 mg;
Carbo 69.9 gr; Sod 283.2 mg; Potas 185.9 mg.

Joan Finney, Kansas State Treasurer

TWO-WAY PARTY CAKE

1 cup butter, softened
2¼ cups sugar
2 eggs
1 teaspoon vanilla extract
3 cups sifted cake flour
½ cup baking cocoa
2 teaspoons soda
1 teaspoon salt
2 cups buttermilk

Cream butter and sugar in mixer bowl until light and fluffy. Blend in eggs 1 at a time. Mix in vanilla. Add sifted dry ingredients alternately with buttermilk, beginning and ending with dry ingredients. Pour into 3 greased and floured 9-inch cake pans. Bake at 350°F. for 30 to 35 minutes or until cake tests done. Remove to wire rack to cool. Spread Cocoa Cream Cheese Frosting between layers and over top and side of cake. Yield: 15 servings.

Approx Per Serving: Cal 334; Prot 4.3 gr; T Fat 13.8 gr; Chol 72.2 mg; Carbo 50.4 gr; Sod 452.6 mg; Potas 123.3 mg.

COCOA CREAM CHEESE FROSTING

⅓ cup butter
9 ounces cream cheese
6 cups sifted confectioners' sugar
1 cup baking cocoa
5 to 7 tablespoons light cream

Cream butter and cream cheese in mixer bowl until light. Add confectioners' sugar and cocoa gradually, beating until fluffy. Add enough cream to make of desired consistency; beat until of spreading consistency. Yield: 15 servings.
Note: Cake may be baked in 9 x 13-inch pan for 55 to 60 minutes and reduce frosting recipe by half to frost top only.

Approx Per Serving: Cal 300; Prot 1.7 gr; T Fat 12.0 gr; Chol 36.0 mg; Carbo 48.6 gr; Sod 95.6 mg; Potas 29.2 mg.

Deana M. (Ebert) Pierson, Hays

COMPANY COCONUT CAKE

1 (2-layer) package white cake mix
½ cup coconut
1 (6-ounce) can cream of coconut
1 (12-ounce) container whipped topping
1 cup coconut

Prepare cake mix according to package directions, adding ½ cup coconut. Bake as directed in greased 9 x 13-inch cake pan. Pierce hot cake with fork. Pour cream of coconut over cake. Refrigerate overnight. Mix whipped topping and 1 cup coconut in bowl. Spread over cake. Flavor improves as cake stands in refrigerator. Yield: 12 servings.

Approx Per Serving: Cal 458; Prot 4.4 gr; T Fat 28.2 gr; Chol 42.1 mg; Carbo 46.7 gr; Sod 443.8 mg; Potas 98.0 mg.

Donna Stirn, Tescott

FASTEST CAKE IN THE WEST

2 cups all-purpose flour
1½ cups sugar
½ teaspoon soda
1 teaspoon cinnamon
½ teaspoon salt
1 (21-ounce) can cherry pie
  filling
¾ cup oil
2 eggs, beaten
1½ cups pecans

Sift dry ingredients into ungreased 9x13-inch cake pan. Add pie filling, oil, eggs and pecans; mix well. Bake at 350°F. for 40 to 45 minutes or until cake tests done. Serve warm with ice cream or cool and frost with cream cheese frosting. Yield: 12 servings.

Approx Per Serving: Cal 463; Prot 4.7 gr; T Fat 25.3 gr; Chol 42.1 mg; Carbo 56.5 gr; Sod 133.9 mg; Potas 120.3 mg.

Melonie Hurst, Chapman

THREE-LAYER ITALIAN CREAM CAKE

½ cup butter, softened
½ cup shortening
2 cups sugar
5 egg yolks
2 cups all-purpose flour
1 teaspoon soda
1 cup buttermilk
1 teaspoon vanilla extract
1½ cups chopped pecans
5 egg whites, stiffly beaten
¼ cup butter, softened
8 ounces cream cheese,
  softened
1 (16-ounce) package
  confectioners' sugar
1 teaspoon vanilla extract
½ cup chopped pecans

Cream ½ cup butter and shortening in mixer bowl until light. Add sugar gradually, creaming until fluffy. Blend in egg yolks 1 at a time. Add sifted flour and soda alternately with buttermilk, mixing well after each addition. Stir in 1 teaspoon vanilla and 1½ cups pecans. Fold in stiffly beaten egg whites. Spoon into 3 greased 8-inch cake pans. Bake at 350°F. for 25 to 30 minutes or until cake tests done. Remove to wire rack to cool. Cream ¼ cup butter and cream cheese in mixer bowl until light. Blend in confectioners' sugar and 1 teaspoon vanilla. Spread between layers and over top and side of cake. Sprinkle ½ cup pecans on top. Yield: 8 servings.

Approx Per Serving: Cal 1165; Prot 12.1 gr; T Fat 61.9 gr; Chol 223.8 mg; Carbo 148.1 gr; Sod 405.3 mg; Potas 339.4 mg.

Amy Graber, Kingman

QUICK LEMON CAKE

1 package one-step angel food
  cake mix
1 can lemon pie filling

Combine dry cake mix and pie filling in mixer bowl; mix until smooth. Spoon into greased and floured 11 x 15-inch cake pan; spread batter evenly. Bake at 350°F. until cake springs back when lightly touched. Yield: 15 servings.

Tammy Keimig, Isabel

Nutritional analysis not available.

PINEAPPLE UPSIDE-DOWN CAKE

2 tablespoons butter
½ cup packed brown sugar
6 slices pineapple
6 maraschino cherries
1 (1-layer) package yellow
  cake mix
⅓ cup unsweetened pineapple
  juice

Microwave butter in round 8-inch glass dish on HIGH (100% power) until melted. Blend in brown sugar. Microwave for 2 minutes or until brown sugar is dissolved. Arrange pineapple slices in dish. Place cherries in centers. Prepare cake mix according to package directions, substituting pineapple juice and water for liquid in directions. Spoon into prepared pan. Cover with paper towel. Microwave on HIGH (100% power) for 9 minutes or until cake tests done, turning dish ¼ turn one time. Invert onto serving plate immediately. Yield: 6 servings.

Approx Per Serving: Cal 408; Prot 2.8 gr; T Fat 7.1 gr; Chol 11.8 mg;
  Carbo 84.1 gr; Sod 458.1 mg; Potas 333.4 mg.
Nutritional information does not include the ingredients required to prepare cake mix.

Lisa Schuetz, Oberlin

POUND CAKE

1 cup butter, softened
3 cups sugar
5 eggs
1 teaspoon baking powder
1 cup milk
3 cups all-purpose flour
½ teaspoon salt
1 teaspoon vanilla extract
½ teaspoon lemon extract

Cream butter and sugar in mixer bowl until light and fluffy. Blend in eggs 1 at a time. Dissolve baking powder in milk. Add to creamed mixture alternately with sifted flour and salt, mixing well after each addition. Mix in flavorings. Pour into greased bundt pan. Bake at 300°F. for 1½ hours. Cool in pan for 5 minutes. Remove to wire rack to cool completely. May glaze if desired. Yield: 16 servings.

Approx Per Serving: Cal 367; Prot 5.1 gr; T Fat 14.1 gr; Chol 116.6 mg;
  Carbo 56.2 gr; Sod 254.9 mg; Potas 69.1 mg.

Kenneth Glenn Family, Cunningham

RIBBON DESSERT CAKE

1 (16-ounce) package fudge
  cake mix
⅓ cup confectioners' sugar
12 ounces cream cheese,
  softened
2 (8-ounce) cartons frozen
  whipped topping, thawed
2 (4-ounce) packages fudge
  instant pudding mix
2½ cups milk

Prepare and bake cake mix in 9 x 13-inch cake pan according to package directions. Cream confectioners' sugar and cream cheese in mixer bowl until light and fluffy. Blend in 8 ounces whipped topping. Spread evenly over cake layer. Prepare pudding mix with milk in bowl, mixing until smooth. Spread over cream cheese layer. Top with remaining whipped topping. Yield: 20 servings.

Approx Per Serving: Cal 333; Prot 4.4 gr; T Fat 16.6 gr; Chol 23.2 mg;
  Carbo 42.7 gr; Sod 358.9 mg; Potas 72.5 mg.

Tim Bell, Atchison

SEVEN-UP CAKE

1½ cups butter, softened
3 cups sugar
5 eggs
3 cups all-purpose flour
¾ cup 7-Up
¼ cup confectioners' sugar

Cream butter and sugar in mixer bowl for 3 minutes. Beat in eggs 1 at a time. Add flour and 7-Up. Beat for 2 minutes. Pour into greased and floured bundt pan. Bake at 350°F. for 1¼ hours. Cool in pan for 10 minutes. Remove to wire rack to cool completely. Dust with confectioners' sugar. Yield: 16 servings.

Approx Per Serving: Cal 420; Prot 4.6 gr; T Fat 19.3 gr; Chol 132.3 mg;
  Carbo 58.6 gr; Sod 230.2 mg; Potas 48.6 mg.

John McKeever, Marysville

SPONGE CAKE

6 egg yolks
10 tablespoons sugar
1 tablespoon lemon juice
1 tablespoon grated lemon rind
½ teaspoon salt
1 cup sifted cake flour
10 egg whites
1 teaspoon cream of tartar
1 tablespoon water
10 tablespoons sugar

Beat egg yolks in mixer bowl until thick and lemon-colored. Add 10 tablespoons sugar, lemon juice, lemon rind and salt; mix well. Sift in flour, folding to mix well. Beat egg whites in bowl until frothy. Sift in cream of tartar; add water. Beat until stiff. Fold in 10 tablespoons sugar. Fold egg whites gently into cake batter. Pour into ungreased tube pan. Bake at 325°F. for 1 hour. Remove to wire rack to cool. Yield: 12 servings.

Approx Per Serving: Cal 158; Prot 5.1 gr; T Fat 2.7 gr; Chol 125.8 mg; Carbo 28.4 gr; Sod 150.9 mg; Potas 67.3 mg.

Nancy L. Presnal, Salina

SUGARLESS CAKE

1 cup raisins
1 cup chopped Jonathan apple
½ cup margarine
1 cup water
1 teaspoon cinnamon
¼ teaspoon nutmeg
1 egg, beaten
1 cup whole wheat flour
1 teaspoon baking powder
1 teaspoon soda
⅛ teaspoon salt
1 teaspoon vanilla extract
1 cup chopped pecans

Bring raisins, apple, margarine, water and spices to a boil in saucepan. Boil for 3 minutes. Cool. Beat in egg. Add sifted dry ingredients, vanilla and pecans; mix well. Spoon into greased and floured 8 x 8-inch cake pan. Bake at 350°F. for 12 minutes or until cake tests done. Remove to wire rack to cool. Yield: 9 servings.

Approx Per Serving: Cal 290; Prot 4.2 gr; T Fat 20.6 gr; Chol 28.1 mg; Carbo 26.1 gr; Sod 294.8 mg; Potas 277.2 mg.

Eileen Meier, Linn

STRAWBERRY CRUNCH CAKE

2 (10-ounce) packages frozen
   sliced strawberries, thawed
⅓ cup packed brown sugar
½ cup chopped pecans
1 teaspoon cinnamon
1 cup butter, softened
1¼ cups sugar
2 eggs
1 cup (8 ounces) sour cream
2 cups all-purpose flour
1 teaspoon baking powder
½ teaspoon soda
½ teaspoon salt
4 teaspoons cornstarch
2 teaspoons lemon juice

Drain strawberries, reserving juice. Mix brown sugar, pecans and cinnamon in bowl; set aside. Cream butter and sugar in mixer bowl until light and fluffy. Blend in eggs. Add sour cream gradually, mixing well. Stir in sifted flour, baking powder, soda and salt. Layer half the cake batter, strawberries, half the brown sugar mixture, remaining batter and remaining brown sugar mixture in greased 9x13-inch cake pan. Bake at 350°F. for 30 to 35 minutes or until cake tests done. Cool. Mix reserved strawberry juice and cornstarch in saucepan. Cook over medium heat until thickened, stirring constantly; remove from heat. Stir in lemon juice. Serve warm over cake. Garnish with whipped cream. Yield: 15 servings.

Approx Per Serving: Cal 638; Prot 3.8 gr; T Fat 19.3 gr; Chol 78.3 mg; Carbo 116.8 gr; Sod 310.3 mg; Potas 385.3 mg.

Karen Hartner, Manhattan

CREAMY WHITE CAKE

1 cup butter, softened
1¾ cups sugar
6 egg whites
¾ cup milk
½ cup water
1 teaspoon vanilla extract
3 cups sifted cake flour
4 teaspoons baking powder
¾ teaspoon salt
½ cup butter, softened
1 egg yolk
2 tablespoons buttermilk
½ teaspoon vanilla extract
3 cups (about) sifted
   confectioners' sugar

Cream 1 cup butter in mixer bowl until light. Add sugar gradually, beating until fluffy. Add egg whites 2 at a time, beating well after each addition. Combine milk, water and 1 teaspoon vanilla in bowl. Add sifted flour, baking powder and salt to creamed mixture alternately with milk mixture, beginning and ending with dry ingredients and mixing well after each addition. Spoon into 2 greased and floured 9-inch cake pans. Bake at 350°F. for 30 to 35 minutes or until cake tests done. Remove to wire rack to cool. Combine ½ cup butter and remaining ingredients in order listed in mixer bowl, blending well. Beat at medium speed for 3 minutes. Add a small amount of additional confectioners' sugar if necessary for desired consistency. Spread between layers and over top and side of cake. Yield: 12 servings.

Approx Per Serving: Cal 556; Prot 4.9 gr; T Fat 24.2 gr; Chol 94.2 mg; Carbo 82.0 gr; Sod 560.1 mg; Potas 85.7 mg.

Karla Sipes, Manter

WHITE CAKE SUPREME

¾ cup shortening
1½ cups sugar
1½ teaspoons vanilla extract
2¼ cups sifted cake flour ·
1 tablespoon baking powder
1 teaspoon salt
1 cup skim milk
5 egg whites, stiffly beaten

Cream shortening and sugar at medium-high speed in mixer bowl for 10 minutes or until light and fluffy. Add vanilla. Add sifted flour, baking powder and salt alternately with milk, beginning and ending with dry ingredients and mixing well after each addition. Fold in stiffly beaten egg whites. Spoon into two 9-inch cake pans lined with greased baking parchment. Bake at 375°F. for 18 to 20 minutes or until cake tests done. Remove to wire rack to cool. Spread Basic Buttercream Frosting between layers and over top and side of cake. Yield: 12 servings.

Approx Per Cup: Cal 318; Prot 3.9 gr; T Fat 14.2 gr; Chol 0.4 mg; Carbo 44.3 gr; Sod 291.2 mg; Potas 72.2 mg.

BASIC BUTTERCREAM FROSTING

3 to 3½ cups confectioners'
   sugar
½ cup shortening
¼ cup water
⅛ teaspoon salt
¾ teaspoon vanilla extract

Combine 3 cups confectioners' sugar and remaining ingredients in mixer bowl. Blend well at low speed. Beat at high speed until smooth, adding confectioners' sugar if necessary for desired consistency. Yield: 4 cups.

Approx Per Cup: Cal 652; Prot 0.0 gr; T Fat 28.0 gr; Chol 0.0 mg; Carbo 104.5 gr; Sod 70.3 mg; Potas 3.2 mg.

Brandi Rathgeber, Kiowa

WHITE VELVET CAKE

½ cup shortening
2½ cups sifted cake flour
1½ cups sugar
1 tablespoon baking powder
1 teaspoon salt
1 cup milk
3 egg whites
1½ teaspoons vanilla extract
¼ teaspoon almond extract
1 recipe confectioners' sugar
   frosting
¼ teaspoon almond extract

Cream shortening in mixer bowl until light. Sift in flour, sugar, baking powder and salt; mix well. Add ¾ cup milk; beat for 2 minutes. Add remaining ¼ cup milk, egg whites, vanilla and ¼ teaspoon almond extract; beat for 1 minute. Spoon into 9x13-inch cake pan. Bake at 350°F. for 40 minutes. Frost with confectioners' sugar frosting flavored with ¼ teaspoon almond extract if desired. Yield: 12 servings.

Approx Per Serving: Cal 405; Prot 3.5 gr; T Fat 12.4 gr; Chol 9.5 mg; Carbo 71.3 gr; Sod 299.0 mg; Potas 70.2 mg.

Brenda Andres, Alta Vista

BOSTON CREAM CANDY

3 cups sugar
1 cup light corn syrup
1½ cups whipping cream
1 teaspoon vanilla extract

Mix all ingredients in saucepan. Bring to a boil, stirring until sugar dissolves completely. Cook to 234 to 240°F. on candy thermometer, soft-ball stage. Remove from heat. Beat until cool. Pour into buttered pan. Let stand until firm. Cut into squares. Yield: 40 ounces.

Approx Per Ounce: Cal 86; Prot 0.1 gr; T Fat 0.0 gr; Chol 0.0 mg; Carbo 22.1 gr; Sod 13.6 mg; Potas 29.2 mg.

Rebecca Walsh, Garden City

CHERRY-CHOCOLATE CANDY

2 cups sugar
⅔ cup evaporated milk
½ cup butter
12 marshmallows
⅛ teaspoon salt
1 cup (6 ounces) cherry chips
1 teaspoon vanilla extract
2 cups (12 ounces) milk
    chocolate chips
¾ cup peanut butter
1 cup salted peanuts, finely
    chopped

Bring mixture of sugar, evaporated milk, butter, marshmallows and salt to a boil in saucepan over medium heat. Boil for 5 minutes; remove from heat. Stir in cherry chips until melted. Add vanilla. Pour into buttered 9x13-inch dish. Cool. Melt chocolate chips in double boiler over hot water. Mix in peanut butter and peanuts. Spread evenly over cherry mixture. Chill until firm. Cut into squares. Yield: 40 pieces.

Approx Per Piece: Cal 101; Prot 1.6 gr; T Fat 6.0 gr; Chol 8.4 mg; Carbo 13.1 gr; Sod 67.8 mg; Potas 37.9 mg.

Marilyn Wallace, Tipton

CHOCOLATE GOOBERS

½ cup butter
½ cup creamy peanut butter
1¼ cups graham cracker
    crumbs
1 cup confectioners' sugar
1 cup (6 ounces) semisweet
    chocolate chips
1 tablespoon shortening

Melt butter and peanut butter in saucepan; blend well. Stir in mixture of cracker crumbs and sugar. Shape into 1-inch balls. Melt chocolate chips with shortening in saucepan over low heat. Dip peanut butter balls into chocolate, coating well. Place on waxed paper. Chill for 1 hour or until firm. Yield: 36 pieces.

Approx Per Piece: Cal 96; Prot 1.4 gr; T Fat 6.8 gr; Chol 7.9 mg; Carbo 8.8 gr; Sod 77.2 mg; Potas 52.5 mg.

Angela Evans, Chapman

VERA'S DIVINITY CANDY

3 cups sugar
1 cup light corn syrup
½ cup water
3 egg whites, stiffly beaten
½ cup chopped pecans
½ teaspoon almond extract

Bring sugar, corn syrup and water to a boil in saucepan over medium heat, stirring until sugar is completely dissolved. Cook over high heat to 250 to 268°F. on candy thermometer, hard-ball stage, stirring occasionally. Pour in very thin stream over egg whites in bowl, beating constantly until mixture is very stiff and loses its luster. Stir in pecans and flavoring. Drop by spoonfuls onto waxed paper or pour ¾ inch thick in buttered dish. Let stand until firm. Yield: 30 ounces.

Approx Per Ounce: Cal 124; Prot 0.5 gr; T Fat 1.4 gr; Chol 0.0 mg;
Carbo 28.4 gr; Sod 12.5 mg; Potas 17.5 mg.

Ann Maring, Bird City

TWO-INGREDIENT FUDGE

2 cups (12 ounces) semisweet
chocolate chips
¾ cup sweetened condensed
milk
64 walnut halves

Melt chocolate chips in double boiler. Blend in condensed milk. Pour into buttered 8x8-inch dish. Chill until firm. Cut into squares. Press walnut half onto each square. Yield: 64 pieces.

Approx Per Piece: Cal 63; Prot 1.4 gr; T Fat 3.7 gr; Chol 3.4 mg;
Carbo 7.7 gr; Sod 8.1 mg; Potas 52.6 mg.

Amanda Brungardt, Manhattan

NOODLE CLUSTERS

2 cups (12 ounces)
butterscotch chips
1 (10½-ounce) package roasted
peanuts
3 cups chow mein noodles

Melt butterscoth chips in saucepan over low heat; remove from heat. Stir in peanuts and noodles. Drop by teaspoonfuls onto waxed paper. Let stand until firm. Yield: 36 pieces.

Approx Per Piece: Cal 125; Prot 3.5 gr; T Fat 9.2 gr; Chol 0.4 mg;
Carbo 9.4 gr; Sod 79.5 mg; Potas 100.8 mg.

Barbie Tollett, Hartford

PEANUT BRITTLE

1 cup (heaping) sugar
½ cup water
½ cup white corn syrup
⅛ teaspoon salt
1 cup raw peanuts
1 teaspoon soda
1 teaspoon vanilla extract

Combine first 4 ingredients in heavy 9-inch skillet. Cook over medium heat, until sugar dissolves, stirring constantly. Cook, uncovered, over high heat to 235°F. on candy thermometer, soft-ball stage. Add peanuts. Cook until amber-colored, stirring constantly; remove from heat. Stir in soda and vanilla. Pour into buttered pan; spread very thin. Cool. Break into pieces. Yield: 8 servings.

Approx Per Serving: Cal 264; Prot 4.7 gr; T Fat 9.0 gr; Chol 0.0 mg;
Carbo 44.3 gr; Sod 213.2 mg; Potas 127.3 mg.

Donald P. Schnacke, Executive Vice President
Kansas Independent Oil and Gas Association, Wichita

PEANUT BUTTER FUDGE

2 cups marshmallow creme
1 cup crunchy peanut butter
1 teaspoon vanilla extract
2 cups sugar
⅔ cup milk

Mix marshmallow creme, peanut butter and vanilla in large mixer bowl. Heat sugar and milk in saucepan over medium heat until sugar dissolves, stirring constantly. Cook to 235°F. on candy thermometer, soft-ball stage. Mix into peanut butter mixture. Spread in buttered 9-inch square dish. Let stand until firm. Cut into squares. Yield: 24 pieces.

Approx Per Piece: Cal 158; Prot 3.0 gr; T Fat 5.6 gr; Chol 1.0 mg;
Carbo 25.7 gr; Sod 73.1 mg; Potas 79.9 mg.

Leslie Thoden, Gardner

CARAMEL AND CEREAL DIPPED MARSHMALLOWS

27 light caramels
½ cup margarine
¼ teaspoon butter flavoring
½ teaspoon burnt sugar
  flavoring
½ cup sweetened condensed
  milk
Large marshmallows
Rice Krispies cereal

Heat first 5 ingredients in saucepan over low heat until melted and smooth, stirring frequently. Dip marshmallows 1 at a time into caramel; roll in cereal to coat. Place on waxed paper to cool.

Nutritional analysis not available.

Tami L. Van Kooten, Phillipsburg

PEANUT BUTTER BALLS

½ cup melted margarine
1 (16-ounce) jar crunchy
  peanut butter
1 (16-ounce) package
  confectioners' sugar
3½ cups crisp rice cereal
1 (8-ounce) milk chocolate
  candy bar
1 cup (6 ounces) semisweet
  chocolate chips
¾ piece paraffin

Beat margarine and peanut butter in bowl until well mixed. Mix in confectioners' sugar. Add cereal; mix well. Shape into 1-inch balls. Chill for 1 hour. Melt chocolate bar, chocolate chips and paraffin in double boiler over hot water; blend well. Dip candy into chocolate with toothpick, coating well. Let stand on waxed paper until firm. Yield: 48 pieces.

Approx Per Piece: Cal 134; Prot 2.0 gr; T Fat 7.4 gr; Chol 0.9 mg;
  Carbo 16.6 gr; Sod 80.8 mg; Potas 66.0 mg.

Terri Lattin, Dearing

ROCKY ROAD CANDY

1 cup (6 ounces) semisweet
  chocolate chips
1 tablespoon butter
1½ cups chopped pecans
2 cups miniature marshmallows
1 cup flaked coconut
2 eggs, beaten
1¼ cups confectioners' sugar
½ teaspoon vanilla extract

Place chocolate chips and butter in large glass dish. Microwave on HIGH (100% power) for 3 minutes or until melted. Stir in pecans, marshmallows and coconut. Blend eggs, confectioners' sugar and vanilla in bowl. Add to chocolate mixture; mix well. Drop by teaspoonfuls onto waxed paper. Chill until firm. May microwave mixture on HIGH (100% power) for 30 seconds if it becomes too stiff to drop. Yield: 24 pieces.

Approx Per Piece: Cal 145; Prot 1.7 gr; T Fat 9.8 gr; Chol 22.6 mg;
  Carbo 14.7 gr; Sod 20.0 mg; Potas 84.6 mg.

Melany Martinek, Garden City

CANDIED PECANS

1½ cups sugar
½ cup orange juice
1 teaspoon grated orange rind
3½ cups pecan halves

Bring sugar and orange juice to a boil in saucepan, stirring constantly until sugar is dissolved. Cook to 234 to 240°F. on candy thermometer, soft-ball stage. Add orange rind and pecans. Stir until cloudy. Spread on waxed paper; separate with fork. Cool. Yield: 16 ounces.

Approx Per Ounce: Cal 253; Prot 2.4 gr; T Fat 18.4 gr; Chol 0.0 mg;
  Carbo 23.2 gr; Sod 0.3 mg; Potas 171.7 mg.

Jenni Watsone, Hillsboro

Glazed Cookies

(O'Lakes Keeper Recipe)

1 cup LAND O LAKES® Butter, softened
3/4 cup sugar
1 teaspoon almond extract
2 cups all-purpose flour
1/2 teaspoon baking powder
1/4 teaspoon salt

Glaze   1 1/2 cup powdered sugar
1 teaspoon almond extract
4 to 5 teaspoons water

Sliced almonds

* Heat oven to 400°. Combine butter, sugar and almond extract in large mixer bowl. Beat at medium speed, scraping bowl often, until creamy (1 to 2 minutes). Reduce speed to low; add all remaining cookie ingredients. Beat until well mixed (1 to 2 minutes).

* Roll dough into 1-inch balls; place 2 inches apart on cookie sheet. Flatten balls to 1/4 inch thickness

with the bottom of a buttered glass dipped in sugar. Bake for 7 to 9 minutes or until edges are very lightly browned. Cool 1 minute; remove from cookie sheets. Cool completely.

* Stir together all glaze ingredients in small bowl with wire whisk. Decorate cooled cookies with glaze and sliced almonds.

Makes 3½ dozen cookies

For baking questions call the
Land O'Lakes Holiday Bakeline:
1-800-782-9606
Nov.1-Dec. 24, 8:00 a.m.-6:00 p.m. (CST)
www.landolakes.com

True.™

LAKES

APPLE-OATMEAL COOKIES

¼ cup margarine, softened
¾ cup packed brown sugar
2 eggs, beaten
1 cup all-purpose flour
¾ cup whole wheat flour
½ teaspoon baking powder
½ teaspoon soda
½ teaspoon cinnamon
¼ teaspoon salt
½ cup quick-cooking oats
1 cup raisins
1¼ cups chopped apples
½ cup chopped pecans

Cream margarine and brown sugar in mixer bowl until light and fluffy. Blend in eggs. Add next 6 sifted dry ingredients; mix well. Mix in oats, raisins, apples and pecans. Drop by spoonfuls onto greased cookie sheet. Bake at 375°F. for 10 minutes. Cool on wire rack. Yield: 60 cookies.

Approx Per Cookie: Cal 50; Prot 0.9 gr; T Fat 1.8 gr; Chol 8.4 mg; Carbo 8.2 gr; Sod 31.4 mg; Potas 49.0 mg.

Kharon Hunter, Topeka

BLACKBERRY BARS

¾ cup margarine, softened
1 cup packed brown sugar
1¾ cups all-purpose flour
½ teaspoon soda
1 teaspoon salt
1½ cups quick-cooking oats
1 (10-ounce) jar seedless
  blackberry preserves

Cream margarine and brown sugar in mixer bowl until light and fluffy. Sift in flour, soda and salt, mixing well. Stir in oats. Press half the mixture into greased 9x13-inch baking pan. Spread preserves over top, spreading to within ¼ inch of edge. Press remaining oats mixture over preserves. Bake at 400°F. for 30 to 35 minutes or until golden brown. Cool. Cut into bars. Yield: 24 bars.

Approx Per Bar: Cal 170; Prot 1.8 gr; T Fat 6.2 gr; Chol 0.0 mg; Carbo 27.5 gr; Sod 180.5 mg; Potas 69.8 mg.

Nikki Miller, Belleville

BUTTERFINGER BARS

1 cup margarine
½ cup sugar
½ cup packed brown sugar
4 cups quick-cooking oats
1 cup (6 ounces) chocolate
    chips, melted
¾ cup creamy peanut butter
½ cup packed brown sugar

Cream margarine, sugar and brown sugar in mixer bowl until light and fluffy. Mix in oats; mixture will be crumbly. Press into greased 9 x 13-inch baking pan. Bake at 350°F. for 15 minutes. Cool. Melt chocolate chips in saucepan over low heat. Blend in peanut butter and brown sugar. Spread over baked layer. Cool. Cut into small bars. Yield: 60 bars.

Approx Per Bar: Cal 101; Prot 1.7 gr; T Fat 6.1 gr; Chol 0.0 mg;
Carbo 11.1 gr; Sod 58.0 mg; Potas 61.6 mg.

Jennifer Park, Smith Center

BROWNIES

4 (1-ounce) squares
    unsweetened chocolate
⅔ cup shortening
⅔ cup sugar
4 eggs
1 teaspoon vanilla extract
1¼ cups all-purpose flour
1 teaspoon baking powder
1 teaspoon salt
1 cup chopped pecans

Melt chocolate and shortening in 3-quart saucepan over low heat; blend well. Stir in sugar, eggs and vanilla. Add dry ingredients; mix well. Stir in pecans. Spread in greased 9 x 13-inch baking pan. Bake at 350°F. for 30 minutes or just until brownies begin to pull from sides of pan. Cool. Cut into 1½ x 2-inch bars. Yield: 36 squares.

Approx Per Square: Cal 110; Prot 1.8 gr; T Fat 8.3 gr; Chol 28.1 mg;
Carbo 8.5 gr; Sod 75.4 mg; Potas 57.5 mg.

Brenda Krehbiel, Colby

EASY BROWNIES

½ cup butter
2 tablespoons baking cocoa
1 cup sugar
2 eggs
¾ cup all-purpose flour
1 teaspoon vanilla extract
½ cup chopped pecans
¼ cup flaked coconut

Melt butter in 9 x 9-inch baking pan. Add remaining ingredients in order listed, mixing well after each addition. Bake at 350°F. for 15 to 20 minutes or until brownies test done. Cool. Cut into squares. Yield: 12 servings.

Approx Per Serving: Cal 218; Prot 2.6 gr; T Fat 12.9 gr; Chol 65.8 mg;
Carbo 24.5 gr; Sod 107.7 mg; Potas 69.8 mg.

Phyllis Thompson, Chanute

BLONDE BROWNIES

⅔ cup margarine
2 cups packed brown sugar
2 tablespoons hot water
2 eggs, slightly beaten
2 teaspoons vanilla extract
2 cups all-purpose flour
1 teaspoon baking powder
¼ teaspoon soda
1 teaspoon salt
1 cup chopped pecans
6 ounces (1 cup) chocolate
   chips

Melt margarine with brown sugar and water in saucepan. Cool. Combine with eggs and vanilla in bowl. Add sifted dry ingredients and pecans gradually, mixing well by hand. Pour into greased 9 x 13-inch baking pan. Sprinkle with chocolate chips. Bake at 350°F. for 25 to 30 minutes or until brownies test done. Cool. Cut into squares. Yield: 24 squares.

Approx Per Square: Cal 228; Prot 2.4 gr; T Fat 11.7 gr; Chol 21.1 mg;
   Carbo 30.5 gr; Sod 184.3 mg; Potas 132.7 mg.

Denise Masterson, Cheney

4-H BROWNIES

1½ cups all-purpose flour,
   sifted
2 cups sugar
¼ cup baking cocoa
1 teaspoon salt
1 cup melted margarine
4 eggs, slightly beaten
2 teaspoons vanilla extract
1 cup chopped pecans
1 cup sugar
¼ cup baking cocoa
¼ cup margarine
½ cup milk
2 tablespoons light corn syrup
⅛ teaspoon vanilla extract
2 to 4 cups confectioners'
   sugar

Sift flour, 2 cups sugar, ¼ cup cocoa and salt into bowl. Add 1 cup melted margarine and eggs; mix well. Mix in 2 teaspoons vanilla and pecans. Pour into greased 9 x 13-inch baking pan. Bake at 350°F. for 35 minutes. Combine 1 cup sugar, ¼ cup cocoa, ¼ cup margarine, milk, corn syrup and ⅛ teaspoon vanilla in saucepan. Cook over low heat until sugar is dissolved, stirring constantly. Cook over medium heat to 234 to 240°F. on candy thermometer, soft-ball stage. Add enough confectioners' sugar to make of desired consistency; beat until smooth. Pour over warm brownies. Cool. Cut into squares. Yield: 36 squares.

Approx Per Square: Cal 231; Prot 1.9 gr; T Fat 9.8 gr; Chol 28.6 mg;
   Carbo 35.8 gr; Sod 145.9 mg; Potas 57.7 mg.

Kaye Sipes, Manter

NO-BAKE THREE-LAYER MINT BROWNIES

¼ cup sugar
5 tablespoons baking cocoa
1 teaspoon vanilla extract
1 egg, beaten
½ cup melted butter
2 cups graham cracker crumbs
1 cup flaked coconut
½ cup butter, softened
2 tablespoons vanilla instant
   pudding mix
3 tablespoons milk
2 cups confectioners' sugar
2 cups chocolate chips
6 tablespoons butter
¼ to ½ teaspoon peppermint
   extract

Blend sugar, cocoa, vanilla and egg in bowl. Add melted butter; mix well. Stir in crumbs and coconut. Press into ungreased 9x13-inch pan. Chill. Blend softened butter with pudding mix, milk and confectioners' sugar in bowl. Spread over crumb layer. Chill for 15 minutes. Melt chocolate chips and 6 tablespoons butter in small glass bowl in microwave. Blend in peppermint flavoring. Spread over confectioners' sugar layer. Chill until firm. Cut into squares. Yield: 36 squares.

Approx Per Square: Cal 179; Prot 1.3 gr; T Fat 12.0 gr; Chol 28.9 mg;
   Carbo 19.0 gr; Sod 132.3 mg; Potas 78.0 mg.

Megan Evans, Lebo

CHOCOLATE CHIP-COCONUT BARS

⅔ cup margarine, softened
1 cup packed brown sugar
1 cup sugar
2 eggs
3 tablespoons water
1 teaspoon vanilla extract
2 cups sifted all-purpose flour
2½ teaspoons baking powder
½ teaspoon salt
1½ cups coconut
1 cup (6 ounces) chocolate
   chips

Combine margarine, brown sugar, sugar and eggs in mixer bowl. Beat at high speed for 2 minutes. Add water and vanilla. Beat for 1 minute. Add sifted flour, baking powder and salt; mix well. Stir in coconut and chocolate chips. Pour into greased 9x13-inch baking pan. Bake at 350°F. for 15 minutes or until light brown. Mixture will rise and then subside. Cool. Cut into bars. Yield: 24 bars.

Approx Per Bar: Cal 215; Prot 2.1 gr; T Fat 9.9 gr; Chol 21.1 mg;
   Carbo 31.1 gr; Sod 160.2 mg; Potas 88.3 mg.

Debra Kay Steinlage, Corning

CINNAMON RAISIN BARS

¼ cup sugar
1 tablespoon cornstarch
1 cup water
2 cups raisins
½ cup butter, softened
1 cup packed brown sugar
1½ cups all-purpose flour
½ teaspoon soda
½ teaspoon salt
1 tablespoon water
1½ cups oats
1 tablespoon water
1 cup confectioners' sugar
¼ teaspoon cinnamon
1 tablespoon milk

Mix sugar and cornstarch in saucepan. Blend in 1 cup water. Add raisins. Cook over medium heat until mixture is thickened. Cool. Cream butter and brown sugar in mixer bowl until light and fluffy. Sift in flour, soda and salt; mix well. Add 1 tablespoon water and oats; mix until crumbly. Press half the oats mixture in greased 9x13-inch baking pan. Spread with raisin mixture. Mix 1 tablespoon water with remaining oats mixture. Pat over raisin layer. Bake at 350°F. for 30 minutes. Cool. Mix remaining ingredients in small bowl. Drizzle over baked layer. Cut into bars. Yield: 72 bars.

Approx Per Bar: Cal 60; Prot 0.6 gr; T Fat 1.4 gr; Chol 4.0 mg;
Carbo 11.6 gr; Sod 38.3 mg; Potas 50.3 mg;

Abby Janssen, Geneseo

MARBLE SQUARES

⅓ cup sugar
8 ounces cream cheese,
   softened
1 egg
¾ cup water
½ cup margarine
1½ (1-ounce) squares
   unsweetened baking
   chocolate
2 cups sugar
2 cups all-purpose flour
2 eggs
½ cup sour cream
1 teaspoon soda
½ teaspoon salt
1 cup chocolate chips

Cream ⅓ cup sugar and cream cheese in mixer bowl until light and fluffy. Blend in 1 egg. Set aside. Bring water, margarine and baking chocolate to a boil in saucepan; mix well. Remove from heat. Add mixture of 2 cups sugar and flour; mix well. Blend in 2 eggs, sour cream, soda and salt. Pour into greased and floured 10x15-inch baking pan. Spoon cream cheese mixture over top. Cut through layers with knife to marbleize. Sprinkle with chocolate chips. Bake at 375°F. for 25 to 30 minutes or until toothpick inserted in center comes out clean. Cool. Cut into squares. Yield: 60 squares.

Approx Per Square: Cal 100; Prot 1.3 gr; T Fat 5.1 gr; Chol 17.7 mg;
Carbo 13.2 gr; Sod 66.0 mg; Potas 53.5 mg.

Jesse Goodman, Bucyrus

FUDGIE SCOTCH SQUARES

1½ cups graham cracker crumbs
1 (15-ounce) can sweetened condensed milk
1 cup (6 ounces) semisweet chocolate chips
1 cup (6 ounces) butterscotch chips
1 cup chopped walnuts

Combine all ingredients in bowl; mix well. Press into greased 9x9-inch baking pan. Bake at 350°F. for 30 to 35 minutes or until brown. Cool for 45 minutes. Cut into 1½-inch squares. Yield: 36 squares.

Approx Per Square: Cal 138; Prot 2.5 gr; T Fat 7.3 gr; Chol 5.4 mg; Carbo 17.8 gr; Sod 47.4 mg; Potas 112.5 mg.

Shawn Schweitzer, Osborne

CARAMELITAS

1 cup all-purpose flour
1 cup oats
¾ cup packed brown sugar
½ teaspoon soda
¼ teaspoon salt
¾ cup melted margarine
1 tablespoon flour
1 (12-ounce) jar caramel ice cream topping
1 cup (6 ounces) chocolate chips
½ cup chopped walnuts

Combine 1 cup flour, oats, brown sugar, soda, salt and melted margarine in mixer bowl. Mix at low speed. Pat into greased 9x13-inch baking pan. Bake at 350°F. for 10 minutes. Blend 1 tablespoon flour with caramel topping in bowl. Sprinkle chocolate chips over baked layer. Drizzle topping over chocolate chips. Top with walnuts. Bake for 20 to 25 minutes longer or until brown. Cool. Cut into bars. Yield: 36 bars.

Approx Per Bar: Cal 150; Prot 1.8 gr; T Fat 8.5 gr; Chol 0.0 mg; Carbo 18.5 gr; Sod 85.8 mg; Potas 86.8 mg.

Kristi Weddle, DuBois, Nebraska

CHOCOLATE CHIP COOKIES

1 cup butter, softened
1½ cup sugar
¾ cup packed brown sugar
3 eggs
1 teaspoon vanilla extract
1 teaspoon black walnut
   flavoring
3¾ cups all-purpose flour
1½ teaspoons salt
1½ teaspoons soda
2 cups (12 ounces) chocolate
   chips

Cream butter, sugar and brown sugar in mixer bowl until light and fluffy. Blend in eggs and flavorings. Sift in dry ingredients; mix well. Stir in chocolate chips. Drop by spoonfuls onto greased cookie sheet. Bake at 350°F. for 10 to 15 minutes or until light brown. Cool on wire rack. Yield: 72 cookies.

Approx Per Cookie: Cal 98; Prot 1.2 gr; T Fat 4.5 gr; Chol 18.4 mg;
   Carbo 14.0 gr; Sod 96.2 mg; Potas 33.0 mg.

Barbara Rezac, Onaga

DATE PINWHEEL COOKIES

8 ounces dates, finely chopped
⅓ cup sugar
⅓ cup water
½ cup chopped pecans
½ teaspoon vanilla extract
½ cup shortening
1 cup packed brown sugar
2 eggs
½ teaspoon vanilla extract
2⅓ cups all-purpose flour
½ teaspoon baking powder
¼ teaspoon soda
¼ teaspoon salt
¼ teaspoon cinnamon

Combine dates, sugar and water in saucepan. Bring to a boil. Cook over low heat for 4 minutes or until thickened, stirring constantly. Remove from heat. Stir in pecans and ½ teaspoon vanilla. Chill. Cream shortening and brown sugar in mixer bowl until light and fluffy. Blend in eggs and ½ teaspoon vanilla. Add sifted dry ingredients; mix well. Roll to 10x18-inch rectangle on floured surface. Spread with date mixture. Roll from long side as for jelly roll; seal edges. Cut into halves crosswise. Chill, wrapped in waxed paper. Slice rolls ¼ inch thick. Place cut side down on greased cookie sheet. Bake at 350°F. for 8 to 10 minutes or until brown. Cool on wire rack. Yield: 72 cookies.

Approx Per Cookie: Cal 59; Prot 0.7 gr; T Fat 2.4 gr; Chol 7.0 mg;
   Carbo 9.1 gr; Sod 15.3 mg; Potas 39.9 mg.

LuAnn Ward, Manhattan

COCONUT JOYS

½ cup margarine
2 cups confectioners' sugar
3 cups flaked coconut
2 (1-ounce) squares semisweet
    chocolate, melted

Melt margarine in saucepan. Stir in confectioners' sugar and coconut. Shape into walnut-sized balls. Make indentation in top of each ball. Freeze until firm. Fill indentations with melted chocolate. Store in airtight container in refrigerator. Yield: 36 cookies.

Approx Per Cookie: Cal 87; Prot 0.3 gr; T Fat 5.3 gr; Chol 0.0 mg;
    Carbo 10.2 gr; Sod 45.9 mg; Potas 28.4 mg.

Auby Ninemire, WaKeeney

FASTNACHTKEUCHLEIN

5 cups all-purpose flour
2 eggs
1 tablespoon melted butter
¼ cup cream
Oil for deep frying
1 cup (or more) confectioners'
    sugar

Combine flour, eggs, butter and cream in bowl; mix well. Let stand, covered, in cool place for 30 minutes or longer. Roll a small amount at a time as thin as possible on floured surface. Cut into 2 x 3-inch strips. Stretch strips carefully, beginning at center; do not tear dough. Keep dough covered to prevent drying. Deep-fry in hot oil until brown on both sides, turning once; do not pierce dough. Drain on paper towels. Cool. Sprinkle with confectioners' sugar. Yield: 120 cookies.
Note: Recipe may be halved.

Approx Per Cookie: Cal 30; Prot 1.0 gr; T Fat 0.7 gr; Chol 10.7 mg;
    Carbo 5.0 gr; Sod 5.0 mg; Potas 9.2 mg.
Nutritional information does not include oil for deep frying.

Jon Grill, Whitewater

FORGOTTEN COOKIES

3 egg whites
1 cup sugar
1¼ teaspoons vanilla extract
⅛ teaspoon salt
1 cup (6 ounces) miniature
    chocolate chips

Beat egg whites in bowl until foamy. Add sugar gradually, beating until stiff. Add vanilla and salt. Fold in chocolate chips gently. Drop by teaspoonfuls onto foil-lined cookie sheet. Place in preheated 350°F. oven. Turn oven off. Let stand in closed oven overnight.
Yield: 30 cookies.

Approx Per Cookie: Cal 56; Prot 0.6 gr; T Fat 2.0 gr; Chol 0.0 mg;
    Carbo 9.9 gr; Sod 14.2 mg; Potas 23.2 mg.

William Morris, Logan

GINGERSNAPS

⅔ cup oil
1 cup sugar
1 egg
¼ cup molasses
2 cups sifted all-purpose flour
2 teaspoons soda
½ teaspoon salt
1 teaspoon cinnamon
1 teaspoon ginger
¼ cup (about) sugar

Combine oil and 1 cup sugar in bowl. Add egg and molasses; mix well. Add sifted flour, soda, salt and spices; mix well. Drop by heaping teaspoonfuls into ¼ cup sugar; coat well. Place on ungreased cookie sheet. Bake at 350°F. for 12 to 15 minutes or until brown. Cool on wire rack. Yield: 24 cookies.

Approx Per Cookie: Cal 144; Prot 1.4 gr; T Fat 6.4 gr; Chol 10.5 mg; Carbo 20.5 gr; Sod 116.2 mg; Potas 44.2 mg.

Beth Bigge, Stockton

HAMBURGER COOKIES

60 vanilla wafers
30 thin mints
½ cup green coconut
1 egg white
1 (2-ounce) bottle of sesame seed

Arrange half the wafers flat side up on cookie sheet. Top with mints. Bake at 350°F. just until mints soften. Sprinkle with coconut; top with remaining wafers flat side down. Brush with egg white; sprinkle with sesame seed. Chill until firm. Yield: 30 cookies.

Approx Per Cookie: Cal 101; Prot 1.2 gr; T Fat 4.0 gr; Chol 3.2 mg; Carbo 15.8 gr; Sod 46.3 mg; Potas 37.2 mg.

Heather Christy, Lebo

LOLLIPOP COOKIES

½ cup sugar
¼ cup butter, softened
2 tablespoons shortening
1 egg
1 teaspoon vanilla extract
1¼ cups flour
½ teaspoon baking powder
½ teaspoon salt
6 milk chocolate stars
6 popsicle sticks

Combine first 5 ingredients in mixer bowl; beat until smooth. Add flour, baking powder and salt; mix well. Drop half the dough by spoonfuls onto ungreased cookie sheet. Flatten lightly. Place 1 star on each cookie; add popsicle stick as for lollipop. Top with remaining dough; press edges to seal. Decorate as desired. Bake at 375°F. for 8 minutes or until light brown. Cool on wire rack. Yield: 6 cookies.

Approx Per Cookie: Cal 331; Prot 4.6 gr; T Fat 16.6 gr; Chol 67.7 mg; Carbo 42.0 gr; Sod 318.2 mg; Potas 74.9 mg.

Erin Taylor, Junction City

MARTIAN COOKIES

½ cup margarine, softened
¾ cup sugar
1 egg
½ teaspoon vanilla extract
½ cup all-purpose flour
½ teaspoon soda
1 teaspoon cinnamon
½ teaspoon salt
1 cup quick-cooking oats
1 cup coarsely shredded
  unpeeled zucchini
1 cup chopped walnuts
½ cup (3 ounces) semisweet
  chocolate chips
½ cup (3 ounces) butterscotch
  chips

Cream margarine at medium speed in mixer bowl for 30 seconds or until light. Add sugar gradually, beating until fluffy. Beat in egg and vanilla. Add sifted flour, soda, cinnamon and salt; mix well. Stir in remaining ingredients. Drop by rounded teaspoonfuls 2 inches apart onto ungreased cookie sheets. Bake at 350°F. for 10 to 12 minutes or until golden brown. Cool on wire rack. Yield: 48 cookies.

Approx Per Cookie: Cal 80; Prot 1.0 gr; T Fat 5.0 gr; Chol 5.3 mg; Carbo 10.8 gr; Sod 55.6 mg; Potas 38.8 mg.

Staci Jackson, Phillipsburg

PEANUT BLOSSOMS

½ cup shortening
½ cup sugar
½ cup packed brown sugar
½ cup peanut butter
1 egg
2 tablespoons milk
1 teaspoon vanilla extract
1¾ cups all-purpose flour
1 teaspoon soda
½ teaspoon salt
½ cup sugar
48 milk chocolate candy kisses

Cream shortening, ½ cup sugar and brown sugar in mixer bowl until light and fluffy. Blend in peanut butter, egg, milk and vanilla. Add sifted flour, soda and salt. Beat at medium speed until smooth. Shape by rounded teaspoonfuls into balls. Roll in ½ cup sugar, coating well. Place on ungreased cookie sheet. Bake at 375°F. for 10 to 12 minutes or until golden brown. Top each cookie immediately with candy kiss; press until cookie edges begin to crack. Cool on wire rack. Yield: 48 cookies.

Approx Per Cookie: Cal 129; Prot 2.0 gr; T Fat 6.9 gr; Chol 7.2 mg; Carbo 15.7 gr; Sod 66.7 mg; Potas 67.6 mg.

Gwen M. Rieck, Burlingame

PECAN SNOWBALLS

1 cup margarine, softened
¼ cup sugar
2 teaspoons vanilla extract
2 cups all-purpose flour
¾ teaspoon salt
1½ cups chopped pecans
1 cup confectioners' sugar

Cream margarine and sugar in mixer bowl until light and fluffy. Add vanilla, flour and salt; mix well. Mix in pecans. Shape into small balls. Place on ungreased cookie sheet. Bake at 300°F. for 40 to 45 minutes or until light brown. Roll in confectioners' sugar, coating well. Cool on wire rack. Yield: 48 cookies.

Approx Per Cookie: Cal 92; Prot 0.9 gr; T Fat 6.5 gr; Chol 0.0 mg; Carbo 8.0 gr; Sod 80.2 mg; Potas 28.4 mg.

Sue Van Allen Kipp, Phillipsburg

PEPPERNUTS

½ cup butter, softened
1 cup sugar
1 cup dark corn syrup
1 cup molasses
2 eggs
7 cups all-purpose flour
2 teaspoons soda
½ teaspoon each salt, pepper
1 teaspoon cinnamon
¼ teaspoon nutmeg
¼ teaspoon cloves

Cream butter and sugar in mixer bowl until light and fluffy. Blend in corn syrup, molasses and eggs. Sift in 1 cup flour, soda, salt, pepper and spices; mix well. Add remaining 6 cups flour; mix well. Chill for 24 hours. Shape into long rolls ¼ inch in diameter. Slice into ½-inch pieces. Place on greased cookie sheet. Bake at 325 degrees for 20 minutes. Cool on wire rack. Store in airtight container. Yield: 64 (¼-cup) servings.

Approx Per Serving: Cal 102; Prot 1.6 gr; T Fat 1.8 gr; Chol 12.3 mg; Carbo 20.1 gr; Sod 62.9 mg; Potas 63.8 mg.

Delores Rieck, Burlingame

POTATO DOUGH KOLACHES

2 packages dry yeast
1 tablespoon sugar
1 cup warm (110 to 115°F.)
   potato water
2 eggs, beaten
1 cup sugar
1½ teaspoons salt
⅔ cup shortening
1 cup mashed potatoes
1 cup evaporated milk
8 to 9 cups all-purpose flour

Dissolve yeast and 1 tablespoon sugar in warm potato water in bowl. Add eggs, 1 cup sugar, salt, shortening, potatoes and evaporated milk; mix well. Add flour 1 cup at a time to kneading consistency, mixing well after each addition. Knead on floured surface until smooth and elastic. Place in greased bowl, turning to grease surface. Let rise, covered, in warm place until doubled in bulk. Shape into balls. Place in greased baking pan. Let rise until doubled in bulk. Make deep indentation in each ball. Fill as desired. Bake at 350°F. for 10 to 15 minutes or until brown. Yield: 48 servings.

Approx Per Serving: Cal 146; Prot 3.3 gr; T Fat 4.2 gr; Chol 12.7 mg;
   Carbo 23.4 gr; Sod 90.5 mg; Potas 57.8 mg.
Nutritional information does not include filling.

Tammy Grace, Haddam

PUMPKIN COOKIES

½ cup butter, softened
1½ cups sugar
1 egg
1 cup cooked pumpkin
1 teaspoon vanilla extract
2½ cups all-purpose flour
1 teaspoon baking powder
1 teaspoon soda
½ teaspoon salt
1 teaspoon nutmeg
1 teaspoon cinnamon
½ cup chopped toasted almonds
1 cup (6 ounces) chocolate
   chips

Cream butter and sugar in mixer bowl until light and fluffy. Blend in egg, pumpkin and vanilla. Sift in dry ingredients; mix well. Fold in almonds and chocolate chips. Drop by teaspoonfuls onto greased cookie sheet. Bake at 350°F. for 15 minutes or until light brown. Cool on wire rack. Yield: 72 cookies.

Approx Per Cookie: Cal 62; Prot 0.8 gr; T Fat 2.7 gr; Chol 7.5 mg;
   Carbo 9.2 gr; Sod 55.4 mg; Potas 27.6 mg.

Cambry Pagenkopf, Pratt

WHOLE WHEAT SNICKERDOODLES

½ cup margarine, softened
1 cup sugar
1 egg
2 cups whole wheat flour
1 teaspoon baking powder
½ teaspoon soda
½ teaspoon salt
½ teaspoon nutmeg
1 tablespoon grated orange rind
2 tablespoons milk
1 teaspoon vanilla extract
2 tablespoons sugar
1 teaspoon cinnamon

Cream margarine and 1 cup sugar in mixer bowl until light and fluffy. Blend in egg. Sift flour, baking powder, soda, salt and nutmeg in bowl; add orange rind. Add to creamed mixture alternately with milk and vanilla, mixing well after each addition. Shape into balls. Roll in mixture of 2 tablespoons sugar and cinnamon. Place on ungreased cookie sheet; flatten slightly. Bake at 375°F. for 8 to 10 minutes or until brown. Cool on wire rack.
Yield: 36 cookies.

Approx Per Cookie: Cal 72; Prot 1.1 gr; T Fat 2.9 gr; Chol 7.1 mg; Carbo 11.0 gr; Sod 83.7 mg; Potas 29.1 mg.

Janelle Hahn, Hesston

KANSAS SUGAR COOKIES

1 cup margarine, softened
1 cup sugar
1 cup confectioners' sugar
1 cup oil
2 eggs
4¼ cups sifted flour
1 teaspoon cream of tartar
1 teaspoon soda
1 teaspoon vanilla extract
1 teaspoon almond or lemon
  extract

Cream margarine, sugar and confectioners' sugar in mixer bowl until light and fluffy. Blend in oil and eggs. Add sifted dry ingredients; mix well. Mix in flavorings. Shape into small balls. Place on ungreased cookie sheet. Flatten with bottom of glass dipped in additional sugar. Bake at 350°F. for 12 minutes or until light brown. Cool on wire rack. Dough may be stored in refrigerator for 1 week. Yield: 48 cookies.

Approx Per Cookie: Cal 140; Prot 1.4 gr; T Fat 8.7 gr; Chol 10.5 mg; Carbo 14.4 gr; Sod 70.9 mg; Potas 15.9 mg.

Karen Horton, Hutchinson

SWEDISH SPRITZ

1 cup butter, softened
⅔ cup sugar
1 teaspoon almond flavoring
1 egg
2½ cups all-purpose flour
⅛ teaspoon baking powder
¼ teaspoon salt

Cream butter and sugar in mixer bowl until light and fluffy. Blend in flavoring and egg. Sift in dry ingredients gradually; mix well. Chill in refrigerator. Pack into cookie press. Press S's and O's onto ungreased cookie sheet. Bake at 350°F. for 3 minutes or until very light brown. Cool on wire rack. Yield: 60 cookies.

Approx Per Cookie: Cal 56; Prot 0.7 gr; T Fat 3.2 gr; Chol 13.7 mg; Carbo 6.2 gr; Sod 48.1 mg; Potas 7.0 mg.

Susan Peterson, Clifton

SUNFLOWER COOKIES

1 cup shortening
1 cup sugar
1 cup packed brown sugar
2 eggs
1 teaspoon vanilla extract
1 teaspoon soda
½ teaspoon baking powder
¼ teaspoon salt
2 cups quick-cooking oats
1 cup flaked coconut
1 cup sunflower seed

Cream shortening, sugar and brown sugar in mixer bowl until light and fluffy. Blend in eggs and vanilla. Add sifted soda, baking powder and salt; mix well. Stir in oats, coconut and sunflower seed. Drop by spoonfuls onto ungreased cookie sheet. Bake at 350°F. for 8 to 10 minutes or until brown. Cool on wire rack. Yield: 36 cookies.

Approx Per Cookie: Cal 154; Prot 2.[...]
Carbo 16.2 gr; Sod 53.7 mg; Pota[...]

Favorite Recipes
MEXICAN WEDDING CAKES

1 cup Butter
1/2 cup Powdered Sugar
1 tsp. Vanilla
2 1/4 cup Flour
1/4 tsp. Salt
3/4 cup finely chopped Nuts

Heat oven to 400°. Mix thoroughly butter, sugar and vanilla. Work in flour, salt and nuts until dough holds together. Shape dough into balls. Place on cookie sheet. Bake 10-12 minutes. While warm, roll in powdered sugar. Yield: 4 doz.

(This depression-era recipe came from Milt's mother. It wouldn't be Thanksgiving at the McDaniels' without Date Pudding! Note that this rich tasting dessert contains no eggs or shortening.)

1 cup Flour
1 cup Sugar
1 tsp. Baking Powder
Pinch of Salt
1/2 cup chopped Dates
1/2 cup chopped Nuts
1 cup Milk
1 1/2 cups Brown Sugar, packed
1 1/2 cups Boiling Water

Preheat oven to 350°. Put first six ingredients in mixing bowl and stir to blend. Set aside. Pour boiling water over brown sugar in 9x13" pan and stir until sugar is dissolved. Stir milk into dry ingredients. Pour batter into hot syrup. Bake about 30 minutes until cake is solid. Serve with whipped topping.

BUTTERMILK PIE

1 cup buttermilk
2 cups sugar
½ cup melted butter
¼ cup all-purpose flour
3 eggs
1 teaspoon vanilla extract
1 unbaked 9-inch pie shell

Combine buttermilk with sugar, butter, flour, eggs and vanilla in bowl; mix well. Pour into pie shell. Bake at 350°F. for 10 minutes. Reduce temperature to 325°F. Bake for 50 minutes or until set and golden brown. Yield: 6 servings.

Approx Per Serving: Cal 617; Prot 7.2 gr; T Fat 28.3 gr; Chol 174.6;
Carbo 85.8 gr; Sod 455.0 mg; Potas 115.7 mg.

Mrs. Wayne Evans, Winfield

PRALINE CHEESECAKE PIE

24 ounces cream cheese,
   softened
1¼ cups packed dark brown
   sugar
2 tablespoons all-purpose flour
3 eggs
1½ teaspoons vanilla extract
½ cup chopped pecans
1 (10-inch) graham cracker
   pie shell
1 cup (8 ounces) sour cream
2 tablespoons sugar
2 teaspoons vanilla extract

Combine cream cheese, brown sugar, flour, eggs and 1½ teaspoons vanilla in bowl; beat until smooth. Stir in most of the pecans. Pour into pie shell. Bake at 350°F. for 30 minutes. Combine sour cream, sugar and 2 teaspoons vanilla in bowl; mix well. Spoon over pie. Sprinkle with remaining pecans. Bake for 10 minutes longer. Yield: 8 servings.

Approx Per Serving: Cal 8
   Carbo 79.0 gr; Sod 414.

uisburg

EASY ALMOND RASPBERRY COOKIES

1 tube (20 ounces) of refrigerated Sugar Cookie Dough
   1 cup chopped Almonds
   1 Tbls. Almond Extract
   1/2 cup Red Raspberry Preserves
   1/4 cup Powdered Sugar
   Preheat oven to 350°F. Remove cookie dough from wrapper and place in mixing bowl. With hands, mix chopped almonds and almond extract into cookie dough.
   Drop spoonfuls of dough two inches apart on cookie sheet. Press lightly floured finger in center to make an indentation. Fill with approximately 1/2 tsp. of raspberry preserves. Bake 15-18 minutes or until cookies are golden brown.
   Remove cookies from oven and place on cooling rack. Decorate top of cookie by sprinkling with powdered sugar. Makes

CHERRY PIE

¾ cup cherry juice
2 tablespoons cornstarch
⅓ cup honey
3 cups sour cherries, drained
1 tablespoon margarine
⅛ teaspoon almond extract
1 cup whole wheat pastry flour
1 cup unbleached flour
½ teaspoon salt
2 tablespoons nonfat dry milk
  powder
¾ cup shortening
⅓ cup low-fat (1%) milk

Blend cherry juice with cornstarch in sauce-pan. Stir in honey. Cook until thickened and clear; remove from heat. Add cherries, marga-rine and almond extract. Mix whole wheat flour, unbleached flour, salt and dry milk pow-der in bowl. Cut in shortening with pastry blender until crumbly. Stir in milk with fork to form dough. Divide into 2 slightly unequal por-tions. Roll larger portion on floured surface. Fit into 9-inch pie plate. Fill with cherry mixture. Roll remaining pastry. Cut into strips. Weave strips into lattice on top of pie. Trim and flute pastry. Place 3-inch wide strip of foil over rim of pastry. Bake at 350°F. for 45 minutes or until brown. Yield: 6 servings.

Approx Per Serving: Cal 630; Prot 9.3 gr; T Fat 31.2 gr; Chol 0.8 mg;
Carbo 82.3 gr; Sod 220.5 mg; Potas 379.5 mg.

Zena Gore Ebert, Pratt

QUICK CHERRY TARTS

18 vanilla wafers
8 ounces cream cheese,
  softened
1 egg
⅓ cup sugar
1 teaspoon almond flavoring
1 (21-ounce) can cherry pie
  filling

Place 1 vanilla wafer in each paper-lined muf-fin cup. Combine cream cheese, egg, sugar and flavoring in mixer bowl; mix until smooth. Place 1 spoonful in each prepared muffin cup. Bake at 375°F. for 10 minutes. Cool. Chill until serving time. Top with pie filling. Yield: 18 tarts.

Approx Per Tart: Cal 122; Prot 1.6 gr; T Fat 5.8 gr; Chol 29.8 mg;
Carbo 16.0 gr; Sod 46.1 mg; Potas 16.2 mg.

Aaron Belland, Garden City

OATMEAL PIE

¼ cup butter
¾ cup packed brown sugar
¾ cup light corn syrup
2 eggs
1 cup oats
¾ cup flaked coconut
1 teaspoon vanilla extract
1 unbaked 8-inch pie shell

Cream butter and brown sugar in mixer bowl until light and fluffy. Add corn syrup, eggs, oats, coconut and vanilla; mix well. Pour into pie shell. Bake at 350°F. for 40 to 45 minutes or until brown. Yield: 6 servings.

Approx Per Serving: Cal 544; Prot 6.3 gr; T Fat 23.8 gr; Chol 107.9 mg; Carbo 78.5 gr; Sod 328.8 mg; Potas 223.9 mg.

Teresa Black, Ottawa

COLORADO PEACH CREAM PIE

½ cup butter
1½ cups all-purpose flour
½ teaspoon salt
4 cups sliced fresh peaches
¼ cup sugar
2 tablespoons all-purpose flour
¾ cup sugar
1 egg
¼ teaspoon salt
½ teaspoon vanilla extract
1 cup (8 ounces) sour cream
⅓ cup sugar
⅓ cup all-purpose flour
¼ cup butter
1 teaspoon cinnamon

Cut ½ cup butter into mixture of 1½ cups flour and ½ teaspoon salt in bowl. Press mixture into 9-inch pie plate. Mix peaches with ¼ cup sugar in bowl. Let stand for several minutes. Combine 2 tablespoons flour, ¾ cup sugar, egg, ¼ teaspoon salt and vanilla in bowl; mix well. Fold in sour cream. Stir into peaches. Pour into pie shell. Bake at 400°F. for 15 minutes. Reduce temperature to 350°F. Bake for 20 minutes longer. Mix ⅓ cup sugar, ⅓ cup flour, ¼ cup butter and cinnamon in bowl until crumbly. Sprinkle over pie. Increase temperature to 400°F. Bake for 10 minutes longer. Yield: 6 servings.

Approx Per Serving: Cal 681; Prot 7.4 gr; T Fat 32.5 gr; Chol 130.0 mg; Carbo 93.2 gr; Sod 579.7 mg; Potas 341.2 mg.

Lou Whipple, Jetmore

PUMPKIN-PECAN PIE

⅓ cup packed brown sugar
2 tablespoons butter
⅓ cup finely chopped pecans
1 unbaked 9-inch pie shell
2 eggs, well beaten
1 cup canned pumpkin
1 tablespoon all-purpose flour
1 cup packed brown sugar
½ teaspoon salt
½ teaspoon cinnamon
½ teaspoon ginger
½ teaspoon allspice
1 tablespoon butter
½ teaspoon vanilla extract
1 cup (½ pint) half and half

Mix ⅓ cup brown sugar, 2 tablespoons butter and pecans in bowl until crumbly. Press gently over bottom of pie shell. Bake at 450°F. for 10 minutes. Reduce temperature to 325°F. Cool. Combine eggs, pumpkin, flour, 1 cup brown sugar, salt, spices, 1 tablespoon butter, vanilla and half and half in bowl; beat until smooth. Pour into partially baked pie shell. Bake at 325°F. for 40 to 45 minutes or until set. Yield: 6 servings.

Approx Per Serving: Cal 518; Prot 6.4 gr; T Fat 26.7 gr; Chol 119.2 mg; Carbo 66.2 gr; Sod 580.9 mg; Potas 388.4 mg.

Crystal Beneda, Oberlin

PUMPKIN ICE CREAM PIE

1½ cups graham cracker crumbs
½ cup melted margarine
¼ cup sugar
1 cup canned pumpkin
½ cup packed brown sugar
½ teaspoon cinnamon
½ teaspoon ginger
¼ teaspoon nutmeg
½ teaspoon salt
4 cups (1 quart) vanilla ice cream, softened

Combine cracker crumbs, margarine and sugar in bowl; mix well. Press into buttered 9-inch pie plate. Chill for 45 minutes. Combine pumpkin, brown sugar, spices and salt in mixer bowl; mix well. Stir in ice cream. Spoon into pie shell. Freeze until firm. Let stand at room temperature for 20 minutes before serving. Yield: 8 servings.

Approx Per Serving: Cal 428; Prot 3.9 gr; T Fat 25.3 gr; Chol 42.2 mg; Carbo 47.3 gr; Sod 433.9 mg; Potas 258.7 mg.

Susan Thole, Stafford

RAISIN-PECAN PIE

3 eggs
1 cup sugar
2 tablespoons margarine
7½ teaspoons lemon juice
⅛ teaspoon salt
½ teaspoon nutmeg
½ teaspoon cinnamon
1 cup raisins
½ cup chopped pecans
1 unbaked 9-inch pie shell

Combine eggs, sugar, margarine, lemon juice, salt and spices in mixer bowl; mix well. Stir in raisins and pecans. Pour into pie shell. Bake at 375°F. for 30 minutes. Yield: 8 servings.

Approx Per Serving: Cal 372; Prot 5.1 gr; T Fat 17.9 gr; Chol 94.8 mg; Carbo 51.3 gr; Sod 235.7 mg; Potas 239.7 mg.

Melinda Martinek, Garden City

STRAWBERRY DELIGHT PIE

2 (3-ounce) packages strawberry gelatin
2 cups boiling water
2 (10-ounce) packages frozen strawberries
2½ cups graham cracker crumbs
½ cup sugar
⅔ cup melted margarine
2 cups confectioners' sugar
12 ounces cream cheese, softened
1 (8-ounce) carton frozen whipped topping, thawed
½ cup chopped pecans

Dissolve gelatin in boiling water in bowl. Stir in strawberries. Chill until partially set. Combine cracker crumbs, sugar and margarine in bowl; mix well. Press over bottom and side of 10-inch pie plate. Cream confectioners' sugar and cream cheese in mixer bowl until light and fluffy. Blend in whipped topping. Add pecans. Spread in prepared pie plate. Spoon partially congealed strawberry mixture over top. Chill until serving time. Yield: 6 servings.

Approx Per Serving: Cal 1175; Prot 12.7 gr; T Fat 62.6 gr; Chol 62.9 mg; Carbo 151.1 gr; Sod 785.8 mg; Potas 449.0 mg.

David Latty, Caldwell

CHOCOLATE ICE CREAM

½ cup baking cocoa
3 tablespoons warm water
6 eggs
3 cups sugar
½ teaspoon salt
2 (4-ounce) packages vanilla
  instant pudding mix
3 tablespoons vanilla extract
2 cups whipping cream
4 cups half and half
10 cups milk

Dissolve cocoa in warm water in cup. Beat eggs in large mixer bowl until thick and lemon-colored. Add mixture of sugar, salt and dry pudding mix gradually, mixing well after each addition. Blend in cocoa mixture and vanilla. Mix in whipping cream. Pour into 1½-gallon ice cream freezer container. Add half and half and milk to fill-line. Freeze according to manufacturer's instructions. Yield: 24 cups.

Approx Per Cup: Cal 349; Prot 7.5 gr; T Fat 17.7 gr; Chol 121.0 mg;
Carbo 43.0 gr; Sod 178.7 mg; Potas 269.0 mg.

Geraldine Orr, Gaylord

PEACH ICE CREAM

2 cups finely, chopped fresh
  peaches
¼ cup sugar
¼ cup water
1 to 2 drops of red food coloring
1 to 2 drops of yellow food
  coloring
1 (15-ounce) can sweetened
  condensed milk
1 cup (½ pint) whipping cream
½ cup toasted sliced almonds

Combine peaches, sugar and ¼ cup water in bowl. Mash peaches. Mix in food colorings. Drain peaches, reserving juice. Add enough water to reserved juice to measure ¾ cup. Combine mashed peaches, juice and condensed milk in bowl; mix well. Pour into freezer tray. Freeze until firm. Spoon into mixer bowl; beat until fluffy. Whip cream in bowl until soft peaks form. Fold whipped cream and almonds gently into ice cream mixture. Return to freezer tray. Freeze until firm. Yield: 8 servings.

Approx Per Serving: Cal 418; Prot 8.0 gr; T Fat 21.4 gr; Chol 63.9 mg;
Carbo 51.6 gr; Sod 90.5 mg; Potas 393.0 mg.

Carl Black, Cottonwood Falls

STRAWBERRY ICE CREAM

2 (3-ounce) packages
   strawberry gelatin
2 cups boiling water
3 cups sugar
4 eggs, well beaten
4½ cups milk
2 cups (1 pint) whipping cream
2 teaspoons vanilla extract
2 (10-ounce) packages frozen
   strawberries, thawed

Dissolve gelatin in boiling water in bowl. Cool. Blend in sugar, eggs, milk, whipping cream and vanilla. Add undrained strawberries; mix well. Pour into ice cream freezer container. Freeze according to manufacturer's instructions. Yield: 16 cups.

Approx Per Cup: Cal 392; Prot 5.9 gr; T Fat 15.1 gr; Chol 112.4 mg;
   Carbo 60.9 gr; Sod 93.6 mg; Potas 204.7 mg.

Angela Straub, Wamego

HOMEMADE VANILLA ICE CREAM

5 eggs, separated
8 cups milk
1 (12-ounce) can evaporated
   milk
2 cups half and half
1½ cups sugar
¼ teaspoon salt
1 tablespoon vanilla extract

Combine egg yolks, milk, evaporated milk, half and half, sugar, salt and vanilla in large bowl; mix well. Beat egg whites in bowl until stiff peaks form. Fold gently into milk mixture. Pour into ice cream freezer container. Freeze according to manufacturer's directions. Yield: 16 cups.

Approx Per Cup: Cal 252; Prot 9.2 gr; T Fat 11.5 gr; Chol 116.8 mg;
   Carbo 28.6 gr; Sod 159.3 mg; Potas 316.4 mg.

Senator Robert V. Talkington, Kansas Senate President

NEW-FASHIONED VANILLA ICE CREAM

1 envelope unflavored gelatin
½ cup milk
2 cups milk
2 cups sugar
3½ cups milk
4 cups (1 quart) whipping
   cream
2 tablespoons vanilla extract

Soften gelatin in ½ cup milk in saucepan. Heat over low heat until gelatin is completely dissolved, stirring constantly. Add 2 cups milk gradually. Stir in sugar until completely dissolved. Pour into ice cream freezer container. Add remaining 3½ cups milk, whipping cream and vanilla. Freeze according to manufacturer's instructions. Yield: 16 cups.

Approx Per Cup: Cal 367; Prot 4.9 gr; T Fat 25.6 gr; Chol 91.9 mg;
   Carbo 31.2 gr; Sod 65.4; Potas 185.6 mg.

Sharon Baroman, Hays

APPLE CRUNCH

1½ pounds tart apples
1 tablespoon light brown sugar
1 teaspoon cinnamon
2 tablespoons cold water
1 cup old-fashioned oats
¼ cup packed light brown sugar
¼ cup whole wheat flour
⅛ teaspoon salt
3 tablespoons melted margarine

Peel and slice apples. Mix 1 tablespoon brown sugar and cinnamon in cup. Alternate layers of apples and cinnamon mixture in buttered 2-quart baking dish. Sprinkle with cold water. Combine oats, ¼ cup brown sugar, flour and salt in bowl. Stir in margarine. Sprinkle over apples. Bake at 375°F. for 50 to 60 minutes or until apples are tender and topping is crisp and brown. Serve warm. Yield: 4 servings.

Approx Per Serving: Cal 335; Prot 4.2 gr; T Fat 11.2 gr; Chol 0.0 mg;
Carbo 58.5 gr; Sod 176.4 mg; Potas 333.8 mg.

Javenia Peters, Formoso

APPLE ROLL

3 cups all-purpose flour
1 teaspoon baking powder
½ teaspoon salt
2 rounded tablespoons
   shortening
1 egg
¾ to ⅞ cup milk
7 cups sliced peeled apples
½ cup sugar
Cinnamon to taste
2¾ cups water
2 cups sugar

Combine flour, baking powder and salt in bowl. Cut in shortening until crumbly. Break egg into measuring cup. Add enough milk to measure 1 cup; mix well. Add to crumb mixture; mix to form dough. Roll to 12 x 18-inch rectangle on floured surface. Sprinkle with apples and mixture of ½ cup sugar and cinnamon. Roll from long side to enclose apples; seal edges. Bring water and 2 cups sugar to a boil in saucepan. Pour into 9 x 13-inch baking dish. Slice apple roll 1½ inches thick. Place slices cut side down in hot syrup. Bake at 350°F. for 1 hour. Yield: 12 servings.

Approx Per Serving: Cal 366; Prot 4.6 gr; T Fat 5.4 gr; Chol 23.6 mg;
Carbo 76.8 gr; Sod 132.0 mg; Potas 142.7 mg.

Marjorie Walton, Goddard

CINNAMON BREAKFAST APPLES

1 cup sugar
1 teaspoon cinnamon
¼ teaspoon nutmeg
5 large Jonathan apples, thinly
 sliced
2 tablespoons water
¼ cup butter
Several drops of red food
 coloring

Mix sugar, cinnamon and nutmeg. Sprinkle over apple slices in large saucepan. Add water and butter. Cook, covered, over medium-low heat for 15 to 20 minutes or until tender, stirring occasionally. Add food coloring if desired. Yield: 4 servings.

Approx Per Serving: Cal 448; Prot 0.6 gr; T Fat 13.1 gr; Chol 35.5 mg;
 Carbo 88.2 gr; Sod 143.3 mg; Potas 295.7 mg.

Jason Weese, De Soto

BUSTER BAR DESSERT

1 (8-ounce) package chocolate
 sandwich cookies
⅓ cup melted margarine
8 cups (½ gallon) vanilla ice
 cream, softened
1 cup salted peanuts
½ cup margarine
2 cups confectioners' sugar
1½ cups evaporated milk
⅔ cup chocolate chips
1 teaspoon vanilla extract

Crush cookies. Mix with ⅓ cup melted margarine in bowl. Press over bottom of 9 x 13-inch dish. Spread ice cream in prepared dish. Sprinkle with peanuts. Freeze until firm. Bring remaining ingredients to a boil in saucepan. Cook for 8 minutes, stirring constantly. Cool. Spread over frozen layer. Freeze until serving time. Yield: 12 servings.

Approx Per Serving: Cal 664; Prot 9.3 gr; T Fat 44.7 gr; Chol 73.4 mg;
 Carbo 61.5 gr; Sod 366.9 mg; Potas 312.2 mg.

Nola Elsasser, Clyde

FRUIT KABOB

3 (½-inch thick) banana slices
3 strawberries
3 grapes
1 pineapple chunk
1 maraschino cherry

Thread banana slices, strawberries and grapes alternately onto wooden skewer. Decorate end of skewer with pineapple chunk and cherry. Serve immediately. Yield: 1 serving.

Approx Per Serving: Cal 71; Prot 0.8 gr; T Fat 0.3 gr; Chol 0.0 mg;
 Carbo 18.0 gr; Sod 1.3 mg; Potas 215.4 mg.

Dalene Peterson, Clifton

DENVER CRUNCH

1 cup margarine
2 cups all-purpose flour
½ cup packed brown sugar
1 cup chopped pecans
1 cup confectioners' sugar
8 ounces cream cheese,
  softened
1 (16-ounce) carton frozen
  whipped topping, thawed
1 (21-ounce) can cherry pie
  filling

Cut margarine into flour, brown sugar and pecans in bowl. Press into 9x13-inch baking pan. Bake at 350°F. until light brown. Stir with fork to crumble. Reserve 1 cup crumbs. Spread remaining crumbs in pan. Cream confectioners' sugar and cream cheese in mixer bowl until light and fluffy. Blend in whipped topping. Layer half the cream cheese mixture, pie filling, remaining cream cheese mixture and reserved crumbs in prepared pan. Chill until serving time. Yield: 12 servings.

Approx Per Serving: Cal 365; Prot 4.7 gr; T Fat 16.4 gr; Chol 21.0 mg; Carbo 51.1 gr; Sod 63.3 mg; Potas 126.0 mg.

Vicki Gruber, Hope

FRUIT PIZZA

1 cup margarine, softened
1½ cups sugar
3 eggs
1 teaspoon vanilla extract
½ teaspoon lemon extract
4½ cups all-purpose flour
1 teaspoon soda
½ teaspoon salt
8 ounces cream cheese,
  softened
2 tablespoons pineapple juice
15 ounces strawberries
1 (16-ounce) can crushed
  pineapple, drained
2 bananas, sliced
1 (11-ounce) can mandarin
  oranges, drained
1 (3½-ounce) package vanilla
  instant pudding mix

Cream margarine and sugar in mixer bowl until light and fluffy. Blend in eggs and flavorings. Add sifted flour, soda and salt; mix well. Chill for 1 hour or longer. Divide into 3 portions. Press into 3 pizza pans. Bake at 350°F. for 12 minutes. Cool. Blend cream cheese and pineapple juice in mixer bowl. Spread over crusts. Combine fruit with pudding mix in bowl; mix well. Spread evenly on pizzas. Chill until serving time. Yield: 30 servings.

Approx Per Serving: Cal 252; Prot 3.7 gr; T Fat 9.9 gr; Chol 33.7 mg; Carbo 38.3 gr; Sod 180.9 mg; Potas 107.9 mg.

Myra Horton, Plevna

MAGIC FRUIT COBBLER

½ cup margarine
1½ cups sugar
1 cup all-purpose flour
2 teaspoons baking powder
¾ cup milk
4 cups sliced peaches

Melt margarine in 9x13-inch baking pan. Combine 1 cup sugar, flour, baking powder and milk in bowl; mix well. Pour into prepared pan. Arrange peaches over top. Sprinkle with ½ cup sugar. Bake at 350°F. for 30 to 50 minutes or until brown. Serve warm. Yield: 12 servings.

Approx Per Serving: Cal 234; Prot 2.0 gr; T Fat 8.4 gr; Chol 2.1 mg; Carbo 39.2 gr; Sod 156.9 mg; Potas 150.0 mg.

Norma Peterson, Topeka

LEMON ANGEL

1 (11-ounce) angel food cake
6 egg yolks
1 cup sugar
⅓ cup lemon juice
1 teaspoon grated lemon rind
1 envelope unflavored gelatin
½ cup cold water
6 egg whites
1 cup whipping cream, whipped

Tear cake into 9x13-inch dish. Combine egg yolks, sugar, lemon juice and lemon rind in double boiler. Cook until thickened, stirring constantly. Soften gelatin in cold water in cup. Stir into egg yolk mixture until dissolved. Cool. Beat egg whites in bowl until stiff peaks form. Fold egg whites and whipped cream gently into cooled egg yolk mixture. Pour over cake. Chill for 4 hours to overnight. Yield: 12 servings.

Approx Per Serving: Cal 336; Prot 8.1 gr; T Fat 10.2 gr; Chol 152.2 mg; Carbo 53.7 gr; Sod 205.2 mg; Potas 110.3 mg.

Glennis Zimmerman, South Haven

LEMON DELIGHT

½ cup margarine
1 cup all-purpose flour
½ cup pecans
8 ounces cream cheese, softened
1 cup confectioners' sugar
1 (8-ounce) carton frozen whipped topping, thawed
2 (6-ounce) packages lemon instant pudding mix
5½ cups milk

Cut margarine into flour and pecans in bowl until crumbly. Press into 9x13-inch baking pan. Bake at 350°F. for 15 to 18 minutes or until brown. Cool. Combine cream cheese, confectioners' sugar and half the whipped topping in mixer bowl; mix until smooth and creamy. Spread over baked layer. Prepare pudding mix with milk in bowl. Let stand until thickened. Spread over cream cheese layer. Top with remaining whipped topping. Chill until serving time. Yield: 20 servings.

Approx Per Serving: Cal 297; Prot 5.0 gr; T Fat 16.5 gr; Chol 22.0 mg; Carbo 34.6 gr; Sod 198.1 mg; Potas 148.5 mg.

Kelli Myers, Manhattan

MISSISSIPPI MUD

1 cup all-purpose flour
½ cup butter, softened
½ cup chopped pecans
1 cup confectioners' sugar
8 ounces cream cheese,
    softened
1 cup whipped cream
1 (4-ounce) package chocolate
    instant pudding mix
1 (4-ounce) package vanilla
    instant pudding mix
2½ cups milk
1 cup whipped cream

Mix flour, butter and pecans in bowl. Press into 9x13-inch baking dish. Bake at 350°F. for 20 minutes. Cool. Cream confectioners' sugar and cream cheese in mixer bowl until light and fluffy. Blend in 1 cup whipped cream. Spread over baked layer. Combine pudding mixes and milk in bowl; mix until smooth. Spread over cream cheese layer. Top with 1 cup whipped cream. Chill until serving time.
Yield: 15 servings.

Approx Per Serving: Cal 342; Prot 4.8 gr; T Fat 22.4 gr; Chol 62.5 mg; Carbo 33.2 gr; Sod 207.2 mg; Potas 132.0 mg.

Vanessa Schmidt, Newton

ORANGE CUSTARD FONDUE

1 (3-ounce) package no-bake
    custard mix
1¾ cups milk
1 (4½-ounce) container
    whipped topping
2 tablespoons orange liqueur
1 tablespoon grated orange rind

Prepare custard mix according to package directions, using 1¾ cups milk and omitting egg yolk. Spoon into bowl. Chill in refrigerator. Fold in whipped topping and liqueur. Sprinkle with orange rind. Serve with bite-sized fresh fruits and cubes of angel food cake.
Yield: 4 to 6 servings.

Oneda M. Jahnke, Woodbine

Nutritional analysis not available.

PAVLOVA

3 egg whites
1½ cups sugar
1 teaspoon cornstarch
1 teaspoon vinegar
½ teaspoon vanilla extract
¼ cup boiling water
1 cup whipping cream, whipped
6 kiwifruit, peeled, sliced

Combine egg whites, sugar, cornstarch, vinegar, vanilla and boiling water in mixer bowl. Beat for 15 minutes. Mound onto parchment lined baking sheet. Bake at 350°F. for 15 minutes. Turn off oven. Let pavlova stand in closed oven for 40 minutes. Place on serving plate. Top with whipped cream and kiwifruit. Garnish with grated chocolate. Yield: 8 servings.

Approx Per Serving: Cal 257; Prot 2.0 gr; T Fat 11.2 gr; Chol 39.6 mg; Carbo 38.6 gr; Sod 28.0 mg; Potas 45.4 mg.
Nutritional information does not include kiwifruit.

Sandra Hill, 1983 IFYE to Kansas from New Zealand

PINEAPPLE SALAD DESSERT

1 cup graham cracker crumbs
4 egg yolks
1 cup crushed pineapple
½ cup sugar
1 (3-ounce) package lemon
  gelatin
4 egg whites
½ cup sugar
½ cup graham cracker crumbs

Place 1 cup cracker crumbs in 9x9-inch dish. Beat egg yolks in saucepan. Add pineapple and ½ cup sugar. Cook until thickened, stirring constantly. Remove from heat. Stir in gelatin until dissolved. Cool. Beat egg whites in bowl until frothy. Add ½ cup sugar gradually, beating until stiff peaks form. Fold gently into gelatin mixture. Spread in prepared dish. Sprinkle ½ cup crumbs over top. Chill until firm.
Yield: 9 servings.

Approx Per Serving: Cal 253; Prot 6.8 gr; T Fat 4.2 gr; Chol 112.4 mg;
Carbo 49.1 gr; Sod 196.4 mg; Potas 164.0 mg.

Estaline Bouray, Hardy, Nebraska

PHILLY VELVET CREAM

1½ cups chocolate wafer
  crumbs
⅓ cup melted margarine
½ cup sugar
8 ounces cream cheese,
  softened
1 teaspoon vanilla extract
2 egg yolks
1 cup semisweet chocolate
  chips, melted
2 egg whites
¼ cup sugar
1 cup whipping cream, whipped
¾ cup chopped pecans

Combine cookie crumbs and margarine in bowl; mix well. Press over bottom of 9-inch springform pan. Bake at 325°F. for 10 minutes. Cream ½ cup sugar, cream cheese and vanilla in mixer bowl until light and fluffy. Blend in egg yolks and melted chocolate. Beat egg whites in bowl until soft peaks form. Add ¼ cup sugar gradually, beating until stiff peaks form. Fold gently into chocolate mixture. Fold in whipped cream and pecans gently. Spoon into prepared pan. Freeze until firm. Place on serving plate; remove side of pan.
Yield: 8 servings.

Approx Per Serving: Cal 531; Prot 6.5 gr; T Fat 46.4 gr; Chol 134.2 mg;
Carbo 27.8 gr; Sod 189.1 mg; Potas 202.0 mg.
Nutritional information does not include chocolate wafer crumbs.

Ron Blinzler, Wichita

TOFFEE DESSERT

2 cups fine graham cracker
  crumbs
¾ cup soda cracker crumbs
½ cup melted margarine
2 (4-ounce) packages vanilla
  instant pudding mix
2 cups milk
4 cups (1 quart) vanilla ice
  cream, softened
1 (4-ounce) carton frozen
  whipped topping, thawed
2 large Butterfinger candy bars,
  frozen

Mix graham cracker crumbs, soda cracker crumbs and margarine in bowl; mix well. Reserve ½ cup crumb mixture. Press remaining crumbs in 9x13-inch dish. Combine pudding mix, milk and ice cream in bowl; mix well. Layer pudding mixture and whipped topping in prepared dish. Crush candy bars. Mix with reserved crumbs in bowl. Sprinkle over whipped topping. Chill until serving time.
Yield: 12 servings.

Approx Per Serving: Cal 439; Prot 5.9 gr; T Fat 23.8 gr; Chol 33.8 mg; Carbo 54.7 gr; Sod 400.6 mg; Potas 232.4 mg.

Jeanice Cress, Humboldt

SURPRISE CUSTARDS

6 egg whites
¼ cup sugar
2 cups milk
⅛ teaspoon salt
1 teaspoon almond extract

Beat egg whites in bowl until frothy. Add sugar, milk, salt and almond flavoring; mix well. Pour through fine strainer into greased custard cups, leaving ¼ inch at top. Place in shallow pan of hot water. Bake at 350°F. for 40 minutes or until knife inserted in center comes out clean. Cool on wire rack. Chill until serving time. Unmold onto serving plates. Top with fresh fruit, banana slices in currant jelly or chocolate or butterscotch sauce with nuts.
Yield: 5 servings.

Approx Per Serving: Cal 122; Prot 7.7 gr; T Fat 3.4 gr; Chol 13.7 mg; Carbo 15.0 gr; Sod 162.1 mg; Potas 195.9 mg.
Nutritional information does not include toppings.

Janet Kiser, Manhattan

BROWNIE PUDDING

1 cup sifted all-purpose flour
¾ cup sugar
2 tablespoons baking cocoa
2 teaspoons baking powder
½ teaspoon salt
½ cup milk
2 tablespoons oil
1 teaspoon vanilla extract
¾ cup chopped walnuts
¾ cup packed brown sugar
¼ cup baking cocoa
1¾ cups hot water

Sift flour, sugar, 2 tablespoons cocoa, baking powder and salt into bowl. Add milk, oil and vanilla; mix well. Stir in walnuts. Pour into greased 8 x 8-inch baking pan. Combine brown sugar, ¼ cup cocoa and hot water in bowl; mix well. Pour over batter. Bake at 350°F. for 45 minutes. Yield: 6 servings.

Approx Per Serving: Cal 441; Prot 6.1 gr; T Fat 16.1 gr; Chol 2.8 mg; Carbo 73.4 gr; Sod 306.9 mg; Potas 295.6 mg.

Jennifer Black, Cottonwood Falls

CARROT PUDDING

1 cup grated carrots
1 cup grated potato
1 cup sugar
1 cup all-purpose flour
1 teaspoon soda
½ teaspoon baking powder
1 teaspoon cinnamon
1 (scant) teaspoon cloves
¼ teaspoon salt
1 cup raisins
1 cup sugar
½ cup cream
¼ cup butter
1 teaspoon vanilla extract

Mix carrots, potato and 1 cup sugar in bowl. Add sifted flour, soda, baking powder, cinnamon, cloves and salt; mix well. Stir in raisins. Spoon into top of double boiler. Cook over hot water for 3 hours. Bring 1 cup sugar, cream and butter to a boil in saucepan. Stir in vanilla. Serve sauce over hot pudding. May double sauce if desired. Yield: 10 servings.

Approx Per Serving: Cal 340; Prot 2.4 gr; T Fat 9.3 gr; Chol 30.0 mg; Carbo 64.6 gr; Sod 221.9 mg; Potas 234.4 mg.

Tamara Walsh, Garden City

CUSTARD

2 eggs
¼ cup sugar
½ teaspoon vanilla extract
⅛ teaspoon salt
2 cups milk

Beat eggs, sugar, vanilla and salt in bowl just until well mixed. Scald milk in saucepan. Add to egg mixture in very fine stream, mixing constantly. Pour into buttered baking dish. Bake at 300°F. until knife inserted in center comes out clean. Yield: 4 servings.

Approx Per Serving: Cal 168; Prot 7.5 gr; T Fat 7.2 gr; Chol 143.5 mg; Carbo 18.6 gr; Sod 161.0 mg; Potas 208.4 mg.

Mary Artz, Council Grove

DATE PUDDING

2 cups packed brown sugar
2 cups water
1 cup dates
¼ cup hot water
1 cup chopped pecans
1½ cups all-purpose flour
1 cup sugar
2 teaspoons baking powder
⅛ teaspoon salt
1 cup milk

Mix brown sugar and 2 cups water in 9x13-inch dish. Mix dates and ¼ cup hot water in small bowl. Add date mixture and pecans to brown sugar mixture. Combine remaining ingredients in bowl; mix well. Pour into prepared dish. Bake at 350°F. for 35 to 40 minutes or until brown. Yield: 12 servings.

Approx Per Serving: Cal 380; Prot 3.6 gr; T Fat 7.9 gr; Chol 2.8 mg; Carbo 77.2 gr; Sod 99.7 mg; Potas 326.9 mg.

Jodi Christiansen, Durham

TEATIME TASSIES

½ cup butter, softened
3 ounces cream cheese, softened
1 cup all-purpose flour
1 tablespoon butter, softened
¾ cup packed brown sugar
1 egg
⅔ cup chopped pecans

Cream ½ cup butter and cream cheese in mixer bowl until light and fluffy. Add flour; mix well. Chill dough overnight. Press dough into miniature muffin cups. Combine remaining ingredients in bowl; mix well. Spoon into prepared muffin cups. Bake at 325°F. for 25 to 30 minutes or until set and brown. Yield: 24 servings.

Approx Per Serving: Cal 122; Prot 1.4 gr; T Fat 8.3 gr; Chol 27.8 mg; Carbo 11.2 gr; Sod 66.1 mg; Potas 55.0 mg.

Susan Moss, Greensburg

Harvest Moon Buffet
(Elegant Buffet)

SALMON PARTY BALL
page 15

ELITE SALAD
page 47

ROAST BREAST OF DUCK
page 95

BROCCOLI AND RICE
page 110

BEETS AND PINEAPPLE
page 109

COTTAGE CHEESE DINNER ROLLS
page 181

PAVLOVA
page 168

"AMBER WAVES OF GRAIN" by Chris Floyd

APPLE-PECAN COFFEE CAKE

1 cup whole wheat flour
½ teaspoon baking powder
½ teaspoon soda
⅛ teaspoon salt
½ cup sugar
¼ cup shortening
1 egg
½ teaspoon vanilla extract
½ cup (4 ounces) sour cream
1 large apple, peeled, chopped
¼ cup crushed pecans
¼ cup packed brown sugar
1 tablespoon butter
½ teaspoon cinnamon

Mix flour, baking powder, soda and salt. Set aside. Cream sugar and shortening in large mixer bowl until light and fluffy. Beat in egg and vanilla. Add half the flour mixture, sour cream and remaining flour mixture, mixing well after each addition. Stir in apple. Spread in greased 8-inch square baking pan. Sprinkle with mixture of pecans, brown sugar, butter and cinnamon. Bake at 350°F. for 25 to 30 minutes or until coffee cake tests done. Serve warm. Yield: 9 servings.

Approx Per Serving: Cal 227; Prot 3.2 gr; T Fat 11.3 gr; Chol 33.4 mg;
Carbo 30.4 gr; Sod 126.1 mg; Potas 125.3 mg.

Robin File, Beloit

CHOCOLATE CHIP-DATE COFFEE CAKE

1 cup chopped dates
1½ cups boiling water
1 teaspoon soda
½ cup margarine, softened
1 cup sugar
2 eggs
1 teaspoon vanilla extract
1½ cups all-purpose flour
½ teaspoon soda
½ cup packed brown sugar
½ cup chopped pecans
1 cup (6 ounces) chocolate
  chips

Combine dates, boiling water and 1 teaspoon soda in bowl. Let stand until cool. Cream margarine and sugar in mixer bowl until light and fluffy. Blend in eggs and vanilla. Add flour and ½ teaspoon soda; mix well. Stir in date mixture. Pour into greased and floured 9x13-inch baking pan. Mix remaining ingredients in bowl. Sprinkle over coffee cake. Bake at 350°F. for 35 to 40 minutes or until golden brown. Yield: 12 servings.

Approx Per Serving: Cal 383; Prot 4.1 gr; T Fat 17.4 gr; Chol 42.1 mg;
Carbo 57.0 gr; Sod 209.9 mg; Potas 231.7 mg.

Bill Graves, Secretary of State

SWEDISH COFFEE RING

1 package dry yeast
¼ cup warm water
¾ cup milk, scalded, cooled
¼ cup sugar
¼ cup margarine, softened
1 egg
½ teaspoon cardamom
½ teaspoon salt
3¼ to 3½ cups all-purpose
  flour
½ cup almond paste
¼ cup packed brown sugar
¼ cup margarine, softened
1 cup confectioners' sugar
1 tablespoon water
½ teaspoon vanilla extract

Dissolve yeast in warm water in large bowl. Add next 6 ingredients and 2 cups flour; beat until smooth. Add enough remaining flour to make dough easy to handle. Knead on floured surface for 5 minutes or until smooth and elastic. Place in greased bowl, turning to grease surface. Let rise, covered, for 1 hour or until doubled in bulk. Blend almond paste, brown sugar and margarine in bowl. Roll dough into 9 x 15-inch rectangle on lightly floured surface. Spread with almond paste mixture. Roll as for jelly roll from long side; seal. Place seam side down on lightly greased baking sheet; shape into ring, sealing ends together. Cut two-thirds through ring at 1-inch intervals with scissors. Turn slices to sides. Let rise, covered, for 40 minutes or until doubled in bulk. Bake at 350°F. for 25 minutes or until brown. Spread with mixture of confectioners' sugar, 1 tablespoon water and vanilla. Yield: 15 servings.

Approx Per Serving: Cal 271; Prot 5.3 gr; T Fat 11.4 gr; Chol 18.6 mg;
Carbo 37.8 gr; Sod 158.3 mg; Potas 130.9 mg.

Kathleen Keiter, Gardner

ORANGE-PECAN MUFFINS

2 cups all-purpose flour
3 tablespoons sugar
1 tablespoon baking powder
½ teaspoon salt
2½ teaspoons grated orange
rind
3 tablespoons melted
  shortening
1 egg, beaten
1 cup milk
1 teaspoon vanilla extract
¼ cup chopped pecans
½ cup confectioners' sugar
2 teaspoons orange juice
½ teaspoon orange extract

Combine first 4 dry ingredients in bowl. Add 2 teaspoons orange rind, shortening, eggs, milk, vanilla and pecans. Mix just until moistened. Fill greased or paper-lined muffin cups ⅔ full. Bake at 425°F. for 20 to 25 minutes or until brown. Combine confectioners' sugar, orange juice, orange extract and remaining ½ teaspoon orange rind in bowl; mix well. Drizzle over muffins. Yield: 12 servings.

Approx Per Serving: Cal 177; Prot 3.7 gr; T Fat 6.7 gr; Chol 23.9 mg;
Carbo 25.8 gr; Sod 186.8 mg; Potas 73.2 mg.

Suzie Martin, Herington

HIGH FIBER BRAN MUFFINS

1 cup stone-ground whole
    wheat flour
1½ cups whole bran cereal
1 teaspoon soda
⅛ teaspoon salt
½ cup raisins
1 egg, slightly beaten
½ cup honey
¾ cup skim milk
2 tablespoons safflower oil

Mix whole wheat flour, bran cereal, soda, salt and raisins in bowl. Add egg, honey, milk and oil; mix just until moistened. Fill greased or paper-lined muffin cups ⅔ full. Bake at 400°F. for 15 to 20 minutes or until brown. May substitute dates for raisins. Yield: 12 muffins.

Approx Per Muffin: Cal 148; Prot 3.6 gr; T Fat 3.1 gr. Chol 21.4 mg; Carbo 31.5 gr; Sod 153.1 mg; Potas 162.2 mg.

Mrs. Dwane L. Wallace, Kansas 4-H Foundation Trustee, Wichita

HONEY MUFFINS

1 cup margarine, softened
1 cup honey
1 egg
1 cup (8 ounces) sour cream
2 cups whole wheat flour
1 teaspoon soda
½ teaspoon salt

Combine margarine and honey in bowl; mix well. Blend in egg and sour cream. Add dry ingredients; mix just until moistened. Fill greased muffin cups ⅔ full. Bake at 400°F. for 12 to 15 minutes or until light brown. Yield: 16 muffins.

Approx Per Muffin: Cal 252; Prot 3.0 gr; T Fat 15.2 gr; Chol 22.1 mg; Carbo 28.6 gr; Sod 271.0 mg; Potas 94.2 mg.

Eloise M. Becker, Osborne

SOUR CREAM WAFFLES

2 cups all-purpose flour
1 teaspoon baking powder
1 teaspoon salt
1 teaspoon soda
2 egg yolks
1 cup (8 ounces) sour cream
1 cup sour milk
2 egg whites, stiffly beaten

Sift dry ingredients together; set aside. Beat egg yolks in mixer bowl until thick and lemon-colored. Add sour cream and sour milk; mix until smooth. Add sifted dry ingredients; beat until smooth. Fold in stiffly beaten egg whites gently. Bake in hot waffle iron using manufacturer's instructions. Yield: 6 waffles.

Approx Per Waffle: Cal 286; Prot 9.1 gr; T Fat 11.6 gr; Chol 106.4 mg; Carbo 35.6 gr; Sod 607.4 mg; Potas 175.0 mg.

Heather Grunewald, Olathe

CHERRY ROSE ROLLS

¾ cup milk
1 package dry yeast
½ cup warm water
1 cup sourdough starter
½ cup melted butter
½ cup sugar
1½ teaspoons salt
3 to 4 cups all-purpose flour
1 (21-ounce) can cherry
  pie filling
1 cup confectioners' sugar
1 teaspoon vanilla extract
1 tablespoon milk

Bring ¾ cup milk just to the simmering point in saucepan. Cool for 10 minutes. Dissolve yeast in warm water. Let stand for 5 minutes. Combine milk, yeast, sourdough starter, butter, sugar and salt in bowl. Add enough flour to form a soft dough. Knead on floured surface for 5 to 8 minutes or until smooth and elastic, kneading in additional flour if necessary to make dough easy to handle. Place in greased bowl, turning to grease surface. Chill, covered, for 2 hours to overnight. Punch dough down. Divide into 24 portions. Roll each to 15-inch rope on floured surface. Coil ropes 2 inches apart on greased baking sheet, tucking ends under. Let rise, covered, in a warm place for 2 hours or until doubled in bulk. Make 1-inch wide indentation in tops of rolls. Fill with pie filling. Bake at 400°F. for 15 to 20 minutes or until golden. Cool. Combine confectioners' sugar, vanilla and 1 tablespoon milk in bowl; mix until smooth. Pipe onto rolls. Yield: 24 rolls.

Approx Per Roll: Cal 179; Prot 2.6 gr; T Fat 4.3 gr; Chol 13.0 mg; Carbo 32.3 gr; Sod 184.7 mg; Potas 38.9 mg.

Beverly Helton, Redfield

CARAWAY PUFFS

1 package dry yeast
1⅓ cups sifted all-purpose flour
¼ teaspoon soda
1 tablespoon butter
1 cup (8 ounces) cream-style
  cottage cheese
¼ cup water
2 tablespoons sugar
1 teaspoon salt
1 egg
2 teaspoons caraway seed
2 teaspoons grated onion
1 cup all-purpose flour

Mix yeast, 1⅓ cups flour and soda in mixer bowl. Heat butter, cottage cheese, water, sugar and salt in saucepan until butter is melted; mix well. Add to flour mixture; mix well. Add egg, caraway seed and onion. Beat at low speed for 30 seconds. Beat at high speed for 3 minutes. Stir in 1 cup flour. Place in greased bowl, turning to grease surface. Let rise, covered, in a warm place for 1½ hours or until doubled in bulk. Shape into 12 balls. Place in greased muffin cups. Let rise, covered, in a warm place for 40 minutes. Bake at 400°F. for 12 to 15 minutes or until brown. Yield: 12 rolls.

Approx Per Roll: Cal 135; Prot 6.0 gr; T Fat; 2.4 gr; Chol 27.9 mg; Carbo 21.5 gr; Sod 258.9 mg; Potas 47.9 mg.

Sherri Belcher, Garden City

KRINGLES

1 package dry yeast
¼ cup warm water
½ cup margarine
2 cups all-purpose flour
1½ tablespoons sugar
3 tablespoons nonfat
  dry milk powder
½ teaspoon salt
1 egg, separated
½ cup warm water
2 tablespoons margarine,
  softened
½ cup packed brown sugar
1 tablespoon almond extract
2 cups plumped raisins

Dissolve yeast in ¼ cup water. Combine ½ cup margarine, flour, sugar, dry milk powder and salt in bowl; blend with pastry blender. Add yeast and egg yolk beaten with ½ cup water; beat for 3 minutes. Chill, covered, for 2 to 48 hours. Cream 2 tablespoons margarine, brown sugar and flavoring in mixer bowl until light. Stir in raisins. Divide dough into 2 portions. Roll into two 6x18-inch rectangles on floured surface. Spread raisin filling in 3-inch strip down center of rectangles. Brush beaten egg white in 1-inch strip down center of filling. Fold sides and ends of dough over filling; seal edges. Shape into U's on greased baking sheets. Bake at 400°F. for 25 minutes. Frost with favorite confectioners' sugar frosting.
Yield: 24 servings.

Approx Per Serving: Cal 138; Prot 2.0 gr; T Fat 5.2 gr; Chol 10.7 mg; Carbo 21.8 gr; Sod 112.8 mg; Potas 125.5 mg.

Bonnie Edwards, Olsburg

STICKY QUICKIE BUNS

1½ cups all-purpose flour
2 packages dry yeast
¾ cup milk
½ cup water
¼ cup sugar
¼ cup butter
1 teaspoon salt
1 egg
1¾ cups all-purpose flour
¾ cup margarine
1 cup packed brown sugar
1 tablespoon corn syrup
1 tablespoon water
1 teaspoon cinnamon
¾ cup pecans

Mix 1½ cups flour and yeast in bowl. Heat milk, ½ cup water, sugar, butter and salt in saucepan until warm. Pour over yeast mixture. Add egg; beat at high speed for 3 minutes. Stir in 1¾ cups flour. Let rise, covered, in a warm place for 30 minutes. Combine margarine and remaining ingredients in saucepan. Heat until margarine is melted; mix well. Pour into 9x13-inch baking dish. Stir down batter. Drop by tablespoonfuls into prepared dish. Bake at 375°F. for 15 minutes. Cool in pan for 1 minute. Invert onto serving platter.
Yield: 15 servings.

Approx Per Serving: Cal 335; Prot 4.7 gr; T Fat 17.6 gr; Chol 28.0 mg; Carbo 40.8 gr; Sod 307.3 mg; Potas 156.2 mg.

Carmen Keeten, Phillipsburg

BATTER-WAY ROLLS

2 packages dry yeast
1½ cups warm water
¼ cup sugar
⅓ cup shortening
1 egg
1½ teaspoons salt
4 cups all-purpose flour

Dissolve yeast in warm water in large mixer bowl. Add sugar, shortening, egg, salt and 2 cups flour. Beat until smooth. Stir in remaining flour. Let rise, covered, in warm place for 30 minutes or until doubled in bulk. Fill greased muffin cups half full. Let rise in a warm place for 30 minutes or until risen to top of muffin cups. Bake at 400°F. for 10 to 15 minutes or until brown. Yield: 18 rolls.

Approx Per Roll: Cal 155; Prot 3.6 gr; T Fat ;4.7 gr; Chol 14.0 mg;
Carbo 24.2 gr; Sod 182.0 mg; Potas 45.6 mg.

Ruth Ann Bigge, Stockton

HARVEST PUMPKIN ROLLS

1 package dry yeast
⅓ cup warm (110°F.) water
2 eggs
1 cup mashed, cooked unsalted
   pumpkin
⅓ cup margarine, softened
⅓ cup honey
1 teaspoon salt
4 to 5 cups all-purpose flour

Dissolve yeast in warm water. Combine eggs, pumpkin, margarine, honey and salt in bowl; mix well. Add yeast and 2 cups flour; beat for 2 minutes. Add enough remaining flour to form soft dough. Let rest on floured surface for 3 to 5 minutes. Knead for 8 to 10 minutes or until smooth and elastic, kneading in remaining flour. Place in greased bowl, turning to grease surface. Let rise, covered, in warm place for 1 hour or until doubled in bulk. Punch dough down. Let rest for 10 minutes. Pinch off a 2-
inch ball of dough; set aside. Divide remaining dough into 10 portions. Shape into pumpkins. Place on greased baking sheet. Garnish top side with plumped raisins to resemble jack-o'-lantern face if desired. Roll reserved dough into inch rope. Cut into 10 pieces for stems. Make indentations in rolls. Place stems in indentations; pinch to seal. Bake at 400°F. for minutes or until golden brown. Yield: 10 rolls.

.4 gr; T Fat 8.0 gr; Chol 50.6 mg;
Potas 152.6 mg.

Christine Steichen and Annette Kiser, Manhattan

approximately 4 dozen cookies.

PUMPKIN BREAD

2 2/3 cups Flour
3 cups Sugar
2 tsp. Baking Soda
2 tsp. Cinnamon
2 tsp. Nutmeg
1 1/2 tsp. Salt
4 Eggs
1 can Pumpkin (2 cups)
1 cup Cooking Oil
2/3 cup Water
1 cup Nuts

Mix first six ingredients together in mixing bowl. In another bowl mix the next four ingredients together, then add to first mixture. Mix well. Add nuts. Pour into greased and floured loaf pans. (Makes 3 regular size loaves or several smaller ones) Bake at 325° for 50 minutes.

Favorite Recipes

AUNT NANCY'S NO FAIL YEAST ROLLS

Melt:

1 stick Butter

Add:

1 cup Scalded Milk

1/2 cup Sugar

1 tsp. Salt

Dissolve:

2 pkgs. Rapid rise Yeast in 1/2 cup Lukewarm Water

Beat 3 Eggs

When milk mixture is cool (If it's too hot, it will kill the yeast), combine above ingredients.

Gradually add:

6 cups Flour, stirring constantly (I like to use 1/2 whole wheat, 1/2 Better for Bread (Pillsbury) and some cracked Wheat Berries for extra texture, but just using white flour will work) Add more flour, if needed, until dough pulls away from plastic mixing bowl.

Cover with damp dishtowel and let rise until double.

Turn out on floured counter, roll out in 1/4" (or less) thin layer. Melt 1/2 stick Butter and spread over top. Cut into triangles, (approx. 5" x 2"), and roll up from base, butter side out. Put rolls on cookie sheets with an inch between them, tips of triangles tucked underneath. Set in warm place to rise again, about an hour. (Rising time will depend on the room temperature. Cool rooms will not allow yeast to work very fast.)

Bake in 350° oven for 15-20 minutes, or until golden brown on edges.

½ teaspoon soda

2 teaspoons salt

4 cups (or more) all-purpose flour

---

solve yeast in water. Scald milk in sauce- Mix with sugar, shortening and salt in . Cool. Add 1 cup flour; beat until th. Add egg, yeast mixture and ½ cup mix well. Stir in baking powder and ½ lour; mix well. Stir in enough remaining to make dough easy to handle. Let rest for nutes. Knead on lightly floured surface for 8 minutes or until smooth and elastic. in greased bowl, turning to grease surface. ise in a warm place until doubled in bulk. h dough down; divide into 3 portions. Let or 5 minutes. Roll each portion into circle oured surface. Cut into 8 wedges. Spread wedge with 1 teaspoon butter. Sprinkle cheese. Roll wedges from wide ends. e into crescents on greased baking sheet. with egg white. Sprinkle with sesame Let rise in a warm place until doubled in Bake at 400°F. for 12 minutes. : 24 rolls.

gr; T Fat 9.1 gr; Chol 24.3 mg; tas 51.6 mg.

Janel Remus, Osborne

---

lve yeast in lukewarm water. Heat cot-heese to lukewarm in saucepan. Combine e cheese, yeast, sugar, eggs, soda and salt l; mix well. Stir in enough flour to make lough. Place in greased bowl, turning to grease surface. Let rise, covered, in warm place for 1½ hours or until doubled in bulk. Punch dough down. Divide into 2 portions. Shape each portion into 12 rolls. Roll in additional flour. Place in 2 greased 8-inch baking pans. Let rise in warm place until doubled in bulk. Bake at 350°F. for 20 minutes or until golden. Brush tops with butter if desired. Yield: 24 rolls.

Approx Per Roll: Cal 114; Prot 5.7 gr; T Fat 1.6 gr; Chol 24.9 mg; Carbo 18.8 gr; Sod 247.3 mg; Potas 54.3 mg.

Sharon Krehbiel, Colby

KANSAS BREAD STICKS

1 package dry yeast
¼ cup warm (115°F.) water
1 tablespoon molasses
½ cup buttermilk
¼ cup cottage cheese
2 tablespoons oil
2 eggs
1 cup whole wheat flour
½ cup rye flour
¼ cup salted sunflower seed
2 tablespoons unprocessed bran
2 tablespoons wheat germ
2 tablespoons sesame seed
1 teaspoon baking powder
¾ teaspoon salt
1 to 1¼ cups all-purpose flour
2 tablespoons Parmesan cheese

Dissolve yeast in mixture of warm water and molasses in large mixer bowl. Add buttermilk, cottage cheese, oil and 1 egg; mix for 2 minutes. Add next 8 dry ingredients; mix well. Add enough all-purpose flour to make a soft dough; mix for 3 minutes. Knead on lightly floured surface or with dough hook for 10 minutes. Place in greased bowl, turning to grease surface. Let rise, covered, in warm place until doubled in bulk. Punch dough down. Divide into 2 portions. Divide each portion into 12 balls. Roll each ball into 10 to 12-inch rope on floured surface. Place 1½ inches apart on greased baking sheets. Let rise, covered, in warm place until doubled in bulk. Brush with 1 egg beaten with 1 tablespoon water. Sprinkle with cheese. Bake at 350°F. for 20 minutes or until golden brown. Yield: 24 sticks.

Approx Per Stick: Cal 158; Prot 5.7 gr; T Fat 9.5 gr; Chol 22.3 mg; Carbo 14.0 gr; Sod 133.3 mg; Potas 166.5 mg.

Cynthia S. Falk, Kansas Wheat Commission, Manhattan

PINEAPPLE WHOLE WHEAT ROLLS

⅓ cup pineapple juice
⅓ cup milk
3 tablespoons oil
3 tablespoons brown sugar
¼ teaspoon salt
1 cup all-purpose flour
1 package dry yeast
1 (8-ounce) can juice-pack crushed pineapple, drained
2 to 2¼ cups whole wheat flour
¼ cup honey
¼ cup butter, melted

Heat first 5 ingredients in saucepan to 120°F. Combine with all-purpose flour and yeast in mixer bowl. Beat at low speed for 30 seconds. Beat at high speed for 3 minutes. Stir in pineapple and enough whole wheat flour to make medium dough. Knead in remaining whole wheat flour on floured surface. Place in greased bowl, turning to grease surface. Let rise, covered, for 1 hour or until doubled in bulk. Punch dough down. Let rest for 10 minutes. Shape into 45 balls. Place 3 balls in each of 15 greased muffin cups. Let rise, covered, for 20 minutes. Bake at 350°F. for 15 minutes. Brush with mixture of honey and butter. Yield: 15 rolls.

Approx Per Roll: Cal 186; Prot 3.7 gr; T Fat 6.4 gr; Chol 10.2 mg; Carbo 30.2 gr; Sod 77.8 mg; Potas 121.2 mg.

Sonya Meeds, Oakley

EARLY COLONIAL BREAD

½ cup yellow cornmeal
½ cup packed brown sugar
1 tablespoon salt
¼ cup oil
2 cups boiling water
2 tablespoons yeast
½ cup warm (110 to 115°F.)
    water
¾ cup whole wheat flour
½ cup rye flour
2 cups bread flour
2 to 2½ cups all-purpose flour

Mix first 4 ingredients in bowl. Stir in boiling water. Let stand until cooled to lukewarm. Dissolve yeast in warm water. Add yeast, whole wheat and rye flours to cornmeal mixture; mix well. Add bread flour and enough all-purpose flour to make medium dough. Knead on floured surface for 6 minutes or until smooth and elastic. Place in greased bowl, turning to grease surface. Let rise, covered, until doubled in bulk. Divide into 2 portions on floured surface. Let rest, covered, for 10 minutes. Shape into loaves; place in greased 5 x 9-inch loaf pans. Let rise until almost doubled in bulk. Bake at 375°F. for 35 minutes or until loaves test done. Cool on wire racks. Yield: 24 servings.

Approx Per Serving: Cal 154; Prot 3.6 gr; T Fat 2.6 gr; Chol 0.0 mg;
    Carbo 28.8 gr; Sod 267.4 mg; Potas 54.7 mg.

Riley and Faye Walters Family, Cassoday

FRENCH HERB BREAD

1 cup buttermilk
¼ cup water
6 tablespoons margarine
1½ cups all-purpose flour
2 tablespoons sugar
1½ teaspoons salt
2 tablespoons dry yeast
1½ cups all-purpose flour
½ cup minced onion
1 tablespoon minced parsley
⅛ teaspoon garlic powder
½ to 1 cup all-purpose flour
1 egg white
2 tablespoons water
Parsley flakes to taste

Heat mixture of buttermilk, ¼ cup water and margarine to 120 °F. in saucepan. Mix 1½ cups flour, sugar, salt and dry yeast in large mixer bowl. Add hot buttermilk mixture. Beat at medium speed for 3 minutes. Stir in 1½ cups flour, onion, parsley and garlic powder. Dough will be sticky. Knead on floured surface until smooth and elastic, adding enough remaining ½ to 1 cup flour as necessary. Place in greased bowl, turning to grease surface. Let rise until doubled in bulk. Roll into 2 rectangles; roll as for jelly roll. Shape into French loaves; place on greased baking sheet. Let rise until doubled in bulk. Brush with mixture of beaten egg white and 2 tablespoons water. Sprinkle with parsley flakes. Bake at 400°F. for 20 minutes or until loaves test done. Cool on wire racks. Yield: 24 servings.

Approx Per Serving: Cal 113; Prot 3.0 gr; T Fat 3.1 gr; Chol 0.2 mg;
    Carbo 18.0 gr; Sod 184.6 mg; Potas 54.1 mg.

Julie Sellers, Florence

HAZEL'S RYE BREAD

1 package dry yeast
½ cup warm water
3 cups rye flour
1 tablespoon aniseed
¾ cup sugar
½ cup grated orange rind
1½ teaspoons salt
2½ cups hot water
¾ cup molasses
5½ to 6 cups all-purpose flour

Dissolve yeast in warm water. Mix rye flour aniseed, sugar, orange rind and salt in large bowl. Add hot water and molasses; mix well. Let stand until cool. Add yeast and enough all-purpose flour to make medium dough. Let rise, covered, in warm place until doubled in bulk. Shape into 3 large or 4 small loaves; place in greased loaf pans. Bake at 300°F. for 15 minutes. Cover with foil. Bake for 1 hour and 15 minutes longer or until loaves test done. Remove to wire rack to cool. Yield: 36 slices.

Approx Per Slice: Cal 194; Prot 0.9 gr; T Fat 0.1 gr; Chol 0.0 mg; Carbo 48.8 gr; Sod 90.4 mg; Potas 83.8 mg.

John Carlin, Governor of Kansas (1979–1987)

RAISIN WHOLE WHEAT LOAVES

2 packages dry yeast
3 cups warm (110 to 115°F.) water
½ cup honey
¼ cup packed brown sugar
2 teaspoons salt
5 cups whole wheat flour
3 to 4 cups all-purpose flour
¾ cup hulled sunflower seed
2 cups raisins
1 tablespoon butter

Dissolve yeast in warm water in small bowl. Add to mixture of honey, brown sugar and salt in large mixer bowl. Beat at low speed until well blended. Add whole wheat flour gradually, beating constantly at medium speed. Add enough all-purpose flour to make medium dough. Knead on floured surface until smooth and elastic, adding sunflower seed, raisins and additional flour as necessary. Place in greased bowl, turning to grease surface. Let rise, covered, in warm place for 1½ hours or until doubled in bulk. Shape into 2 loaves on floured surface; place in greased 5 x 9-inch loaf pan. Let rise, covered, in warm place for 1 hour or until doubled in bulk. Bake at 350°F. for 50 minutes or until brown. Remove from pans to wire rack. Brush tops with butter. Cool. Yield: 24 slices.

Approx Per Slice: Cal 253; Prot 7.1 gr; T Fat 2.9 gr; Chol 0.0 mg; Carbo 53.7 gr; Sod 184.1 mg; Potas 271.8 mg.

Dawn Linsey, Lebo

WHOLE WHEAT BANANA BREAD

1 cup sugar
½ cup melted margarine
1 cup mashed bananas
⅓ cup water
2 eggs, slightly beaten
1 cup all-purpose flour
1 cup whole wheat flour
1 teaspoon soda
½ teaspoon salt
½ cup chopped pecans

Blend sugar and margarine in large bowl. Add bananas, water and eggs; mix well. Add sifted flours, soda and salt gradually, mixing well after each addition. Fold in pecans. Pour into 5 x 9-inch loaf pan greased on bottom only. Bake at 350°F. for 55 to 65 minutes or until toothpick inserted in center comes out clean. Cool in pan for 10 minutes. Remove to wire rack to cool completely. Cool completely before slicing. Store, tightly wrapped, in refrigerator. Yield: 12 servings.

Approx Per Serving: Cal 267; Prot 4.2 gr; T Fat 12.5 gr; Chol 42.1 mg; Carbo 36.6 gr; Sod 261.7 mg; Potas 159.4 mg.

Randy Straub, Wamego

CHRISTMAS BREAD

1 cup raisins
½ cup orange juice
2 packages quick-rising yeast
½ cup warm water
½ cup sugar
1 teaspoon salt
1 cup butter
½ cup milk
1 (8-ounce) jar citron
2 eggs
2 teaspoons lemon extract
½ teaspoon mace
6 cups all-purpose flour
1 recipe buttercream frosting

Heat raisins in orange juice in saucepan until warm. Remove from heat; cover. Let stand until cool. Dissolve yeast in warm water in large bowl. Let stand until foamy. Stir in sugar and salt. Melt butter in saucepan over low heat. Stir in milk. Cool. Add to yeast mixture with raisins, citron, eggs, lemon flavoring, mace and half the flour; mix well. Add remaining flour 1 cup at a time, mixing well after each addition. Knead on floured surface for 5 to 7 minutes or until smooth and elastic. Place in greased bowl, turning to grease surface. Let rise, covered, in warm place until doubled in bulk. Punch dough down. Let rise, covered, in warm place until doubled in bulk. Shape into 2 French-style loaves; place on greased baking sheet. Let rise in warm place until doubled in bulk. Bake at 350°F. for 25 to 30 minutes or until loaves test done. Remove to wire rack to cool. Frost with a buttercream frosting. Yield: 24 servings.

Approx Per Serving: Cal 259; Prot 4.5 gr; T Fat 8.7 gr; Chol 45.4 mg; Carbo 41.3 gr; Sod 220.0 mg; Potas 124.1 mg.
Nutritional information does not include frosting.

Claudia Harris Mirabella, Bellevue, Nebraska

CRANBERRY-DATE BREAD

1 cup fresh cranberries
⅓ cup water
¼ cup sugar
1 (8-ounce) package
  chopped dates
1 cup chopped walnuts
1 cup boiling water
⅓ cup shortening
2 cups all-purpose flour
2 teaspoons baking powder
¾ teaspoon salt
½ cup sugar
1 container Egg Beaters
1 teaspoon vanilla extract

Bring cranberries, ⅓ cup water and ¼ cup sugar to a boil in saucepan; reduce heat. Simmer for 3 minutes or until cranberries pop. Cool. Combine dates, walnuts, boiling water and shortening in bowl; stir until shortening melts. Mix flour, baking powder, salt and ½ cup sugar in large bowl. Make well in center of mixture. Add cranberry and date mixtures, Egg Beaters and vanilla; mix until moistened. Pour into greased 4½x8½-inch loaf pan. Bake at 350°F. for 65 minutes. Cool in pan for 10 minutes. Remove to wire rack to cool completely. Yield: 12 servings.

Approx Per Serving: Cal 312; Prot 6.2 gr; T Fat 13.0 gr; Chol 0.0 mg;
    Carbo 47.2 gr; Sod 195.1 mg; Potas 224.4 mg.

Mr. and Mrs. Bob Collins, Stark

CRANBERRY-PECAN LOAF

2 cups all-purpose flour
1½ teaspoons baking powder
½ teaspoon soda
1 egg
¼ cup shortening
¾ cup orange juice
1 (½x1-inch) piece
  orange rind
1 teaspoon salt
1 cup sugar
½ cup pecans
1 cup cranberries

Sift flour, baking powder and soda into bowl. Combine egg, shortening, orange juice, orange rind, salt and sugar in blender container. Process until smooth. Add pecans and cranberries. Process just until pecans and cranberries are chopped. Add to flour mixture; mix just until moistened. Pour into greased 5x9-inch loaf pan. Bake at 350°F. for 25 to 30 minutes or until loaf tests done. Remove to wire rack to cool. Yield: 12 servings.

Approx Per Serving: Cal 234; Prot 3.3 gr; T Fat 9.0 gr; Chol 21.1 mg;
    Carbo 36.0 gr; Sod 259.0 mg; Potas 95.5 mg.

Shannon Roloff, Iola

EASY CHEESE BREAD

3¾ cups buttermilk baking mix
2 cups shredded Cheddar
  cheese
2 tablespoons poppy seed
⅛ teaspoon red pepper
1¼ cups milk
1 egg, beaten

Combine baking mix, cheese, poppy seed and red pepper in bowl; toss until well mixed. Add milk and egg; stir for 2 minutes. Pour into greased 5x9-inch loaf pan. Bake at 350°F. for 55 to 60 minutes or until loaf tests done. Remove to wire rack to cool. Yield: 15 servings.

Approx Per Serving: Cal 206; Prot 7.2 gr; T Fat 9.7 gr; Chol 34.6 mg;
    Carbo 22.0 gr; Sod 509.7 mg; Potas 69.9 mg.

Julie Brooks, Norton

OATMEAL BREAD

1 cup quick-cooking oats
½ cup packed brown sugar
½ cup whole wheat flour
1 tablespoon salt
2 tablespoons margarine
2 cups boiling water
1 package dry yeast
½ cup warm water
5 cups all-purpose flour

Mix first 5 ingredients in large bowl. Add boiling water. Cool to lukewarm. Add yeast dissolved in warm water; mix well. Add flour; mix well. Knead on floured surface for 8 minutes or until smooth and elastic. Place in greased bowl, turning to grease surface. Let rise, covered, for 1 hour or until doubled in bulk. Shape into 2 loaves; place in greased loaf pans. Let rise, covered, for 1 hour or until doubled in bulk. Bake at 375°F. for 25 minutes or until loaves test done. Cool on wire rack. Yield: 24 servings.

Approx Per Serving: Cal 143; Prot 3.7 gr; T Fat 1.5 gr; Chol 0.0 mg;
    Carbo 28.4 gr; Sod 280.3 mg; Potas 67.6 mg.

Patrick Sullivan, Rose Hill

PEANUT BUTTER-OATMEAL BREAD

1½ cups sifted all-purpose flour
1 cup sugar
1 tablespoon baking powder
½ teaspoon salt
½ cup chunky peanut butter
1 cup oats
1 egg, beaten
1 cup milk

Sift flour, sugar, baking powder and salt into bowl. Cut in peanut butter until crumbly. Add oats, egg and milk; stir just until moistened. Pour into greased 5x9-inch loaf pan. Bake at 350°F. for 1 hour. Cool on wire rack.
Yield: 12 servings.

Approx Per Serving: Cal 230; Prot 6.5 gr; T Fat 7.2 gr; Chol 23.9 mg;
    Carbo 36.1 gr; Sod 196.6 mg; Potas 140.7 mg.

Lisa Leuthold, Manhattan

PUMPKIN RIBBON BREAD

1 cup mashed cooked pumpkin
½ cup oil
2 eggs
1½ cups sugar
1⅔ cups all-purpose flour
1 teaspoon soda
½ teaspoon salt
½ teaspoon cloves
½ teaspoon cinnamon
1 cup chopped pecans
6 ounces cream cheese,
  softened
⅓ cup sugar
1 tablespoon all-purpose flour
1 egg
2 teaspoons grated orange rind

Mix pumpkin, oil and 2 eggs in bowl. Add 1½ cups sugar, 1⅔ cups flour, soda, salt and spices; mix well. Stir in pecans. Beat cream cheese with ⅓ cup sugar, 1 tablespoon flour, 1 egg and orange rind in small bowl. Pour ¼ of the batter into each of 2 greased and floured 3½ x 7½-inch loaf pans. Spread cream cheese mixture over batter. Top with remaining batter, covering cream cheese mixture. Bake at 325°F. for 1½ hours or until toothpick inserted in center comes out clean. Cool in pans for 10 minutes. Remove to wire rack to cool completely. Store in refrigerator. Yield: 24 servings.

Approx Per Serving: Cal 206; Prot 2.9 gr; T Fat 11.5 gr; Chol 39.5 mg; Carbo 23.9 gr; Sod 104.5 mg; Potas 76.9 mg.

Luella Fuhrman, Moran

STRAWBERRY BREAD

1½ cups all-purpose flour
½ teaspoon salt
½ teaspoon baking powder
2 teaspoons cinnamon
1 cup sugar
2 eggs, slightly beaten
1 (10-ounce) package
  frozen strawberries, thawed
10 tablespoons oil
¾ cup chopped pecans

Mix flour, salt, baking powder, cinnamon and sugar in bowl. Add eggs, undrained strawberries and oil; mix well. Mix in pecans. Pour into 2 greased and floured 3½ x 7-inch loaf pans. Bake at 350°F. for 1 hour. Serve warm or cold, plain or with butter or strawberry cream cheese. Yield: 20 servings.

Approx Per Serving: Cal 197; Prot 2.2 gr; T Fat 11.7 gr; Chol 25.3 mg; Carbo 22.0 gr; Sod 68.1 mg; Potas 67.3 mg.

Linda Rowe, Scranton

VASIOPETA
(Greek New Year's Bread)

2 packages dry yeast
¼ cup warm (115°F.) water
2 cups warm (115°F.) milk
1 teaspon salt
3 cups all-purpose flour
1 cup sugar
4 eggs
3 egg yolks
½ cup unsalted butter, melted
1 teaspoon grated lemon rind
7 to 8 cups all-purpose flour
1 egg
2 tablespoons water

Dissolve yeast in warm water in large bowl. Add milk, salt and 3 cups flour; mix well. Let rise, covered, in warm place for 1½ hours or until doubled in bulk. Add sugar, 4 eggs, egg yolks, butter and lemon rind; beat with wooden spoon. Stir in enough flour to make soft dough. Knead on floured surface until smooth and elastic. Place in greased bowl, turning to grease surface. Let rise, covered with damp cloth, for 1 hour or until doubled in bulk. Divide into 2 portions. Cut 1 portion into 3 portions; roll each into 15-inch rope. Braid together; pinch ends and tuck under. Place in greased 5 x 9-inch loaf pan. Repeat with remaining dough. Let rise, covered, for 45 minutes or until doubled in bulk. Brush with 1 egg beaten with 2 tablespoons water. Bake at 350°F. for 45 minutes or until loaves test done. Cool on wire rack. Yield: 24 servings.

Approx Per Serving: Cal 314; Prot 8.7 gr; T Fat 7.0 gr; Chol 98.8 mg; Carbo 53.3 gr; Sod 114.9 mg; Potas 112.4 mg.

Heath Rupp, Hays

WHOLE WHEAT WALNUT BREAD

1 cup sifted all-purpose flour
2 teaspoons baking powder
¼ teaspoon salt
½ teaspoon cinnamon
¼ teaspoon nutmeg
¼ teaspoon allspice
½ cup whole wheat flour
¼ cup butter, softened
¾ cup sugar
2 eggs
⅔ cup milk
½ teaspoon vanilla extract
½ cup chopped walnuts

Sift all-purpose flour, baking powder, salt and spices together. Stir in whole wheat flour. Cream butter and sugar in bowl until light and fluffy. Add eggs 1 at a time, mixing well after each addition. Add dry ingredients alternately with milk and vanilla, mixing well after each addition. Stir in walnuts. Pour into greased loaf pan. Bake at 350°F. for 55 minutes or until loaf tests done. Cool in pan for 10 minutes. Remove to wire rack to cool completely. Yield: 12 servings.

Approx Per Serving: Cal 189; Prot 4.0 gr; T Fat 8.7 gr; Chol 55.9 mg; Carbo 25.0 gr; Sod 163.5 mg; Potas 82.7 mg.

Kelli Schultz, St. Francis

MILO DOUGHNUTS

2 cakes compressed yeast
¼ cup warm water
1½ cups milk
¼ cup shortening
½ cup sugar
2 teaspoons salt
2 eggs
4 to 5 cups all-purpose flour
2 cups milo flour
Oil for deep frying
1 pound confectioners' sugar
¼ cup (about) milk

Dissolve yeast in warm water in bowl. Heat 1½ cups milk to scalding in saucepan. Stir in shortening, sugar and salt. Cool to lukewarm. Add milk mixture and beaten eggs to yeast. Add 2½ cups all-purpose flour; beat until smooth. Stir in milo flour and enough remaining all-purpose flour to make a soft dough. Let rise, covered, in warm place for 10 minutes. Knead on floured surface until smooth and elastic, kneading in up to ½ cup flour. Place in greased bowl; brush with melted shortening. Let rise, covered, for 1 hour. Punch dough down. Let rise, covered, in warm place for 45 minutes. Roll on lightly floured surface. Cut with floured doughnut cutter. Let stand for 20 to 30 minutes. Deep-fry in 365°F. oil until golden. Drain on paper towel. Mix confectioners' sugar with ¼ cup milk. Dip hot doughnuts in glaze. Drain on wire rack. Make milo flour by processing milo in blender until finely ground. Sift to remove unprocessed particles. Yield: 36 doughnuts.

Approx Per Doughnut: Cal 140; Prot 2.4 gr; T Fat 2.4 gr; Chol 15.7 mg; Carbo 27.4 gr; Sod 128.4 mg; Potas 42.1 mg.
Nutritional information does not include milo or oil for deep frying.

Jeff Casten, President, Kansas Grain Sorghum Producers Association, Quenemo

BUTTERMILK PANCAKES

2 cups all-purpose flour
2 teaspoons baking powder
1 teaspoon salt
2 tablespoons sugar
½ teaspoon soda
2 eggs, slightly beaten
1½ cups buttermilk
¼ cup melted shortening

Sift dry ingredients into bowl. Combine eggs, buttermilk and shortening. Add to dry ingredients; stir just until mixed. Batter will be lumpy. Bake on hot greased griddle until bubbles appear; turn. Bake until golden. Serve hot. Yield: 6 pancakes.

Approx Per Pancake: Cal 302; Prot 8.7 gr; T Fat 11.7 gr; Chol 85.5 mg; Carbo 39.6 gr; Sod 634.1 mg; Potas 148.6 mg.

Levi Metcalf, Caldwell

Prairie Potluck
(Potluck Supper)

CROCK•POTS OF BEAN SOUP
page 23

LIME SHERBET SALAD
page 193

HOT CHICKEN SALAD
page 194

HAM LOAF
page 194

BARBECUE GREEN BEANS
page 195

HIGH FIBER BRAN MUFFINS
page 177

OATMEAL CAKES
page 195

"FLINT HILLS FENCE POST" by Kris Kobiskie

LIME SHERBET SALAD

8 (3-ounce) packages lime
  gelatin
8 cups boiling water
4 cups cold water
1 gallon lime sherbet
8 cups crushed pineapple,
  drained
3 (16-ounce) packages
  miniature marshmallows
2 cups finely chopped pecans

Dissolve gelatin in boiling water in large container. Add cold water and sherbet; stir until sherbet is almost melted. Add pineapple, marshmallows and pecans; mix well. Pour into 12 x 18-inch pan. Chill until firm. Cut into serving portions. Yield: 50 servings.

Approx Per Serving: Cal 283; Prot 2.9 gr; T Fat 4.1 gr; Chol 0.3 mg;
   Carbo 61.5 gr; Sod 60.4 mg; Potas 111.4 mg.

Rock Springs 4-H Center, Junction City

SLOPPY JOE

15 pounds ground beef
¾ cup vinegar
2 cups tomato juice
10 cups catsup
6 medium onions, chopped
1 large green bell
  pepper, chopped
8 cups chopped celery
½ cup margarine
¼ cup packed brown sugar
3 tablespoons salt
3 tablespoons chili powder
4 large potatoes, peeled, grated

Brown ground beef in large skillet, stirring until crumbly; drain. Add vinegar, tomato juice and catsup; mix well. Pour into large roasting pan. Sauté onions, green peppers and celery in margarine in skillet. Add brown sugar, salt, chili powder and potatoes; mix well. Mix with ground beef mixture in roasting pan. Bake at 325 to 350°F. for 1 hour, stirring frequently. Serve as desired. Yield: 60 servings.

Approx Per Serving: Cal 279; Prot 20.6 gr; T Fat 18.2 gr; Chol 76.6 mg;
   Carbo 7.5 gr; Sod 513.3 mg; Potas 406.0 mg.

Ledona Dowell, Cuba

HAM LOAF

10 pounds ground ham
10 pounds ground beef
24 eggs, well beaten
1½ cups packed brown sugar
¾ cup prepared mustard
2 tablespoons pepper
¼ teaspoon salt
16 cups soft bread crumbs
4 cups catsup
1½ cups chopped onions
6 cups catsup
2 cups barbecue sauce
1½ cups packed brown sugar

Mix ground ham, ground beef, eggs, 1½ cups brown sugar, mustard, pepper, salt, bread crumbs, 4 cups catsup and onions in large mixer container. Mix for 5 to 6 minutes or until well mixed. Divide between two 12 x 22-inch baking pans. Shape mixture in each pan into 5 or 6 loaves. Bake at 350°F. for 1½ to 2 hours. Blend remaining 6 cups catsup, barbecue sauce and 1½ cups brown sugar in large bowl. Pour over loaves. Bake for 30 minutes longer.
Yield: 120 servings.

Approx Per Serving: Cal 220; Prot 11.8 gr; T Fat 12.2 gr; Chol 86.9 mg;
    Carbo 15.6 gr; Sod 436.7 mg; Potas 267.8 mg.

Rock Springs 4-H Center, Junction City

HOT CHICKEN SALAD

24 pounds chopped cooked
    chicken
16 pounds celery, chopped
4 pounds toasted almonds
1½ cups chopped onions
30 cups mayonnaise
3 cups lemon juice
2 tablespoons pepper
12 pounds cheese, shredded
3 (16-ounce) packages potato
    chips, crushed

Combine chicken, celery, almonds and onions in large container; mix well. Add mixture of mayonnaise, lemon juice and pepper; toss until well mixed. Divide among eight 12 x 20-inch baking pans. Layer cheese and potato chips over top. Bake at 350°F. for 25 minutes or to 140°F. on meat thermometer.
Yield: 192 servings.

Approx Per Serving: Cal 558; Prot 27.9 gr; T Fat 46.5 gr; Chol 96.8 mg;
    Carbo 8.7 gr; Sod 511.6 mg; Potas 557.4 mg.

K-State Union, Kansas State University

BARBECUED GREEN BEANS

3 pounds bacon, chopped
6 medium onions, chopped
6 cups catsup
6 cups packed brown sugar
1 cup barbecue sauce
3 (number 10) cans
    green beans, drained

Cook bacon and onions in large skillet until brown, stirring frequently. Mix in catsup, brown sugar and barbecue sauce. Place green beans in 12 x 18-inch baking pan. Pour bacon mixture over beans. Bake at 250°F. for 2 hours. Yield: 120 servings.

Approx Per Serving: Cal 148; Prot 3.9 gr; T Fat 8.0 gr; Chol 8.0 mg;
    Carbo 18.3 gr; Sod 413.1 mg; Potas 187.1 mg.

Rock Springs 4-H Center, Junction City

OATMEAL CAKES

4 cups quick-cooking oats
5 cups boiling water
2 cups shortening
4 cups packed brown sugar
4 cups sugar
8 eggs
1 teaspoon vanilla extract
5⅓ cups sifted all-purpose flour
4 teaspoons soda
2 teaspoons salt
2 cups chopped pecans
4 cups raisins
4 cups packed brown sugar
½ cup margarine
4 cups coconut
2 cups chopped pecans
2 cups cream

Mix oats with boiling water in bowl. Let stand for 20 minutes. Cream shortening, 4 cups brown sugar and sugar in large bowl. Beat in eggs and vanilla. Add oats and sifted flour, soda and salt; mix well. Stir in 2 cups pecans and raisins. Pour into greased baking pans. Bake at 350°F. for 25 to 30 minutes or until cakes test done. Mix 4 cups brown sugar, margarine, coconut, 2 cups pecans and cream in bowl. Spread over hot cakes. Broil for 3 minutes or until bubbly. Yield: 80 servings.

Approx Per Serving: Cal 335; Prot 3.1 gr; T Fat 15.4 gr; Chol 33.2 mg;
    Carbo 48.5 gr; Sod 134.1 mg; Potas 214.1 mg.

Corinne Clark, Clinton, Missouri

CREAM CHEESE BROWNIES

6 (8-ounce) bars semisweet
  baking chocolate
2¼ cups butter
9 cups sugar
24 eggs, beaten
6 cups all-purpose flour
2 tablespoons baking powder
1 tablespoon salt
1 tablespoon almond extract
4 tablespoons vanilla extract
6 cups chopped pecans
3 cups sugar
36 ounces cream cheese,
  softened
1½ cups butter, softened
12 eggs, beaten
¾ cup all-purpose flour
2 tablespoons vanilla extract

Heat chocolate, 2¼ cups butter and 9 cups sugar in large saucepan over low heat until sugar dissolves, stirring constantly. Beat in 24 eggs and sifted 6 cups flour, baking powder and salt. Stir in almond flavoring, 4 tablespoons vanilla flavoring and pecans. Pour ⅔ of the chocolate batter into 2 greased 18 x 30-inch baking pans. Cream 3 cups sugar, cream cheese and 1½ cups butter in mixer bowl. Beat in 12 eggs. Stir in ¾ cup flour and 2 tablespoons vanilla flavoring. Drizzle over chocolate batter in baking pans in marbled pattern. Drizzle remaining ⅓ of the chocolate batter over top. Bake at 350°F. for 25 to 30 minutes. Cool completely before cutting. Cut each pan into 128 bars by making 8 x 16 cuts. Yield: 256 bars.

Approx Per Bar: Cal 142; Prot 2.1 gr; T Fat 8.8 gr; Chol 76.1 mg;
  Carbo 15.3 gr; Sod 83.1 mg; Potas 49.5 mg.

K-State Union, Kansas State University

PEANUT BUTTER COOKIES — ROCK SPRINGS 4-H CENTER

4 cups margarine, softened
4 cups sugar
2¾ cups packed brown sugar
8 eggs
4 cups peanut butter
11 cups all-purpose flour
4 teaspoons soda
2 teaspoons salt

Cream margarine, sugar and brown sugar in large mixer bowl until light and fluffy. Beat in eggs. Blend in peanut butter. Add sifted dry ingredients; mix well. Drop by teaspoonfuls onto greased cookie sheet. Flatten lightly with fork. Bake at 300°F. for 10 to 12 minutes or until golden brown. Cool on wire rack. Yield: 144 cookies.

Approx Per Cookie: Cal 164; Prot 3.2 gr; T Fat 9.1 gr; Chol 14.0 mg;
  Carbo 18.3 gr; Sod 145.6 mg; Potas 73.9 mg.

Bill Riley, Executive Director, Kansas 4-H Foundation, Manhattan

PUMPKIN SQUARES

32 cups all-purpose flour
16 cups quick-cooking oats
16 cups packed brown sugar
16 cups margarine
32 (16-ounce) cans pumpkin
24 cups sugar
64 eggs
31 (14-ounce) cans evaporated
  milk
5 tablespoons plus
  1 teaspoon salt
10 tablespoons plus
  2 teaspoons cinnamon
5 tablespoons plus
  1 teaspoon ginger
2 tablespoons plus
  2 teaspoons cloves
16 cups chopped pecans
16 cups packed brown sugar
4 cups margarine

Mix flour, oats, 16 cups brown sugar and 16 cups margarine in very large container. Press into sixteen 12 x 20-inch baking pans. Bake at 350°F. for 15 minutes. Blend pumpkin, sugar, eggs, evaporated milk, salt and spices in very large container. Pour about 2 quarts of the mixture into each pan. Bake for 20 minutes. Sprinkle mixture of pecans, 16 cups brown sugar and 4 cups margarine over pumpkin layers. Bake for 20 minutes longer. Cut each pan into 34 servings. Yield: 512 servings.

Approx Per Serving: Cal 271; Prot 4.5 gr; T Fat 10.0 gr; Chol 39.7 mg; Carbo 35.9 gr; Sod 232.3 mg; Potas 246.6 mg.

K-State Union, Kansas State University

SUGAR COOKIES

4 cups butter
4 cups sugar
8 eggs
1 tablespoon vanilla extract
1 teaspoon lemon extract
1 teaspoon salt
3½ tablespoons baking powder
9 cups all-purpose flour

Cream butter, sugar and eggs in large mixer container. Add flavorings, salt, baking powder and flour; mix well. Drop by teaspoonfuls onto greased cookie sheets. Flatten with glass dipped in additional sugar. Bake at 350°F. for 8 to 10 minutes or until golden brown. Remove to wire rack to cool. Yield: 300 cookies.

Approx Per Cookie: Cal 50; Prot 0.6 gr; T Fat 2.7 gr; Chol 14.6 mg; Carbo 5.7 gr; Sod 50.7 mg; Potas 6.3 mg.
Nutritional information does not include sugar for flattening cookies.

Jeanne Dowell, Randolph

Quantities to Serve 100

Baked beans . . . . 5 gallons
Beef . . . . 40 pounds
Beets . . . . 30 pounds
Bread . . . . 10 loaves
Butter . . . . 3 pounds
Cabbage for slaw . . . . 20 pounds
Cakes . . . . 8 cakes
Carrots . . . . 33 pounds
Cauliflower . . . . 18 pounds
Cheese . . . . 18 pounds
Chicken for chicken pie . . . . 40 pounds
Coffee . . . . 3 pounds
Cream . . . . 3 quarts
Fruit cocktail . . . . 1 gallon
Fruit juice . . . . 4 (No. 10) cans
Fruit salad . . . . 20 quarts
Ham . . . . 40 pounds
Hamburger . . . . 30 to 36 pounds
Ice Cream . . . . 4 gallons
Lettuce . . . . 20 heads
Meat loaf . . . . 24 pounds
Milk . . . . 6 gallons
Nuts . . . . 3 pounds
Olives . . . . 1¾ pounds
Oysters . . . . 18 quarts
Pickles . . . . 2 quarts
Pies . . . . 18 pies
Potatoes . . . . 35 pounds
Potato salad . . . . 12 quarts
Roast pork . . . . 40 pounds
Rolls . . . . 200 rolls
Salad dressing . . . . 3 quarts
Scalloped potatoes . . . . 5 gallons
Soup . . . . 5 gallons
Sugar cubes . . . . 3 pounds
Tomato juice . . . . 4 (No. 10) cans
Vegetables . . . . 4 (No. 20) cans
Vegetable salad . . . . 20 quarts
Whipping cream . . . . 4 pints
Wieners . . . . 25 pounds

Substitution Chart

	Instead of:	Use:
Baking	1 teaspoon baking powder	¼ teaspoon soda plus ½ teaspoon cream of tartar
	1 tablespoon cornstarch (for thickening)	2 tablespoons flour or 1 tablespoon tapioca
	1 cup sifted all-purpose flour	1 cup plus 2 tablespoons sifted cake flour
	1 cup sifted cake flour	1 cup minus 2 tablespoons sifted all-purpose flour
	1 cup fine dry bread crumbs	¾ cup fine cracker crumbs
Dairy	1 cup buttermilk	1 cup sour milk or 1 cup yogurt
	1 cup heavy cream	¾ cup skim milk plus ⅓ cup butter
	1 cup light cream	⅞ cup skim milk plus 3 tablespoons butter
	1 cup sour cream	⅞ cup sour milk plus 3 tablespoons butter
	1 cup sour milk	1 cup milk plus 1 tablespoon vinegar or lemon juice or 1 cup buttermilk
Seasoning	1 teaspoon allspice	½ teaspoon cinnamon plus ⅛ teaspoon cloves
	1 cup catsup	1 cup tomato sauce plus ½ cup sugar plus 2 tablespoons vinegar
	1 clove of garlic	⅛ teaspoon garlic powder or ⅛ teaspoon instant minced garlic or ¾ teaspoon garlic salt or 5 drops of liquid garlic
	1 teaspoon Italian spice	¼ teaspoon each oregano, basil, thyme, rosemary plus dash of cayenne
	1 teaspoon lemon juice	½ teaspoon vinegar
	1 tablespoon mustard	1 teaspoon dry mustard
	1 medium onion	1 tablespoon dried minced onion or 1 teaspoon onion powder
Sweet	1 1-ounce square chocolate	¼ cup cocoa plus 1 teaspoon shortening
	1⅔ ounces semisweet chocolate	1 ounce unsweetened chocolate plus 4 teaspoons granulated sugar
	1 cup honey	1 to 1¼ cups sugar plus ¼ cup liquid or 1 cup corn syrup or molasses
	1 cup granulated sugar	1 cup packed brown sugar or 1 cup corn syrup, molasses or honey minus ¼ cup liquid

Equivalent Chart

	When the recipe calls for:	Use:
Baking Essentials	½ cup butter	1 stick
	2 cups butter	1 pound
	4 cups all-purpose flour	1 pound
	4½ to 5 cups sifted cake flour	1 pound
	1 square chocolate	1 ounce
	1 cup semisweet chocolate pieces	1 6-ounce package
	4 cups marshmallows	1 pound
	2¼ cups packed brown sugar	1 pound
	4 cups confectioners' sugar	1 pound
	2 cups granulated sugar	1 pound
Cereal & Bread	1 cup fine dry bread crumbs	4 to 5 slices
	1 cup soft bread crumbs	2 slices
	1 cup small bread cubes	2 slices
	1 cup fine cracker crumbs	28 saltines
	1 cup fine graham cracker crumbs	15 crackers
	1 cup vanilla wafer crumbs	22 wafers
	1 cup crushed cornflakes	3 cups uncrushed
	4 cups cooked macaroni	1 8-ounce package
	3½ cups cooked rice	1 cup uncooked
Dairy	1 cup freshly grated cheese	¼ pound
	1 cup cottage cheese	1 8-ounce carton
	1 cup sour cream	1 8-ounce carton
	1 cup whipped cream	½ cup heavy cream
	⅔ cup evaporated milk	1 small can
	1⅔ cups evaporated milk	1 13-ounce can
Fruit	4 cups sliced or chopped apples	4 medium
	1 cup mashed banana	3 medium
	2 cups pitted cherries	4 cups unpitted
	3 cups shredded coconut	½ pound
	4 cups cranberries	1 pound
	1 cup pitted dates	1 8-ounce package
	1 cup candied fruit	1 8-ounce package
	3 to 4 tablespoons lemon juice plus 1 teaspoon grated rind	1 lemon
	⅓ cup orange juice plus 2 teaspoons grated rind	1 orange
	4 cups sliced peaches	8 medium
	2 cups pitted prunes	1 12-ounce package
	3 cups raisins	1 15-ounce package

When the recipe calls for:	Use:
Meats 4 cups chopped cooked chicken 3 cups chopped cooked meat 2 cups cooked ground meat	1 5-pound chicken 1 pound, cooked 1 pound, cooked
Nuts 1 cup chopped nuts	4 ounces, shelled 1 pound, unshelled
Vegetables 2 cups cooked green beans 2½ cups lima beans or red beans 4 cups shredded cabbage 1 cup grated carrots 1 4-ounce can mushrooms 1 cup chopped onion 4 cups sliced or chopped raw potatoes 2 cups canned tomatoes	½ pound fresh or 1 16-ounce can 1 cup dried, cooked 1 pound 1 large ½ pound, fresh 1 large 4 medium 1 16-ounce can

Measurement Equivalents

1 tablespoon = 3 teaspoons
2 tablespoons = 1 ounce
4 tablespoons = ¼ cup
5 tablespoons + 1 teaspoon
   = ⅓ cup
8 tablespoons = ½ cup
12 tablespoons = ¾ cup
16 tablespoons = 1 cup
1 cup = 8 ounces or ½ pint
4 cups = 1 quart
4 quarts = 1 gallon
	6½ to 8-ounce can = 1 cup
	10½ to 12-ounce can = 1¼ cups
	14 to 16-ounce can (No. 300) = 1¾ cups
	16 to 17-ounce can (No. 303) = 2 cups
	1-pound 4-ounce can or 1-pint 2-ounce can
	   (No. 2) = 2½ cups
	1-pound 13-ounce can (No. 2½) = 3½ cups
	3-pound 3-ounce can or 46-ounce can
	   = 5¾ cups
	6½-pound or 7-pound 5-ounce can (No. 10)
	   = 12 to 13 cups

Metric Equivalents

Liquid	Dry
1 teaspoon = 5 milliliters 1 tablespoon = 15 milliliters 1 fluid ounce = 30 milliliters 1 cup = 250 milliliters 1 pint = 500 milliliters	1 quart = 1 liter 1 ounce = 30 grams 1 pound = 450 grams 2.2 pounds = 1 kilogram

NOTE: *The metric measures are approximate benchmarks for purposes of home food preparation.*

Index

Essence of Kansas!

Kansas 4-H Foundation
116 Umberger Hall, KSU
Manhattan, KS 66506

Please send _____ copies of **Essence of Kansas!** at $10.00 per copy plus $2.00 per book ordered for shipping and handling.

I enclose an additional donation for Kansas 4-H of $_____

Name _____

Address _____

City _____ County _____ State _____ Zip _____

Enclosed you will find names and addresses for gift cookbooks.
I understand you will enclose a gift card with my name for each gift cookbook.

Essence of Kansas!

Kansas 4-H Foundation
116 Umberger Hall, KSU
Manhattan, KS 66506

Please send _____ copies of **Essence of Kansas!** at $10.00 per copy plus $2.00 per book ordered for shipping and handling.

I enclose an additional donation for Kansas 4-H of $_____

Name _____

Address _____

City _____ County _____ State _____ Zip _____

Enclosed you will find names and addresses for gift cookbooks.
I understand you will enclose a gift card with my name for each gift cookbook.